PORTRAITS AND PROSPECTS

PORTRAITS
AND
PROSPECTS

BRITISH AND IRISH DRAWINGS AND WATERCOLOURS
FROM THE COLLECTION OF

THE ULSTER MUSEUM, BELFAST

PUBLISHED BY
THE ULSTER MUSEUM, BELFAST
IN ASSOCIATION WITH THE
SMITHSONIAN INSTITUTION TRAVELING EXHIBITION SERVICE

1989

Published on the occasion of an exhibition organized by the Smithsonian
Institution Traveling Exhibition Service (SITES) and the Ulster Museum.

ISBN 0-900761-23-7

Portraits and Prospects:
British and Irish Drawings and Watercolours
from the Collection of the Ulster Museum, Belfast.

ULSTER MUSEUM PUBLICATION No. 264

COVER:
Erskine Nichol (1825–1904): *Paddy at Versailles* 1856 (detail),
Watercolour and bodycolour, catalogue number 55.

FRONTISPIECE:
John Henry Fuseli (1741–1825): *Portrait of Mrs Fuseli in a Red Cap* 1794
Watercolour, bodycolour and white chalk, catalogue number 7.

Printed in Northern Ireland by W. & G. Baird Ltd.

Contents

BRITISH EMBASSY
WASHINGTON, D.C. 20008
TELEPHONE: (202) 462-1340

FROM THE AMBASSADOR

4 November 1988

FOREWORD FROM THE BRITISH AMBASSADOR

PORTRAITS AND PROSPECTS
BRITISH AND IRISH WATERCOLOURS FROM THE ULSTER MUSEUM, BELFAST

I am delighted to welcome this very fine exhibition of works
from the Ulster Museum, Belfast, not only because it represents
two centuries of distinguished artists from Britain and
Ireland, but also because it is the outcome of several years
of close collaboration between the Ulster Museum and the
Smithsonian Institution's Travelling Exhibition Service. I
have no doubt that in the course of its travels around the
United States, it will bring much pleasure to those who see
it. I hope that it will also encourage them to visit Northern
Ireland so as to discover its cultural richness at first hand.

Antony Acland

Compiler's Acknowledgements

The idea for this travelling exhibition came from Mr Donald McClelland of the Smithsonian Institution Traveling Exhibitions Service, on his first visit to the Ulster Museum in 1986. Enthusiastic support and co-operation has been received from the Director of the Ulster Museum, Mr John C. Nolan, and the Keeper of Art, Mr Ted Hickey. Special thanks is due to the British Council for a generous grant. Our paper conservator, Mr Pat McBride, has examined and treated every item in the exhibition before its dispatch to the United States. Valuable input came from the Keeper of Design and Exhibition Services, Mr Roy Service, and his staff, in particular Mrs Sandra Neill, and Mr James Hanna, who has designed the layout and typography of this catalogue. The colour photographs were taken by our photographers, Mr Bill Anderson-Porter, Mr Bryan Rutledge and Mr Michael McKeown. The catalogue has been printed by an Ulster firm, Messrs W & G Baird Ltd. The material which forms the text of the catalogue is the result of many years' study and research with the Ulster Museum's collection. I gratefully acknowledge the help I have received over the years from my colleagues in the Department of Art, particularly Dr Brian Kennedy, Miss Eileen Black and Miss Anne Millar. I was able to do much useful research on the Ulster Museum's drawings and watercolours in February 1987, during my tenure as Visiting Fellow at the Yale Center for British Art, where I appreciated the comments of Mr Patrick Noon and Dr Scott Wilcox. Finally, the largest share of acknowledgement must go to the countless scholars and curators in other institutions with whom I and my predecessors have been corresponding for as long as we have been working on the collections, and whose advice and insight illuminate the individual catalogue entries.

Martyn Anglesea
Curator of Prints and Drawings
Department of Art
Ulster Museum

Acknowledgements

We at the Smithsonian Institution Traveling Exhibition Service are pleased to be able to bring to the United States the exhibition *Portraits and Prospects: British and Irish Drawings and Watercolours from the Ulster Museum, Belfast.* This exhibition will provide many Americans with an opportunity to observe closely examples of the various artistic movements and points of view that form one of the great traditions in Western art. *Portraits and Prospects* spans the eighteenth through the twentieth century, a period in British and Irish history marked by enormous economic and social change. It was a time of contrast as well as a continuity. While new intellectual currents and artistic movements prevailed throughout Europe, the artists of Britain and Ireland retained a sense of their own unique, cultural heritage.

The drawings and watercolours in the exhibition were selected jointly by Martyn Anglesea, Curator of Prints and Drawings at the Ulster Museum, Belfast and Donald McClelland, Exhibition Coordinator and Curator, Smithsonian Institution Traveling Exhibition Service. Mr Anglesea's scholarly catalogue will contribute much towards the study of British/Irish art, and Mr McClelland's essay will provide readers with a fuller understanding of the period under discussion.

We are deeply grateful to The British Council for its generous assistance in supporting the exhibition's American tour. Our special thanks go to John Nolan, Director of the Ulster Museum, Belfast, for his continued interest in the exhibition's development and organization. Others in Belfast who participated significantly in the preparation of the exhibition are the designer of the exhibition catalogue, Mr James Hanna, and Miss H. A. Stevenson of the British Council.

I also would like to extend our special gratitude to His Excellency Sir Antony Acland for his thoughtful statement, and for the assistance of the Cultural Attaché, James Daniel, and Carmel McGill, Northern Ireland Cultural Exchange Officer.

Staff from the Smithsonian Institution Traveling Exhibition Service assisted at every juncture. We express recognition in particular to: Linda Bell, Assistant Director for Administration; Lee Williams, Registrar; Andrea Stevens, Publications Director; Gregory Naranjo, Research Associate; Marci Silverman and Michelle Fayer, Exhibition Assistants. We also are grateful to Walter Sorrel and Karen Fort from the Smithsonian's Office of Exhibits Central.

Portraits and Prospects begins its United States tour in August 1989. We would like to thank the staffs at each of the host museums for their efforts and support on behalf of this important cultural undertaking. Through collaborations such as these, we can continue to bring exhibitions of excellence from abroad to enthusiastic audiences across the United States.

ANNA R COHN
Director, SITES

Foreword

DONALD R. McCLELLAND

There is an intimate and natural view of people and their environment that forms the character of British and Irish art of the 19th and early 20th centuries. This vision is most apparent in the medium of works on paper, such as those presented in this exhibition. The paintings and drawings reflect the discoveries of the natural world and its evolutionary process, rejecting the lavish and grand view typically found in academic art. However, these works are not devoid of an expressive attitude, for they are filled with whimsy and wit. In portraiture particularly, one finds an inner perception of the subject that contains his or her spiritual as well as physical essence.

British and Irish art can often be readily distinguished from that of the rest of Europe, most specifically when it addresses the unique landscape and social climate of the island's isolation. Nature is portrayed with reason and common sense; a strong narrative tradition is seen in scenes of everyday life which bespeak triumph as well as hardship. For this reason alone we owe a considerable debt to the artists in this exhibition for recording their landscape. Through their perceptive documentation, we can readily note both physical changes to the landscape as well as to those of social interaction.

Toward the end of the 18th century, British and Irish artists began to break away from the traditional technique of outlining, in which lines which were carefully drawn and then filled in with colour. The new technique began with a brief sketch and utilized a series of watercolour washes, which when applied sparingly, produced works of great sophistication and charm, possessing the most subtle beauty in colour, complexity, and form. Often, by combining gentle colours with the whitish paper on which they were painted, the images produce an effect in which light appears to come from within the paper itself. The British/Irish landscape, with its mystical atmosphere, can be effectively captured with this technique. This may explain why watercolour is an essentially British/Irish art form.

To those who have not worked in watercolour, many of the examples we see may at first appear to be not much more than coloured sketches. Because of the apparent simplicity with which watercolour paintings are made, not always readily evident are the special challenges inherent in the medium: wet paper can buckle and ripple, colours in washes can merge and become muddy, underdrawing may show through layers of pigment, and mistakes are not easily masked. By examining the construction of a watercolour where very little can be hidden from view, we may not only experience the artist at work and his mastery of the medium, but also catch a glimpse of his creative nature.

This exhibition provides the viewer an opportunity to compare works by academy trained artists with those of naïve artists, whose endearing scenes show popular subjects. Family groups, domestic interiors, and views of homes, large and small, were lovingly recorded by these individuals. They painted what they knew and cared for, subjects seldom considered or studied by the more professional artists of the day. The interior views were consciously rendered, placing emphasis on familiar objects, wall and floor colours, and the arrangement of furniture and pictures. Much of the social history of 19th-century Britain and Ireland can be visually confirmed by these intimate and, we assume, accurate views of daily life. Families kept their paintings in folios or albums and brought them out for periodic reminiscences, not dissimilar to today's family traditions of viewing picture albums or home movies.

As the age of enlightenment began to find expression, professional artists embraced new opportunities to document natural history and far-away places. Watercolour was the perfect medium for recording exotic flowers, fruits, and animals, as well as topographical works showing the wonders of the world, such as those of ancient Rome, India, China, and North America.

The artists George Petrie (1789–1866), Andrew Nicholl (1801–1886), and John Piper (b. 1903) represent a cross-section of British/Irish watercolourists. Through their works, we may better understand the extraordinary breadth of draughtsmanship and British and Irish heritage present in all of the many artists displayed.

The son of a Scottish miniature painter who settled in Ireland, George Petrie was active during the first half of the 19th century. He was a draughtsman, artist, antiquarian, linguist, musician, and a member of one of the most versatile groups of Irish intellectuals. He represented the embodiment of an era marked with a serious interest in anything Irish, no matter what period, origin, or movement of thought, for Irish intellectuals considered their homeland the best hope for the future. It was largely due to Petrie that Irish Christian archaeology became a serious study.

Petrie left an impressive number of brilliantly executed watercolours of Irish buildings and landscapes. Among these is his topographical view of the country, *The Eagle's Nest, Killarney* (catalogue number 33, figure 1), in which he combined his artistic and poetic vision with the exactness of draughtsmanship.

Among the most talented of Irish landscape painters was Andrew Nicholl. His work lends special insight into the landscape of the island. Born in Belfast, Nicholl worked as an apprentice to a printer in the city. We can detect the precision of the printer's craft in Nicholl's landscapes of the Antrim Coast. Having never formally trained in an academy or with a specific artist, Andrew Nicholl might be considered self-taught, yet he was eventually elected an associate of the Royal Hibernian Academy in 1837.

Like Petrie, Nicholl was seriously interested in Irish antiquities as well as the botanical and topographic aspects of Ireland. Nicholl's *A Bank of Flowers, with a View of Bray, Co. Wicklow* (catalogue number 41, figure 2) represents a fresh quality in the observance of nature. This and many similar subjects often utilized wild flowers painted in the foreground to form a screen through which we dimly perceive a landscape. It is as if we are lying on our stomachs, like hares, watching as the world marches by. The paintings have a sharpness of vision and naïvité that is entirely captivating.

Nicholl, together with Petrie, contributed to a volume entitled *Picturesque Sketches* (printed in Dublin in 1835) which contains some of the finest landscape and coastal scenery of Ireland. These folios of prints, based on Nicholl's watercolours and drawings, include views of the familiar romantic sites from one end of Ireland to the other. It is hardly surprising that the first revival of Celtic ornament was inspired by the embellishments of a book published by George Petrie in the 1840s. The most handsome of these was undoubtedly the binding on Petrie's famous work, the *Ecclesiastical Architecture of Ireland* (published in 1845).

John Piper's view of *Bladon* (catalogue number 77, figure 3) owes more to the artist's keen observation of nature than to the antiquities that would have inspired his predecessors. Perhaps too, the

FIGURE 1.
George Petrie (1790–1866)
The Eagle's Nest, Killarney.
Watercolour over pencil on white paper. (no. 33)

FIGURE 2.
Andrew Nicholl (1804–1886)
A Bank of Flowers, with a View of Bray, Co. Wicklow.
Watercolour on white paper. (no. 41)

FIGURE 3.
John Piper (1903–) *Bladon.* 1945.
Pen, black ink and watercolour on white paper.
(no. 77)

drawing reflects the artist's interest in black-and-white photography. On the edge of the park of Blenheim Palace, the village of Bladon conjures all sorts of images: Sir Winston Churchill was born in the palace and was buried in the village. Yet, these connotations aside, the artist chose Bladon for the special character of the vale – memorable for its many effects of light and mood, with its stretch of river, the countryside, and the rather obscure, unidentified small house. And it is the lush green of the summer grass; the yellows, feathery grays, and purple blacks of the vegetation in winter; the foregrounds of pale warm distances of misted trees; and hills punctuated with cool light that inspires his work.

John Piper began his education in 1926 at the Richmond School of Art and continued at the Royal College of Art in London. Soon thereafter, he became an art critic for *The Listener* and *The Nation*. His early work was nonrepresentational. Later he came under the influence of surrealism before reverting to an art form that could best be described as romantic naturalism.

During the Second World War, Piper recorded the war's devastating effects on Britain. It was, perhaps, at this time that his own personal style developed. Watercolour became his favourite medium, no doubt because it best suited his mystical approach to the subject and was convenient for use out of doors. If one is walking in the remote northern fields of Britain on a partly cloudy day, it is indeed rather like being absorbed into one of Piper's dappled watercolours with their streaks, smudges, and ripples of silvery white.

By choosing watercolour and drawing as media for conveying their impressions of Britain and Ireland, the artists in this exhibition provide us the opportunity for a more intimate view of portraiture and landscape painting. In addition, they present to us in ways both eloquent and sensitive the thoughts and visions that we continue to enjoy to this day.

Introduction

A SURVEY OF THE ULSTER MUSEUM'S COLLECTION OF DRAWINGS AND WATERCOLOURS

Martyn Anglesea

Among the national museums of the British Isles, the Ulster Museum is a comparatively young institution. It and the Ulster Folk and Transport Museum were constituted as the national museums of Northern Ireland as recently as 1961. But the Ulster Museum's roots go back to the first museum in Belfast, founded in 1831 by the Belfast Natural History and Philosophical Society, a group of enthusiastic amateurs, mainly medical men and lawyers, akin to so many such founders in the growing industrial centres of Britain and America. Belfast had been the centre of political radicalism in Ireland at the time of the aborted 1798 rebellion. Already industrialised, with thriving cotton mills and shipyards, after about 1830 cotton gave way to linen, and Belfast became the largest linen-producing centre in the world. In the period of political impotence between the Act of Union with Britain in 1801, and the first Parliamentary Reform Act of 1830, Belfast intellectuals devoted themselves to "useful knowledge", of which the Linen Hall Library and the Museum were typical products of the spirit of the age.

The Museum inherits the collections of the Belfast Natural History and Philosophical Society, which relate, however, to archaeology and natural history rather than to art. Indeed, Belfast in the nineteenth century could be called (and was called frequently by its natives) an art-starved city, in contrast to Dublin, Glasgow, Liverpool and other comparable centres. But there were some brave pioneers. A Belfast Association of Artists, founded in 1836, was a short-lived affair which managed to hold only three annual exhibitions. More successful was the Society for the Promotion of the Fine Arts in Belfast, founded in 1843, which held large exhibitions for about twenty years. Some remarkable men were involved in this Society, including the future diplomat Lord Dufferin, the naturalist William Thompson, the architect Sir Charles Lanyon, the politician James Emerson Tennent (the main patron of Andrew Nicholl, who is represented in this exhibition, numbers 39-42), the surgeon Dr James Moore (also represented, numbers 48-49) and the ill-fated cotton-manufacturer, Francis McCracken, who was one of the earliest patrons of the English Pre-Raphaelite painters. A Government School of Design was set up in 1849, but lasted only until 1855. Between then and 1870, when the Belfast School of Art was revived, practically the sole institution which could be called artistic (only just!) was the stationery firm of Marcus Ward's, under its art director John Vinycomb, suppliers of sweetly-sentimental Christmas cards to the British Empire. It was only after years of agitation, mainly by the Belfast Art Society and the Ulster Arts Club, that the Corporation was persuaded in 1890 to open a small art gallery on the upper floor of the Central Library in Royal Avenue in the City Centre. In 1912 it was decided to move all the collections to a new building on a site in the Botanic Gardens, adjacent to the Queen's University, in Belfast's attractive southern suburb. Building operations, halted by the First World War, progressed slower than was hoped, and only one wing of the ambitious design was opened in 1928. Until 1961 the Museum continued to be called the Belfast Municipal Museum and Art Gallery. In the affluent

1960s, the remaining three sides of the courtyard were completed to a new design by Francis Pym of London, which was officially opened in 1972, effectively quadrupling the size of the Museum.

Like the National Museum of Wales in Cardiff, the Ulster Museum is multi-disciplinary, having five curatorial departments under one roof (art, antiquities, botany and zoology, geology, local history). During the 1960s, the collecting policy of the art department was outlined in its present form. Priority is given to building up a collection of international modern art, of which the Museum has the finest public holding in Ireland. The collection of continental old-master paintings is deliberately kept small, since in the present climate competition with the well-established and distinguished collection of the National Gallery of Ireland in Dublin is unrealistic. On the other hand, the historical collections of Irish art are being steadily developed, and encompass painting and sculpture, drawings and prints, silver, glass, ceramics, furniture, costume and textiles. The 1972 building contains a students' room for the study of the prints and drawings collection, and a drawings and watercolours gallery where selections from the collection are displayed. Compared with collections like the Whitworth Art Gallery of Manchester University, or Leeds City Art Gallery, or Newcastle-upon-Tyne, the collection is not particularly large, numbering approximately 3,000 drawings and watercolours. Belfast has not been fortunate enough to receive a substantial collection like the Agnes and Norman Lupton Bequest at Leeds. But the collection is a good representation of British and Irish watercolours and drawings from about 1700 to the present day.

The first group of drawings to be given to the Museum were received in an odd way. They were given in 1896 by the then curator, a painter named James F Johnston (see under Fuseli, numbers 6-10) who mysteriously disappeared whilst swimming at Helen's Bay, and then just as mysteriously turned up again. His gift included the ten drawings by Fuseli which are still the pride of the collection, but then must have been at the nadir of fashionability. Five of them are included in this exhibition. Johnston's gift also contained a group of fifty-two drawings by Edward Duncan (1803-82), most of which appear to have been done on a tour of France in 1835. There are views of Boulogne, Paris, Metz and Strasbourg, and some beautiful free watercolour sketches of French peasants (number 45).

During the early decades of the twentieth century, acquisition of drawings and watercolours was haphazard. In 1905, the W A Sandby Bequest allocated to Belfast five Paul Sandby watercolours, of which the best are *Edwinsford, Carmarthenshire* and *View near the Wood-Yard, Windsor Great Park* (number 2), and the rest tend to be slapdash late works. It was not until 1967 that Sandby's impressive nocturne, *Caernarvon Castle by Moonlight* (number 3), was bought. A large watercolour by William Lee-Hankey, *The Confession*, a genre piece in the style of Bastien-Lepage, was bought from the Belfast Art Society's annual exhibition of 1909. Two pencil drawings of Paris by Henry Edridge arrived in 1910, and pleasant watercolours by George Barrett junior (*Westminster*) and Clarkson Stanfield (*Dover Beach*) were bought in 1912. In 1913 an impressionistic watercolour, *Corner of the Lake*, by William Mark Fisher, was bought from the Belfast art dealer, William Rodman. Fisher, born in Boston of an English father and an Irish Catholic mother, settled in England in 1872 and became a member of the New English Art Club. This appears to have been the first acquisition of a watercolour by a reputable living artist. Also in 1913, a splendidly detailed night view of the interior of *Diocletian's Palace, Split*, painted in 1855 by the German expatriate Carl Haag, was bought. In 1919 a local collector, James Stirling, bequeathed some drawings by Cipriani, Millais and Angelica Kauffmann (the last a somewhat optimistic attribution), and an attractive pencil drawing of a man in a riding habit, then attributed to George Morland, which seems more likely to be by Thomas Rowlandson. Other drawings and watercolours which entered the collection before 1920 include works by David Cox, Tom Collier, Rev William Gilpin, Copley Fielding, Louis Haghe, John Linnell, J W North, John Skinner Prout, Anthony Carey Stannus, Thomas Stothard and Sir David Wilkie.

The 1920s and 1930s, a period when good-quality English watercolours could be bought from London dealers for what appear now to be ridiculously low sums, was the period when the British Museum, the Victoria and Albert Museum and many provincial British museums and art galleries built up distinguished collections in this field. It was also the era when the private collectors, Paul Oppé, Iolo Williams and L G Duke, did most of their buying. Several works formerly in Duke's collection eventually came to the Ulster Museum (see numbers 5 and 17). In this inter-war period Belfast acquired many good English watercolours, a surprisingly large number through Belfast dealers such as Rodman's, but also through the respectable London galleries, Walker's, Palser's and the Fine Art Society. A modest watercolour by Peter de Wint was bought from Rodman's in 1926. Prominent among the watercolours bought in London are an early Girtinesque *Harlech Castle* by Cotman (number 28: Walker's 1935), which appears to date from between 1800 and 1803, John Robert Cozens's *Capo di Bove* (number 13: Walker's 1938), which probably came from the collection of William Beckford, Francis Towne's *Trees and Rocks, Ambleside* (number 16: Fine Art Society 1936), Edward Dayes's *Dunfermline Abbey* (Palser 1937), based on a sketch by the antiquarian James Moore in his sketchbooks of his Scottish tour, now in the Yale Center for British Art, a delicate Michael Angelo Rooker watercolour of *Hyde Park* (number 12: Palser 1937), Samuel Hieronymus Grimm's *St Paul's Cathedral from St George's Fields*, dated 1770 (Fine Art Society 1935), Rowlandson's *Tour in Flanders*, dated 1792 (number 14: Fine Art Society 1935), John Warwick Smith's *Naples from the Arinelli* (Walker's 1938), Thomas Shotter Boys's *King's Palace, Brussels* (number 38: Palser 1938), and David Roberts's *Church of San Jago, Xeres* (number 36: Palser 1937) which was lithographed by Boys as plate VI of Roberts's *Picturesque Sketches in Spain*.

In 1928 the Museum acquired a large bequest of indifferent nineteenth century pictures collected by Sir Robert Lloyd Patterson, a Belfast flax-merchant. On the advice of the Contemporary Art Society and the critic Frank Rutter, it was decided to sell most of these, and to use the proceeds as a fund for the purchase of contemporary works of art. Important items, mostly oil-paintings, by Sickert, Spencer Gore, Duncan Grant, Vanessa Bell, Stanley Spencer, William Roberts and others were bought at this period. Of course, the Museum was then still under the jurisdiction of the Belfast City Council, of which a puritanical element yielded to objections from members of the public about the alleged immodesty of a nude *Mother and Child* by Wilson Steer, which had been bought from the Leicester Galleries with the Lloyd Patterson Fund, on the advice of the Contemporary Art Society. The Council's view prevailed, and the nude was exchanged with the Leicester Galleries for a Wilson Steer oil painting and three drawings, which included Steer's watercolour *Haweswater*, and the impressive portrait of an unknown man by Gerald Brockhurst (number 71).

Amongst the watercolours acquired locally between the wars, mention must be made of the group of nine excellent watercolours by Birket Foster, collected by Sir Frederick Cleaver (of Robinson and Cleavers' department store) and bequeathed in 1936. These range in size from tiny vignettes to large gallery watercolours. Two are included here (numbers 53 and 54). The best example of a Victorian gallery watercolour in the collection, too large to be included, is Henry Gastineau's enormous Turneresque view of *Glenarm, Co Antrim*, dated 1859, which was bequeathed to the Museum in 1938. It resembles an oil-painting in its heavy gilded frame, and makes the Antrim Coast look like the Mediterranean.

The two most striking watercolours acquired during the Second World War were the

Irish-born Mulready's *Giving a Bite* (number 31), of which other versions in watercolour and oil are in the Victoria and Albert Museum, and Cornelius Varley's sombre *Ruins of Kerry House, Lixnaw, Co Kerry* (number 26: Fine Art Society 1943). The latter is signed and dated 1842, many years after the Irish tour of 1808 when Varley made his original sketch (which was with Colnaghi's in 1973). After the end of the War, the Museum, along with many others in the United Kingdom, received its quota from the War Artists' Advisory Committee. This included a number of drawings by the popular Belfast artist William Conor (1884-1968), of which *Men of the Home Front* is in this exhibition (number 68). Other War Artists stationed in Northern Ireland were Edward Ardizzone, Robert Scanlan and Vivian Pitchforth, and the Museum received two watercolours done by Edward Bawden with the Indian Army in the Sudan. The Museum's first Turner watercolour arrived in 1948, the middle-period *Beeston Castle* (number 25), from the Nettlefold Collection which was distributed amongst museums throughout the United Kingdom. To this was added in 1951 an early "blue drawing", perhaps showing *Beachy Head* (number 24), from Turner's period of working in Dr Monro's studio. The collection still lacks any of Turner's late work in watercolour, though the Museum has owned his late oil painting *Dawn of Christianity: the Flight into Egypt* since 1912. In the late 1940s works were acquired by Charles Conder (a lunette on silk, *In the Shadow of Pan*), Peter de Wint, Anthony Devis (a puzzling watercolour of *Olivares and La Brisca*, number 4, by an artist who seems never to have travelled in Spain or anywhere else abroad), Samuel Palmer (a late work influenced by his father-in-law John Linnell), two more Copley Fieldings, two drawings by Thérèse Lessore from the Sickerts' Trust, an atypical watercolour by Russell Flint, and a good well-preserved Samuel Prout watercolour of the *Chapel in the Chateau d'Amboise* (number 29: Fine Art Society 1948), of which a lithograph was published in 1839, and of which another version was with Spink in 1975.

The Contemporary Art Society continued (as they still continue) occasionally to give the Museum watercolours and drawings as well as paintings and sculpture. John Nash's *Farm at Kimble*, given by the Society in 1948, was joined in 1951 by *View of the Plain* (number 72), which was bought in London. Two of Charles Ginner's tightly-executed watercolours, *Storm over Clearbury Ring* (number 68) and *Hampstead Study* were given by the Society in 1946. Robert Bevan's *Tapster Water* (number 63) was bought in 1954.

Like the 1930s, the 1950s decade was another period of extensive addition to the collection, English watercolours still being comparatively cheap on the London market. Acquisitions made at this time include the following: two delicate drawings of *Near Rydal Hall* and *Peamore Park* (no 17) by John White Abbott, Francis Towne's best pupil (Fine Art Society 1953 and 1955); a small but good-quality watercolour *Feeding the Chickens*, by Helen Allingham, given locally in 1950; two watercolours by William James Müller, one of which, *Xanthus from the Theatre* (no 43) derives from that artist's expedition to Lycia in 1841; a large watercolour of *Rouen* by Samuel Austin; two watercolours by Hercules Brabazon Brabazon, one of *Sousse* (number 51) and one of *Venice*; Sir John Gilbert's *Don Quixote and Rosinante* (R·E Abbott 1956); *The Link Boy*, an impressive figure-watercolour bought in 1952 as a William Henry Hunt, of which the attribution is now doubted; a Thomas Hearne sepia of *Caister Castle*; Hugh William "Grecian" Williams's sepia of *Lake Avernus* (number 22), his only known dated work of 1816; a fine stormy scene by Nicolas Pocock; Thomas Walmsley's *Mouth of the Suir*; a scene on the Rhine by William Callow; a view of *Lincoln Cathedral* by Albert Goodwin; good examples by the minor artists William Pearson, Thomas Sunderland (*Ullswater*) and Sir William Pilkington (*Convent of Franciscans on the Palatine Hill*, number 23); a rare flowerpiece dated 1769 by Mary Moser, one of the two original female members of the Royal Academy; and a curious royalist *Allegory of the Napoleonic Wars* by Henry

Singleton (1766-1839), bought locally in 1959. David Cox and his followers were now well represented. The best of the Museum's five watercolours by Cox, *The Snowstorm* (number 30), was bought from the Fine Art Society in 1954. Of Cox's followers, there are four watercolours by Tom Collier, four by Edmund Wimperis (as well as a splendid oil landscape), two large breezy landscapes by the Dublin-born Claude Hayes, *A Windmill in Sussex* (number 61) and *Across the Common*, and two small but good-quality watercolours by Alfred William Rich.

During the late 1960s and early 1970s, the Ulster Museum expanded greatly, both with the extension to the building, and a fivefold increase in staff. In the last fifteen years, while a collection of contemporary prints has been steadily built up, acquisitions in the field of drawings and watercolours have been more selective. Works by Irish artists or with Irish connexions are sought after. Outstanding examples of watercolours by English artists but with Irish content are Edward Burra's sinister *Dublin Street Scene* of 1948 (too large for this exhibition), bought from the Hamet Gallery in 1970, and Richard Hamilton's early, textually-loaded illustration to Joyce's *Ulysses*, *Bronze by Gold* (number 84), also of 1948, bought from Anthony d'Offay in 1980. A curious and very rare example of Irish primitive art of the eighteenth century, William Miller's *George Whitefield preaching in the Timber Yard at Lurgan* (number 1), was bought in London in 1969. The earliest known accurate Irish topographical landscapes by an Irish artist, the two remarkable gouache views on vellum of the *East and West Prospects of the Giant's Causeway*, painted about 1740 by the obscure but highly competent Susanna Drury (active 1733-1770), were bought at Sotheby's in 1971 (as they are on vellum, a highly hygroscopic substance, they are never lent out). A very early example of Rose Barton's work, *St Patrick's Close, Dublin* (number 60), dated 1881, was bequeathed in 1968. In 1971 were bought Adam Buck's charming portrait of a little girl with a skipping rope, *Annie Charlotte Hill* (number 21), and two works by obscure artists of Irish origin: James Forrester's *Powerscourt Waterfall* (number 5), and the *Rock of Fennor on the Boyne* by James George Oben (number 27). Forrester, originally from Dublin, spent the period from 1755 to his death in 1776 in Rome, while Oben, whose real name was O'Brien, changed his name on moving to London, as a Germanic-sounding name made his works more saleable. Two views of *Belturbet, Co Cavan*, by the amateur watercolourist John Nixon, were bought in 1974, to be followed by a lot more from a very extensive collection of Nixon drawings which was sold in London. *Magilligan Mountain* is included here (number 15). An Anthony Devis drawing of *Dublin Bay* was bought in 1977, and in the same year, Francis Wheatley's landscape with a ruined abbey, painted in 1798, which was subsequently identified as *Furness Abbey, Lancashire* (number 18).

Finally, we must consider the large groups of drawings and watercolours, mainly by local artists, which give every collection its uniqueness. At Belfast, foremost among these are Andrew Nicholl (1804-86) and his amateur pupil Dr James Moore (1819-83). Of Nicholl, whose works are now frequently seen on the London art market, the Museum holds some 250 separate items, as well as three volumes of sketches of Irish Antiquities. There is an exceptionally interesting series of 113 early views of the Antrim Coast, painted in 1828 while Nicholl was only twenty-four. (Numbers 39 and 40 are from this series). After 1830, as a protégé of the Belfast MP, Sir James Emerson Tennent, Nicholl was taken to London, where his style changed completely (see numbers 40-42). Nicholl spent the years 1846-1850 in Ceylon, where Emerson Tennent was appointed Colonial Secretary. An artist of rather uneven quality, Nicholl at his best can achieve subtle effects reminiscent of Copley Fielding, de Wint and John Glover. Nicholl's best pupil, Dr James Moore, by whom the Museum holds over 400 watercolours, was an eminent Belfast surgeon. While studying medicine at Edinburgh University in the late 1830s, Moore became acquainted with the Scottish artists John Thomson, Erskine Nicol and Sam Bough. He corresponded with Bough for the rest of his life, and it is Bough's style that he followed. Moore was in the habit of taking a sketch pad and a water-colour box everywhere on his wide travels, and the subjects in the collection cover Ireland, England, Scotland, France and part of Germany. Moore was more successful as a rapid sketcher than Nicholl (see numbers 48 and 49). Nicholl's other talented amateur pupil, the Rev Narcissus Batt (1824-98), is represented by ten albums containing 550 drawings in pen and ink, mainly of British and continental architecture.

In 1975 a surprise bequest was received, consisting of the entire contents of the studio of Kenneth Shoesmith (1890-1939), a maritime painter and poster-designer who, having been an officer in the Royal Mail Line, left the sea in 1918 and worked as a commercial artist for shipping lines. His work is beautifully atmospheric and nostalgic. A touring exhibition was assembled in 1978, and travelled to Liverpool, Southampton, Hull, Glasgow and other seaports. Since then the staff of the Museum have received a steady stream of enquiries from ship-enthusiasts all over the world. From over 350 paintings and drawings, Shoesmith's watercolour of *Cranes, Baker Street* is included here (number 70).

An important discovery was made in 1976, when a series of 170 large watercolours of *The Birds of Ireland*, by the forgotten ornithological painter Richard Dunscombe Parker (1805–81), was rescued from one of the stores. They had been bequeathed to the Museum by the artist's sister in 1932. A gentleman farmer from near Cork, Parker was a sportsman and a naturalist, and his paintings of birds compare favourably with Audubon's. As they were bound in a book for over a century, they are in pristine condition. All of them were put on exhibition in the Museum in 1980. Unfortunately the watercolours are too large to be included in this exhibition.

In spite of the current political troubles in Northern Ireland, the Ulster Museum continues to fulfil an important function in the community, and the collections continue to grow and to be conserved. It will be readily appreciated that, as a representative collection, there are still yawning gaps. Except for a very few Italian and Dutch drawings, it contains no drawings earlier than the beginning of the eighteenth century, and consequently has none of Francis Place's Irish drawings of the 1680s. As yet there are no works of Alexander Cozens, Thomas Girtin, mature Cotman or late Turner, none of Henry Moore's drawings, nor any of the excellent Irish watercolours of William Pars. But it is to be hoped that these gaps will eventually be filled, and that this distinguished collection will in future be better known than hitherto. This selection of eighty-four items can give only a taste of the collection's richness.

Abbreviations

ABBREVIATIONS USED IN THE TEXT
(for bibliographical abbreviations see GENERAL BIBLIOGRAPHY)

ARA   Associate of the Royal Academy.

ARCA   Associate of the Royal College of Art.

ARHA   Associate of the Royal Hibernian Academy.

BAS   Belfast Art Society (later UAA and RUA).

BM   British Museum.

b.   bottom.

bt   bought.

c   circa.

c.   centre.

CBE   Companion of the Order of the British Empire.

Exh   exhibited.

l.   left.

NEAC   New English Art Club.

NGI   National Gallery of Ireland (Dublin).

No   number.

NWCS   "New" Society of Painters in Water-Colours (later the Royal Institute of Painters in Water-Colours, RI).

OWCS   Old Water-Colour Society's Club (Annual Volume).

PRONI   Public Record Office of Northern Ireland.

r.   right.

RA   Royal Academy (London); Royal Academician.

RBA   Royal Society of British Artists.

RE   Royal Society of Painter-Etchers and Engravers.

Ref   reference.

Rep   reproduced.

RHA   Royal Hibernian Academy (Dublin).

RI   Royal Institute of Painters in Water-Colours (formerly the "New" Water-Colour Society, NWCS).

ROI   Royal Institute of Oil-Painters.

RSA   Royal Scottish Academy (Edinburgh).

RSW   Royal Scottish Society of Painters in Water-Colours.

RUA   Royal Ulster Academy (formerly BAS and UAA).

RWS   Royal Society of painters in Water-colours (formerly the "Old" Water-Colour Society, OWCS).

t.   top.

UAA   Ulster Academy of Arts (formerly BAS; afterwards RUA).

UAC   Ulster Arts Club.

VAM   Victoria and Albert Museum (London).

WILLIAM MILLER of Lurgan
Died Lurgan, Co Armagh 1779

An amateur artist, one of the few genuine primitive painters of 18th century Ireland, Miller was described by Malcomson (1827) as "a respectable woollen draper, although he was not a Methodist", and by Pigott (1906) as a cambric manufacturer in Lurgan. He was the son of William Miller who died in 1756, and he married Sarah Hope, a Quaker, in 1760. He invented and constructed a human figure which uttered articulate sounds and called out the hours of the clock, which fascinated John Wesley who met Miller on two visits to Lurgan. So many people came to see it that it seriously disrupted Miller's textile business, so he dismantled it and put it away. He also painted flowers and portraits on glass, and a picture of an angel with a text from Revelation which hung over the pulpit of the First Methodist Chapel in Lurgan in 1778. Miller is believed to have died comparatively young, and his will was proved in 1779. His son Joseph became a medical doctor in Lurgan.

---

1. George Whitefield preaching in the Timber Yard at Lurgan, 12 July 1751. (no. 1267).

Gouache on white laid paper, the figures cut around and bent forward.
33 × 43.5 cms / 13 × 17".

Bought: London, Sotheby's 3 Nov 1969.

Exh Irish Portraits 1969 (Supplement).

Ref Strickland II p. 115.

Rep Eifion Evans: *Daniel Rowland and the Evangelical Revival in Wales* Edinburgh, Banner of Truth Trust 1985.

Inscribed on clouds, cut out and pasted onto the sky:
"But he that receiveth the seed in good ground, is he yt. heareth / The Word, and understandeth it, which also beareth fruit, etc. Math.XIII.23.
Which seed becometh a tree, so that the / Birds of the air, come and lodge in the branches thereof, / And he shall be like a tree planted by the / Rivers of water that bringeth forth his fruit / in his season, his leaf also shall not wither, etc. Psal.13.
Happy the Manna-fattned soil, where, free / from stones & choaking thorns, perpetual streams / of Grace celestial glad – / In such, the Word heav'n sown, With grateful sap replete, becomes a tree. / Pierced through the clouds, its Verdant Top Aspires, / with smiling vigour to the starry host, / Up, through the glowing myriads it ascends / From strength to strength it grows; the heavenly path in lustre doth increase, 'till High at last / High ov'r the Galaxy, with Saphires pav'd, / The beaming portals of the Heav'n of Heav'ns, / Wide ope'd; Up sprightly it ascends, and in / her crystal bosom spreads its beautious boughs. Such vegetives shall never fade, where they, / in glory consumate, do lovely smile / Quaffing immortal sweet; Empyrean dew, which falls incessant from the showery arch / (Of choicest heav'nly tint) that clips the throne / Of majesty supream. Celestial Birds / the paradisal vegetive admires.

Thrones, Princedoms, Virtues, Powers, their voices raise / the vast expanse of the Empyrean Rings / with Hallelujah; Whilst each fruitful branch / A golden harp sustains, heav'n tun'd to play / Angelick harmony, each spray intent / On the percussion of the sounding wire, / In joyous tremor, sympathetick moves / And sweets odereferous sheds, which straight ascends / (Mixing with Melody) the Throne divine, / A thankful incense to the Filian Lamb / The worthy subject of Celestial Praise".
On a separate paper, originally framed below the painting:
"The Revd Mr. Geo. Whitefield preaching in the timber yard at Lurgan, Friday July 12: 1751 on 2 Corint 13 Chap. 5 Ver. Examine...whether you be in the faith:
Thus Whitefield preached to the attentive throng, / Expounding Faith divine. He did not stand, / As children statue-like their lessons read: / But with facility and action's grace / Noteless he spake correct. / In Philosophick quirks spent not his breath / Deducing duty foreign to the mode / Of Sacred Volume: Clearly he set forth / Where faith in Christ and love to bounteous Heav'n / Possess the soul thenceforth must freely spring / All virtuous deeds. And as religion's good / To all capacities of men shou'd reach, / He therefore aimed not the learned ear / to tickle, or the million to perplex; / Extensive as the subject was design'd, / All understood, / So plain, (yet nobly simple) was his style / 'Till all instructed then the sublime he / Employs, and mov'd himself, the audience moves; / Aplause and admiration seiz'd they stand / Convinc'd, transported, bursting into tears, / Concious of guilt the Divine Mercy charms, / To the bright object their affections move, / And Christ but heard before, they're now constrained to love".

A man in the left foreground carries in his shoulder-pouch a book marked "P[ilgrim's] Progress", while an old woman in the centre of the crowd offers a bottle, presumably whiskey, labelled "P[ilgrim's] Injury".

Pigott (1906) describes this picture: "[Miller] made a very extraordinary picture of George Whitefield preaching in a timber yard at Lurgan, the multitude of eager faces around him said to be likenesses of the Lurgan people of that day - amongst others, a well-known idiot woman is easily distinguished. The faces and figures are cut out and placed in a frame; the text from which he preached being printed; altogether forming a very remarkable picture".

This is the only work by Miller at present identified. The lengthy inscriptions and the Miltonic blank verse are possibly Miller's own compositions, and they suggest a first-hand account of Whitefield's preaching. Whitefield visited Ireland only once, and his preaching in Lurgan on 12 July 1751 (the anniversary of the Battle of the Boyne) has probably no connexion with Orangeism as the day was not celebrated as Orangeman's Day until much later. A "scale of importance" is used, making the figure of Whitefield at least five times the size of the other figures, even though he stands at the back of the crowd. The likeness of Whitefield is good: he was really cross-eyed, as is shown in the portraits by Wollaston (c 1742), Nathaniel Hone, Russell (c 1770), and by his nickname of "Dr Squintum". (See J F Kerslake: *Early Georgian Portraits: National Portrait Gallery*, 2 vols HMSO 1977). Kerslake p. 307 refers to a crudely-painted group attributed to John Collet, showing Whitefield preaching in the open air, perhaps at Moorfields, which was sold from the Hughes-Stanton collection, London, Philip Son and Neale, 18 Sept 1956 (271).

George Whitefield (born Gloucester 1714: died Newburyport, Massachusetts 1770): preacher; joined the Society of Methodists while an undergraduate at Oxford in 1735, but split with Wesley in 1741 over doctrinal differences, Whitefield adhering to the Calvinist idea of predestination, while Wesley believed in the Arminian doctrine of free will. Whitefield set up the Moorfields Tabernacle in 1741, and in 1748 became chaplain to the Countess of Huntingdon. Like Wesley, he travelled widely in the British Isles and the American Colonies on preaching tours. He was a popular preacher and threw his large congregations into tearful hysteria. His Calvinistic approach achieved particular fruition in Wales.

Bibliography:
Strickland, Irish Portraits, Hewitt.
John Wesley: *Journal* 26 April 1762, 14 June 1773.
James Stuart: *Historical Memoirs of the City of Armagh* 1819.
John Malcomson: *Memoir of Margaret Malcomson* the Methodist Magazine 1827.
William Jackson Pigott (Miller's great grandson): Ulster Journal of Archaeology July 1906.
T J Malcomson in the Lurgan Mail 21 Nov 1969 p. 18.

PAUL SANDBY
Born Nottingham 1731; died Bayswater 1809

The most important English topographical draughtsman of the 18th century, Paul Sandby used (mistakenly) to be called "the father of English watercolour". He and his elder brother Thomas were employed in the military drawing office in the Tower of London, and in 1746 Paul was engaged as draughtsman on the survey of roads in the Scottish Highlands following the rebellion of 1745. From 1751 he lived at Windsor with his brother, who was Deputy Ranger of Windsor Great Park. In 1769 he was a foundation member of the Royal Academy. About 1770 he toured Wales with Sir Watkin Williams Wynn and again with Joseph Banks. Sandby was chief drawing master at the Royal Military Academy, Woolwich, from 1768 to 1796 when he resigned in favour of his son. He practiced etching and introduced the aquatint technique to England. Most of his pupils were amateurs, but they did include the professionals Rooker, Paul Sandby Munn, Schnebbelie, Harding and Cleveley.

---

2. View near the Wood-Yard, Windsor Great Park. (no. 851).

Watercolour with lead white on white paper
65.7 × 37.7 cms / 14¾ × 25⅞".
W A Sandby bequest 1905.

There is a horizontal join in the paper four inches from the top. The upper strip is wove paper, while the larger lower sheet is laid. White paint is confined to the figures on the left.

Bruce Robertson (verbally 1987) dated this watercolour to the mid 1790s, and remarked on its closeness to two Sandby watercolours in the Yale Center for British Art: *The Woodyard, Windsor Great Park*, c 1792 (Robertson 1985 no. 126) and *Southeast View of the Cheesecake House in Hyde Park* 1797 (Robertson 1985 no. 128). In the latter the top 5.4 cms strip of the watercolour was painted on the mount.

Sandby painted a series of views in and near the woodyard while convalescing from an illness in 1792. Four of these are in the Royal Collections at Windsor (Oppé nos 91-94). Oppé commented that these were "in the loose, late sketching style, outline largely eliminated, softness replacing sharpness, and the scene studied and represented for light and atmosphere rather than form". Two woodyard subjects were exhibited at the Royal Academy in 1793. Another watercolour, *Part of the Woodyard in Windsor Gt Park looking to the North - 1792*, 7¼ × 11⅛", was in the sale of Sandby's remaining works on 3 May 1811 (11), and was exhibited by Bill Thompson in *Fifty Watercolour Drawings* at the Albany Gallery, May-June 1986 (3). It is now in Leicester Museum and Art Gallery. Robertson (1985 p. 11) makes the point that although Sandby's style in the 1790s seemed old fashioned in comparison to John Robert Cozens and John Warwick Smith, who had returned from Italy with new techniques, he was still experimenting with new methods of delineating trees in these landscapes in Windsor Forest and Hyde Park. The woodyard sketches have a sense of intimacy which is lacking in the large bodycolour views of Windsor Forest which Sandby was producing from about 1780.

Ball (letter 2 May 1976) states that the group showing a girl with mother carrying child also appears in one of Sandby's pictures of Nottingham Castle. A large dog lies at the extreme bottom edge near the right hand corner.

Bibliography:
Redgrave, Roget, DNB, Graves RA, Graves S of A, Graves BI, Cundall, Windsor, Hughes, Binyon, VAM, Williams, RA 1934, Nettlefold, Hardie, Mallalieu, Clarke, NGI.
William Sandby: *Paul and Thomas Sandby* 1892.
A P Oppé: *The Drawings of Paul and Thomas Sandby in the Collection of His Majesty the King at Windsor Castle* Phaidon 1947.
Peter Hughes: *Paul Sandby and Sir Watkin Williams Wynn* Burlington Magazine July 1972 p. 459.
Johnson Ball: *The Ancestry, Lives and Connections of the brothers Thomas and Paul Sandby* unpublished PhD thesis, University of Nottingham 1964.
Julian Faigan: *Paul Sandby Drawings* Sydney, Australian Gallery Directors' Council 1981.
Johnson Ball: *Paul and Thomas Sandby, Royal Academicians: an Anglo-Danish saga of art, love and war in Georgian England* London and Edinburgh, Charles Skilton 1985.
New Haven, Yale Center for British Art: *The Art of Paul Sandby* catalogue by Bruce Robertson 1985.
Luke Herrmann: *Paul and Thomas Sandby* Batsford and VAM 1986.
Bruce Robertson: unpublished PhD thesis on Paul and Thomas Sandby, Yale University 1987.

3. Caernarvon Castle by moonlight, with a fire within the Town Walls. 1794. (no. 846).

Watercolour and bodycolour on brown tinted paper
37.6 × 54 cms / 14⅞ × 21¼".

Inscribed on rock in foreground: "Caernarvon Castle / P. Sandby 1794".

Bought: London, Leger Galleries, Feb 1967.

The Eagle Tower is seen from the opposite side of the River Seiont. An additional sailing boat right of centre has been partially erased but its outline is clearly visible. Dr Ball (letter 2 May 1976) pointed out that the figure group is similar to that in Sandby's *The Rainbow - Scene in Windsor Forest*.

A Sandby watercolour of the same view but in the daytime is in the Whitworth Art Gallery, Manchester (rep. Ball 1985 pl 106). The Walker Art Gallery, Liverpool, contains another daytime view (rep. Ball pl 122).

An oil painting of *Caernarvon Castle* in Manchester City Art Gallery (343), formerly attributed to Sandby, shows the Castle from a different angle and is said to depict a fire which took place in 1791. This has been reattributed to Joseph Wright of Derby – see David H Solkin: *A 'Caernarvon Castle by Night' by Joseph Wright of Derby* Burlington Magazine April 1977 p. 284.

The 8th aquatint in Sandby's *Views in North Wales* (1776), showing the Castle by moonlight, and an aquatint of a daytime view in *Views in Wales* (1777) correspond in viewpoint to the Manchester City Art Gallery painting rather than to this dramatic bodycolour.

ANTHONY DEVIS

Born Preston, Lancashire 1729; died Albury, Surrey 1816

Anthony Devis was a younger half-brother of the portrait painter Arthur Devis, and was the uncle of Thomas Anthony Devis. From the 1740s he worked as a drawing master in London, exhibiting at the Free Society of Artists in 1761 and 1763, and won the premium of the Society of Arts in 1763. He exhibited at the Royal Academy in 1772 and 1781. In 1780 he retired for the rest of his life to Albury House near Guildford. Here he built a domed studio on a hill, which was known as "Mushroom Hall". Devis himself, the first man in the village to carry an umbrella, was known to the local children as "Man Mushroom". Devis travelled widely in the British Isles, and possibly went to Italy in 1783-4 with a pupil, William Assheton of Cuerdale Hall. His landscape drawings are characterised by pale washes and a tendency to draw leaves like bunches of bananas.

---

4. Olivares and La Brisca. (no. 772).

Grey wash and watercolour over pencil on white laid paper
Overall: 36 × 52.2 cms / 14 × 20½".
Painted area: 30.7 × 43.5 cms / 12 × 17½".
Ruled pen-line around painted area.
Inscribed in pencil, top margin: "Olivares"; in ink "Le Brixa" "vol 2 p.5"; bottom margin, b.r., in pencil: "6".
Bought: London, Fine Art Society, 1948.

Though he travelled extensively in England, Wales, Scotland and perhaps Ireland, there is no definite evidence that Devis ever went abroad, except for his possible Italian tour with Assheton in 1783-4. There are, however, a few drawings by him of scenes in Italy and Spain. This is a fresh, well preserved example.

Two Devis drawings in the British Museum are comparable in style and may belong to the same series. One of these (1908-2-14-2) had an inscription, since removed: "Vol. 2nd. p.49. Verona". The other (1908-2-14-1) was inscribed: "Part of Granada in Spane vol 1. p.4. St. Helena Ye Great Tower & Church". It is not known to what work the page references allude, but they seem to be copies done from sketches by another hand, rather like Edward Dayes's improvements of the Scottish sketches of the antiquarian James Moore. Andrew Wilton (letter 18 Sept 1972) pointed out that the views are extremely generalised and do not argue any first-hand knowledge of the places. It was quite common for artists of this period to make views of places where they had never been. Paul Sandby's Irish views were all made from sketches done on the spot by the Hon. Mr Dawson, later Lord Portarlington. There are also Italian views by Sandby, who never visited Italy.

Another Devis drawing, *Alcantara in Andalusia*, blue and grey wash 9 × 12", was with Abbott and Holder, London, in February 1977 (list 169 no. 107). None of these drawings are listed in Pavière's catalogue (1950).

Bibliography:
Edwards, Redgrave, Binyon, Graves RA, Graves S of A, Williams, Hardie, Mallalieu.
Sydney H Pavière: *Biographical Notes on the Devis Family of Painters* Walpole Society XXV 1936-7 p 117.
Sydney H Pavière: *The Devis Family of Painters* 1950.
Preston, Harris Museum and Art Gallery: *Drawings by Anthony Devis* 1950.

9

JAMES FORRESTER
Born Dublin? 1730; died Rome 1776

Forrester, like Robert Crone, was an obscure Irish artist in the circle of Richard Wilson. In 1747 he was a pupil of Robert West in St George's Lane, Dublin, and won premiums from the Dublin Society in 1747 and 1750. In 1752 he won the first prize for drawing at the St George's Lane School and left for Italy soon after. He was first noted in Rome by Hayward in 1755. The *Stato delle Anime* of 1758 records him as living in the same house as Louis Gabriel Blanchet. He sent a large landscape to the Royal Academy in 1761, and three landscapes to the Society of Artists in Dublin in 1765. Forrester etched most of the plates in Peter Stephens's *One Hundred and Fifty Views in Italy*, first published in 1762. He was one of the artists criticised by Hackert for too closely imitating Claude and Gaspard Dughet. His recognised oeuvre is very small, including two large moonlight landscapes dated 1766, belonging to Earl Fitzwilliam, two drawings in the Victoria and Albert Museum and a drawing of *Ariccia* in Brinsley Ford's collection. Forrester remained in Rome until his death. There is a monument to him in Santa Maria del Popolo on which the epitaph describes him: "Pictor. Amoenioris. Picturae, Argutii, Clarus".

---

5. The Falls of Powerscourt. (no. 1037).

Pen, black lead, brown and grey washes, heightened with white, on buff laid paper
39.3 × 26.5 cms / 15½ × 10⅜".
Inscribed on original mount (partly cut away): "Powerscourt Ireland Co Carlow" (sic: Powerscourt is actually in Co Wicklow).

Bought: London, Colnaghi's 1971.

Provenance. Bonham's June 1952 (as Sandby); bought L G Duke; Duke collection D2753; sold Sotheby's 22 Oct 1970 (77) bought Colnaghi.

Exh. Colnaghi's Feb-March 1971 (19).

This drawing was incorrectly attributed to Paul Sandby when it entered L G Duke's collection in 1952, and later Iolo Williams suggested Forrester's authorship. Comparison with the two VAM drawings and with the Brinsley Ford drawing satisfied Duke that Williams's attribution was sound. Duke dated the drawing before Forrester's leaving of Ireland for Italy about 1752-5. Duke was liable to be optimistic over his attributions. In any case, this is an interesting mid 18th century drawing of an Irish scene.

Duke wrote in his manuscript catalogue: "The two drawings in the V&A and one belonging to Mr Brinsley Ford are unquestionably by the same hand and they display Forrester's Italianate manner.

"My drawing is not at first sight by the same hand, but a very careful comparison with the drawing of a waterfall in the V&A gives plenty of grounds for supposing that my drawing is in Forrester's Irish and pre-Italianate manner. Points to note are: (a) Closely similar treatment of the ground in the foreground. (b) Similar touch in the cliffs in both drawings. (c) Both drawings heightened with white, though my drawing is the more faded. (d) Identical borders - clearly the artist's own mounts. (e) The cut inscription on my mount may be in the same hand as the name Forrester on the V&A mount. My own conclusion, which Mr Jonathan Mayne of the V&A considers to be probably correct, is that both drawings are by the same hand, - one pre-Italianate and the other Italianate. A similar change in style is noticeable in the drawings of Jonathan Skelton, who spent only the last five years of his life in Italy."

The waterfall, the highest in the British Isles, in the demesne at Powerscourt was evidently an object of sublime or picturesque interest at this date, and was one of the sights of the "Wicklow Tour" which could be made by carriage from Dublin. Though less ambitious, this drawing has some of the feeling of the large watercolours of Downton Castle Park painted later in the century by Thomas Hearne for Richard Payne Knight. It is feasible that the young and talented Forrester could have come to the notice of Viscount Powerscourt, who then may have commissioned him to make drawings of his Park. The absence of any comparable Irish material known to be by Forrester makes it impossible to reach a definite conclusion.

Bibliography:
Strickland, Williams, Mallalieu, VAM.
L G Duke: manuscript records in possession of Dudley Snelgrove (photocopies in Ulster Museum files).
Brinsley Ford: *The letters of Jonathan Skelton* Walpole Society XXXVI 1956-8 p 59.
London, Kenwood House: *British Artists in Rome 1700-1800* June-Aug 1974 (119).

11

JOHN HENRY FUSELI
Born Johann Heinrich Füssli, Zurich 1741; died London 1825

The Swiss-born Fuseli was the second son of Johann Caspar Füssli, painter and collector, who forced him to study for the Zwinglian ministry. Accordingly he studied theology with the anglophile Professor J J Bodmer, and was ordained, along with his friend the physiognomist Johann Caspar Lavater. Both had to flee the country after denouncing a corrupt magistrate. Fuseli was expelled from holy orders and worked for a time in Berlin as a translator. In this capacity he came to England in 1764, taught himself English by watching plays at Drury Lane, and published the first English translation of Winckelmann. In 1768 he met Reynolds who encouraged him to study art. The banker Thomas Coutts paid for him to go to Italy.

He studied in Rome 1770-78 under Anton Raffael Mengs, and was the centre of an international group of artists including Sergel, Banks, Runciman, Abildgaard, Romney, Northcote and John Brown. He then briefly revisited Zurich and returned to London, where he was elected ARA in 1788, RA in 1790, Professor of Painting at the Royal Academy 1799-1805 and 1810, and Keeper of the Royal Academy Schools from 1804 to his death. Fuseli was a linguist, an art-historian and a formidable intellectual, frequenting the circles of Blake, William Roscoe, William Godwin and Mary Wollstonecraft. He died in the Countess of Guildford's house at Putney Heath, and is buried in St Paul's Cathedral.

---

6. *Woman at a Dressing Table.* (no. 788).

Pen, grey wash, watercolour and white over pencil on white laid paper.
22.2 × 17.6 cms / 8¾ × 7".
Inscribed on verso: "F. est au desespoir de ne pouvoir pas ["pre" crossed out] terminer un dessin plus digne du Portef[euil] de Mr. la P que ceux qu'il a eu l'honneur de lui transmettre ajant [sic] à se rendre ["aujourd'hui" crossed out] tout de suite à la maison de Campaigne d'un ami et de partir de là immediatement pour la France".

Given by James F Johnston 1896.

Exh Zurich, Schweizerisches Institut für Kunstwissenschaft 1958-9.

Ref Schiff 1958 no. 29.

Schiff: *Oeuvrekatalog* no. 1097 as *Mrs Fuseli am Toilettentisch*.

The Ulster Museum has ten drawings by Fuseli, all of which were given in 1896 by Johnston, a former curator. Five of these have been identified by Schiff as portraits of Fuseli's wife, Sophia Rawlins of Bath-Easton, whom he married on 30 July 1788, when she was 18 and he 47. She outlived him. Schiff writes: "during the first ten years of his marriage (1790-1800) he drew many portraits of his wife. From these we can trace her gradual transition from the lovely young wife to a domineering virago, as well as the changing hair fashions of the time". (*Fuseli, Lucifer and the Medusa* essay in Hamburg/London/Paris catalogue 1974 p 15.

This drawing is dated 1792 by Schiff, and the French inscription on the back is cited as perhaps the only proof of a journey to France made by Fuseli in 1792, in the company of the radical bookseller Joseph Johnson (see note on no. 10) and Mary Wollstonecraft, to see the effects of the French Revolution.

Bibliography:
DNB, Cundall, Binyon, Williams, VAM, RA 1934, Redgrave Dict, Redgrave Cent, Hardie, Mallalieu.
Henry Fuseli: *Lectures on Painting* 1801 and later editions.
John Knowles: *Life and Writings of John Henry Fuseli* 1831.
J Timbs: *Anecdote Biography* 1862.
Paul Ganz: *Die Zeichnungen Hans Heinrich Füsslis* Zurich 1949.
Nicholas Powell: *The Drawings of Henry Fuseli* 1951.
Frederick Antal: *Fuseli Studies* 1956.
Gert Schiff: *Zeichnungen von Johann Heinrich Füssli* Zurich 1959.
Hugh Macandrew: *Henry Fuseli and William Roscoe* Liverpool Bulletin 8, 1959-60.
W R Jeudwine: *Some Unpublished Drawings by Henry Fuseli* Apollo LXX 1959 p 180.
Gert Schiff: *Johann Heinrich Füsslis Milton-Galerie* Zurich 1963.
Fuseli e Milton Sele Arte 12, March-April 1964 pp 20-22.
Auckland, New Zealand, City Art Gallery: *A Collection of Drawings by Henry Fuseli* 1967.
A Fuseli Find (the Dunedin Fuselis) the Connoisseur CLXVIII 1968.
Zurich, Kunsthaus: *Johann Heinrich Füssli Gemälde und Zeichnungen* May-July 1969.
Review of Zurich Exhibition: Burlington Magazine CXI 1969.

Peter Tomory: *The Life and Art of Henry Fuseli* 1972.
Gert Schiff: *Johann Heinrich Füssli Oeuvrekatalog* 2 vols
  Zurich 1973.
Hamburg, Kunsthalle; London, Tate Gallery; and Paris,
  Petit Palais: *Fuseli* 1974–5.
New Haven, Yale Center for British Art: *The Fuseli Circle
  in Rome* catalogue by Nancy L Pressly 1979.

7. *Mrs Fuseli in a Red Cap*. 1794. (no. 791).

Watercolour with white chalk over pencil on white
wove paper
34.3 × 21.3 cms / 13½ × 8¾".
Dated on shawl "Aug 94".
On verso, faint pencil sketches of women.

Given by James F Johnston 1896.

Exh Zurich, Schweizerisches Institut für Kunstwissenschaft
1958-9.
Zurich 1969 (209).
Hamburg, London, Paris 1974-5 (5).

Ref Schiff 1958 no. 30.
Jeudwine 1959 p 80.
Tomory 1972 pl 203.
Schiff: *Oeuvrekatalog* 1973 no. 1099.

Schiff identified this portrait as Fuseli's wife (see note on no. 6). It is perhaps the most striking portrait drawing in the group. The curls of powdered hair are picked out in white chalk.

8. *Milton when a boy, instructed by his mother.* (no. 793).

Pen, sepia and grey wash over pencil on white laid paper
43 × 30.4 cms / 17 × 12″.
Watermark: "J WHATMAN".

Given by James F Johnston 1896.

Exh Zurich, Schweizerisches Institut für Kunstwissenschaft 1958-9.

Ref Schiff 1958 no. 26.
Schiff: *Miltongalerie* 1963.
Sele Arte March-April 1964 p 20.
Macandrew 1959-60.
Schiff: *Oeuvrekatalog* 1973 no. 1031.

This is dated by Schiff c 1796-8 (letter 18 July 1958). A drawing in the Fitzwilliam Museum, Cambridge (Ricketts and Shannon Bequest 2161) shows the same model. Schiff, *Oeuvrekatalog* no. 1031, points out a resemblance between Milton's mother and a drawing of Mrs Fuseli in the Hornby Library, Liverpool (*Oeuvrekatalog* no. 1110).

There were apparently at least three oil versions of this subject. One was in Fuseli's *Milton Gallery*, no. 38, and later belonged to his friend Sir Francis Burdett; Burdett-Coutts sale, Christie's 4 May 1922 (22) as "Milton being taught to read by his mother. Under an archway the mother is seen caressing her son and holding a book" (55 × 45½″) bought Chapman 40 guineas. This version is now in the Hotel Euler, Basle (Schiff: *Oeuvrekatalog* no. 916).

A picture 50 × 40″, which was claimed to be the *Milton Gallery* version was sold at Sotheby's 5 Dec 1928 (155), property of Mrs Aubrey le Blond. Another version, 36⅛ × 28½″, was painted by Fuseli for the Liverpool banker William Roscoe, and was sent to Liverpool in November 1800 along with a pendant entitled *Return of Milton's Wife, pleading and imploring his pardon*. Presumably Roscoe passed both to his seventh son Henry (1799-1836); they were given to the Walker Art Gallery, Liverpool, in 1914 by Henry's son Sir Henry Enfield Roscoe FRS (1833-1915) (Schiff: *Oeuvrekatalog* no. 917).

A stipple engraving by J Perry in the British Museum seems to stand midway between the Liverpool painting and this Belfast drawing. It is square-headed, the child crosses his right leg over his left, the mother wears a bow on the front of her head and does not wear bracelets; there is also a window in the background which is different from that in the Liverpool painting. The engraving may therefore be after a lost *Milton Gallery* version. The picture may also have been engraved by Moses Haughton.

9. *Two women with fans, walking in a garden.* (no. 792).

Pencil, sepia wash, watercolour and white on white
laid paper
38.1 × 24.5 cms / 15 × 9⅝″.
On verso, four pencil sketches of women.
Watermark "J Larking 1796".
Inscribed b.l. "MEAΔOWC" (Greek delta for D).

Dated b.r. "Aug. 95".

Given by James F Johnston 1896.

Exh Zurich, Schweizerisches Institut für Kunstwissenschaft
1958-9.

Ref Schiff 1958 no. 31.
Jeudwine 1959 p 180.
Schiff: *Oeuvrekatalog* 1973 no. 1067, dated 1795.

In 1958 Schiff dated this drawing c 1796–1800, and since the inscribed date predates the watermark by one year, he suggested that this must have been added by a later hand.

The proportions of the figures and the long lines show Fuseli's debt to the Italian mannerists. The diaphanous draperies of the distant woman are sexually explicit.

10. *Three courtesans with extravagant hairstyles.* 1807. (no. 787).

Watercolour and bodycolour over pencil on white paper
Irregular, 22.1 × 18.1 cms / 8¾ × 7⅛".
Watermark "M.J.L. 1806" under Prince of Wales' feathers.
Dated "June 07".
Inscribed on recto: "Scala Coeli" "Mrs F.M."

The drawing is on a used envelope, hence the address and postmarks on the verso: "Mr Johnson St Paul's Churchyard".
Stamped twice with postmarks: "8 o'clock morn. 16 My. 1807".
Inscribed twice on verso "Neurotics".
The foldmarks of the envelope are visible, and a section missing on the right hand side still adheres to the back of the paper.
Given by James F Johnston 1896.

Exh Zurich: Schweizerisches Institut für Kunstwissenschaft 1958-9.
Zurich 1969 (269).

Ref Schiff 1958 no. 40.
Gert Schiff: *Füssli, Puritain et Satanique* l'Oeuil LXIII March 1960 p 24.
Schiff: *Oeuvrekatalog* 1973 no. 1446.

Schiff *Oeuvrekatalog* p 344 cites this as an example of one of Fuseli's mild obsessions, hair-fetishism. One of the ladies is identified as "Mrs F.M." As to the hairstyles, Schiff writes: "Eine von diesen Frisuren ist reichtes, perlendurchwirktes Rokoko, eine andere hat grotesk-phallischen Charakter".

The address on the envelope is that of Joseph Johnson (see also note on no. 6), a bookseller whose shop in St Paul's Churchyard was the centre of a circle of radical intellectuals with whom Fuseli was friendly from about 1780 onwards.

An aura of mystery surrounds James F Johnston, who gave the ten Fuseli drawings to the Ulster Museum in 1896. He was a painter who exhibited with the Ramblers' Sketching Club and the Belfast Art Society, sending local views in an impressionist style. Up to 1890 he kept an artists' materials shop in the Queens' Arcade. From 1890 to 1896 he was the curator of the newly-opened Art Gallery on the top floor of the Public Library in Royal Avenue. On 23 July 1896 reports appear in the Belfast papers of Johnston's disappearance while swimming at Helen's Bay, Co Down. Some boys found his clothes on the beach but dragging operations failed to discover his body. Johnston was no swimmer and it was assumed that he had taken a cramp and drowned. However, he re-appeared three months later, as the Belfast News-Letter of 23 October 1896 states: "The Librarian (Mr Elliott) announced that a former curator of the library, Mr J F Johnston, was anxious to present some of his pictures to the Art Gallery, and that the chairman and the deputy-chairman had inspected them, and had approved of the acceptance of a certain portion of them. The committee unanimously accepted the gift, and desired that their acknowledgements should be tendered to Mr Johnston". Johnston's gift also included the series of sketches by Edward Duncan (see no. 45).

JOHN FLAXMAN
Born York 1755; died London 1826

Arguably the greatest of the English neoclassical sculptors, and perhaps the only one with a European reputation, Flaxman was the son of a "modeller" of the same name. He was delicate as a boy, but later became sufficiently robust to take on the strenuous craft of sculpture. He exhibited at the Free Society of Artists from 1767 and entered the Royal Academy Schools in 1769. In 1770 he was exhibiting portraits in wax. Flaxman spent the years 1787-94 in Italy, mainly in Rome. His reputation was established with a marble group *The Fury of Athamas*, commissioned by the Earl-Bishop of Derry for his house at Ickworth, Suffolk. On his return to England, Flaxman was elected ARA in 1797 and RA in 1800. He was employed extensively as a designer by Wedgwood, and many of his designs for silver were executed by Paul Storr. In 1810 he was appointed Professor of Sculpture to the Royal Academy. Most of Flaxman's major works are church monuments. A large collection of his models and drawings is at University College, London.

---

11. *Swedenborgian subject?* (no. 779).

Brush-line, pen and grey wash on white paper
35 × 48.8 cms / 13¾ × 19⅛".
Spurious signature in pencil, b.l. "W. Blake".
Given by Mrs Edith M Wheeler, Thornhill Gardens, Marlborough Park, Belfast 1922 (697-1922).

This was given to the Museum as a drawing by William Blake, but was recognised as by Flaxman by Edward Croft-Murray of the British Museum, who saw it in 1971.

Dr David Bindman, Westfield College, London (letter 18 Dec 1984) dates this drawing sometime before Flaxman's journey to Italy in 1787. It seems to belong to a large group of subjects derived from the writings of the Swedish philosopher and mystic Emanuel Swedenborg (1688-1772), and apparently shows a man renouncing his worldly goods before being escorted to heaven by an angel. Only the upper half of the figure of the angel is modelled; the rest of the drawing is left in line only. The whole composition is contained in a lunette. The angel bears some similarity to the angel in Flaxman's monument to *Sarah Morley*, 1784, in Gloucester Cathedral, while the lunette composition using only two figures is seen in his monument to *Mary Lushington*, 1799, in Lewisham Church (rep. Whinney 1964 pl 145). The two supporting angels resemble the hovering angels on the right of Flaxman's large drawing *Get Thee Behind Me, Satan*, brush-line and grey wash, in the Yale Center for British Art (B1977-14-6/68).

Two drawings with comparable subjects are in the Fitzwilliam Museum, Cambridge: *A Soul appearing before the Judges in Hades* and *The Ascent of a Soul into Heaven*, both pen and wash, c 1783. Both are in the Hamburg catalogue, 1979. The Heim Gallery catalogue, 1976, contains other examples (nos 35-39).

David Irwin, 1979, devotes pp 116-18 to a discussion of Flaxman's interest in Swedenborg. The Swedish savant never intended to found a church of his own, but believed that his mystical teachings could be absorbed by all Christian denominations. It was only after his death in 1772 that the Swedenborgian or "New Church" developed. In 1784 Flaxman joined the Theosophical Society, then newly established for the purpose of translating, publishing and promoting Swedenborg's writings. He attended its meetings in the Middle Temple, and in the same year lent some of Swedenborg's books to William Hayley, the biographer of Cowper and friend of Blake. But though Flaxman was sympathetic to the aims of the New Church (founded while he was away in Italy) he was never a member, remaining a devout Anglican all his life. He drew some illustrations to Swedenborg's *Arcana Coelestia* and *Christian Religion*. The library of the Swedenborgian Society in London still has Flaxman's own copy of the first edition of the *Arcana* (1749), and a volume of treatises and indexes to Swedenborg which belonged to him.

A contrary view of Swedenborg's influence on Flaxman is given in an essay by H W Janson on *Thorwaldsen and England* in *Thorwaldsen: Untersuchungen zu seinem Werk und zur Kunst seiner Zeit*, edited by G Bott, Cologne 1977, p. 11.

Bibliography:
Cunningham, DNB, Binyon, Gunnis, Williams, VAM, Redgrave, RA 1934, Hardie.
John Flaxman: *Lectures on Sculpture* 1829.
The Drawings of John Flaxman in University College Gallery 1876.
The Classical Compositions of John Flaxman 1879.
W G Constable: *John Flaxman 1755-1826* 1927.

Margaret Whinney: *Flaxman and the Eighteenth Century* Journal of the Warburg and Courtauld Institutes 1956 pp 269-82.

David Irwin: *Flaxman: Italian Journals and Correspondence* Burlington Magazine June 1959 pp 212-17.

Iolo A Williams: *An Identification of some early drawings by John Flaxman* Burlington Magazine June 1960 pp 246-50.

Margaret Whinney: *Sculpture in Britain 1530-1830* Harmondsworth 1964.

David Irwin: *English Neoclassical Art* 1966.

Margaret Whinney and Rupert Gunnis: *The Collection of Models by John Flaxman RA at University College* 1967.

Robert R Wark: *Drawings by John Flaxman in the Huntington Collection* San Marino, California 1970.

Sarah Symmons: *John Flaxman and Francisco Goya: Infernos Transcribed* Burlington Magazine Sept 1971 p. 822.

London, Royal Academy and VAM: *The Age of Neoclassicism* Council of Europe Exhibition 1972.

Norah Gillow: *Some Flaxman drawings at York* Preview (York Art Gallery Quarterly) XXVI April 1973.

Sarah Symmons: *French copies after Flaxman's outlines* Burlington Magazine Sept 1973 p. 591.

Homan Potterton: *Irish Church Monuments* Belfast 1975.

London, Heim Gallery: *John Flaxman* 1976.

Robert Essick and Jenijoy LaBelle: *Flaxman's Illustrations to Homer* New York 1977.

David Irwin: *John Flaxman 1755-1826. Sculptor, Illustrator, Designer* Trefoil Books (Zwemmer) 1979.

New Haven, Yale Center for British Art: *The Fuseli Circle in Rome* catalogue by Nancy L Pressly 1979.

Hamburg, Kunsthalle: *John Flaxman: Mythologie und Industrie: Kunst um 1800* exhibition arranged with the British Council, catalogue section by David Bindman et al., Prestel 1979.

G E Bentley Jr.: *Flaxman in Italy: a letter reflecting the Anni Mirabiles 1792–93* Art Bulletin LXIII no. 4, Dec 1981 p. 658.

MICHAEL "ANGELO" ROOKER
Born London 1743; died London 1801

Along with Thomas Hearne and the Sandbys, Rooker was one of the foremost topographical or antiquarian draughtsmen of 18th century England. He learnt engraving from his father Edward Rooker, and later attended the St Martin's Lane Academy. He then received some lessons from Paul Sandby, who gave him the nickname "Angelo". In 1769 he was a student in the Royal Academy Schools, and in 1770 was elected ARA. Rooker was a competent engraver, but abandoned it when his sight began to fail. For many years he was principal scene painter at the Haymarket Theatre. In 1778 he commenced a series of sketching tours throughout England. Rooker's work is among the most sophisticated and controlled of any English watercolourist.

---

12. *View in Hyde Park.* (no. 1647).

Watercolour on white paper
21.9 × 30.8 cms / 8¾ × 12⅛".
Signed b.r. "MRooker".

Bought: London, Palser Gallery 1937.

Ref Conner 1984, Appendix 3: *Check-list of Michael Angelo Rooker's drawings and watercolours in British public collections* p. 179.

Conner 1984 p. 103 says: "The London-based draughtsman was not restricted to street scenes or views of grand buildings. The lodges and cottages in Hyde Park were favourite sketching subjects in the late eighteenth century, for here, within half-an-hour's walk of Westminster or Charing Cross, were eminently Picturesque buildings in a rural setting".

Rooker, Hearne and Paul Sandby all painted watercolours of the Cake House in Hyde Park in 1797 and 1798 (see Conner 1984 pp 104-5). This view of a cottage or farm in Hyde Park shows an artist sitting sketching under a tree, and a coach travelling along one of the roadways. The setting appears completely rural as the Park had not yet been landscaped.

The Ulster Museum has another watercolour of a London park in the 18th century, Samuel Hieronymus Grimm's *St Paul's Cathedral from St George's Fields,* 1770 (no. 1644). This also shows details of traffic along the roadways in the park.

Bibliography:
Redgrave Dict, Redgrave Cent, DNB, Binyon, Cundall, Graves RA, Graves S of A, Williams, VAM, Windsor, RA 1934, Roget, Hughes, Nettlefold, Hardie, Mallalieu, Clarke, NGI.
Obituary: The Gentleman's Magazine May 1801 p. 480.
Joseph Farington: *Diary* edited by Kenneth Garlick and Andrew Macintyre, Yale University Press 1978.
MSS and typescript papers: British Museum, Department of Prints and Drawings 1964-12-12-3, items 1-16.
Sybil Rosenfeld: *A Georgian Scene-Painter at Work* British Museum Quarterly XXIV 1969 nos 1-2 pp 33-6.
Patrick Conner: *A View of the first St Mary's* Hornsey Historical Bulletin 23 1982 pp 10-11.
Patrick Conner: *Michael Angelo Rooker in East Anglia* OWCS LVII 1982 pp 48-52.
Patrick Conner: *Michael Angelo Rooker* Batsford and VAM 1984.

John Robert Cozens
Born London 1752; died London 1797

The son of Alexander Cozens (c 1717-86), John Robert Cozens is one of the greatest figures in English watercolour painting. He exhibited at the Incorporated Society of Artists in 1767 and the Royal Academy in 1776, but his main work was done on two continental tours, the first with Richard Payne Knight in 1776-9, and the second with William Beckford in 1782-3. He discovered a new style of poetic landscape in Switzerland and Italy. In 1794 Cozens became insane, and was befriended by Dr

Thomas Monro, the specialist in mental diseases who was also an amateur artist. The "Monro School" in which Girtin and Turner studied was largely engaged in copying Cozens's drawings. Constable considered him "all poetry, the greatest genius that ever touched landscape". Towards the end of his life Cozens may have visited the Lake District with his pupil Thomas Sunderland, but he suffered a relapse and died insane in the care of Dr Monro.

---

13. *Capo di Bove.* (no. 767).

Watercolour over pencil on white laid paper
31.2 × 28.1 cms / 12¼ × 11".
Figure "3" or "5" inscribed in pencil, t.l.
Mounted on thin card.
Inscribed on back of mount, c. "Capo di Bove"; in pencil, in a later hand, "J.R.Cozens".

Bought: London, Walker's Galleries 1938.

Ref Bell and Girtin 1935 p. 70.

The Mausoleum of Caecilia Metella, a well-known landmark on the Appian Way outside Rome, was known in the 18th century as the *Capo di Bove* (literally "ox-head") because of its frieze of ox-skulls and festoons.

Three J R Cozens drawings of this subject were in William Beckford's sale, Christie's 10 April 1805, and are listed by Bell and Girtin as follows:
"(A) 351. View of the Capo di Bove. Drawing 14¼ × 10¾"; Beckford (6) 'touched with great spirit'. Bt. Edridge £5.5.0.; coll. Frank W. Keen, sold Christie's 10 Nov 1933 (11) (Mausoleum in centre, on right a wall with doorway; to left walls of Rome and Campagna in distance).
(B) 352. Beckford (48) 'morning scene'; anonymous buyer £5.10.0.
(C) 353. Beckford (86) 'delicately finished'; bt. Hoare £3.15.0."
Bell's addendum (Walpole Society XXVII 1947 p. 10) amplifies the information on (B) and, as Evelyn Joll has pointed out (letter 7 March 1974), strongly suggests that this is the Ulster Museum drawing 767: "352". View of the Capo di Bove (B) (The Mausoleum of Caecilia Metella on the right surmounting a hanging mass of ruins and attached to a battlemented wall; trees and rough undergrowth in front, sunrise sky). Drawing (12¼ × 11") collection of Ernest R Innes Esq., Christie's 13 Dec 1935 (24).

This, as the title in the middle of the back shows, was the Beckford drawing. It is of an unusual shape and size, but may have been cut down."
These details agree with this watercolour which was bought from Walker's in 1938, and it can be concluded that it originated on Cozens's second visit to Italy in 1782-3 in the entourage of William Beckford. Joll adds: "The suggestion that the drawing may have been cut seems quite plausible in view of the slightly strange way that the composition tails off on the right-hand edge, but I would not like to say for certain".
Beckford left Cozens in Naples on 10 September 1782, where he remained, as Thomas Jones wrote in his *Memoirs*, "a free Agent and loosed from the Shackles of fantastic folly and Caprice". Beckford and the rest of his party travelled on to Rome, whence Cozens followed alone, arriving about 11 December. He remained in Rome until 15 September 1783, when he set off for England alone. He may have met Beckford again in Geneva to receive commissions based on the drawings he had made in his sketchbooks. The commissioned drawings, such as this, were worked on in Cozens's studio after his return to London. Beckford broke off relations with Cozens about the end of 1783, calling him "an ungrateful scoundrel" (Farington's *Diary* 17 June 1797). See also Boyd Alexander: *England's Wealthiest Son; a Study of William Beckford* London 1962.
Beckford's collection of Cozens drawings was sold at Christie's on 10 April 1805 as "a capital and truly valuable collection of original Highly Finished Drawings, the whole executed by that eminent Artist the younger Cozens, during a Tour through the Tyrol and Italy, in company with an amateur of distinguished taste". Though not one of Cozens's most spectacular Italian views, this is a good quiet

example of the atmosphere he could evoke using only a limited range of greys and blues. There is no corresponding drawing in the surviving seven "Beckford Sketchbooks" sold at Sotheby's in 1973.

Bibliography:
Edwards, Redgrave, DNB, Roget, Cundall, Graves RA, Graves S of A, Windsor, RA 1934, Nettlefold, Hardie, Williams, Mallalieu, NGI,
F Gibson: *Alexander and John Robert Cozens* the Studio 1917.
London, Burlington Fine Arts Club: *John Robert Cozens* catalogue by C F Bell, T Girtin and A P Oppé 1923 (the copy in the VAM Library has additional material).
C F Bell and T Girtin: *The drawings and sketches of John Robert Cozens* Walpole Society XXIII 1935; *Additions* XXVII 1947.
C F Bell: *Notes on sketchbooks of John Robert Cozens* unpublished typescript, VAM Library.
A P Oppé: *Alexander and John Robert Cozens* 1952 (the copy in the VAM Library has additional material by C F Bell).
Leeds Arts Calendar 8/27, Autumn 1954 p. 8.
Manchester, Whitworth Art Gallery, and London, VAM: *Watercolours by John Robert Cozens* catalogue by Francis Hawcroft 1971.
Christopher Neve: *Two journeys in monochrome: J R Cozens at the Whitworth* Country Life 11 March 1971.
London, Sotheby's: *Seven Sketchbooks of John Robert Cozens* (i.e. the Beckford Sketchbooks, then belonging to the Duke of Hamilton) sale catalogue with introduction by Anthony Blunt, 29 Nov 1973.
Anthony Blunt: *Recorders of vanished Naples: II. John Robert Cozens* Country Life 30 Aug 1973 p. 588.
Francis Hawcroft: *Grand Tour sketchbooks of John Robert Cozens 1782-83* Gazette des Beaux-Arts, March 1976.
Michael Clarke and Nicholas Penny, eds. : *The Arrogant Connoisseur: Richard Payne Knight* University of Manchester 1982.
New Haven, Yale Center for British Art: *The Art of Alexander and John Robert Cozens* catalogue by Andrew Wilton 1980.
Kim Sloane: *Alexander and John Robert Cozens: the poetry of landscape* Art Gallery of Ontario in association with Yale University Press 1986.

Thomas Rowlandson

Born Old Jewry, London 1756; died Adelphi, London 1827

The son of a bankrupt textile merchant, Rowlandson became a student at the Royal Academy Schools in 1771, and at the age of 16 was sent to some relations in Paris for two years. On his return he exhibited a biblical scene at the Royal Academy in 1775, and later some portraits and landscapes. During the 1780s and 1790s Rowlandson made many British and continental tours, sometimes accompanied by his friends Henry Wigstead and John Nixon. In 1789 he received a legacy from an aunt, which he is supposed to have gambled away, thus forcing himself to fall back on his talent for caricature, at which he was extremely prolific. Rowlandson produced many caricature etchings and illustrated *The Tours of Dr Syntax* and several other works for Ackermann including *The Microcosm of London*. Samuel Howitt was his brother-in-law.

---

14. *A tour in Flanders*. 1792. (no. 844).

Pen and watercolour on white laid paper
20.5 × 30.4 cms / 8 × 12".
Signed b.c. "Rowlandson 1792".

Bought: London, Fine Art Society 1935.

A drawing inscribed with the title *Posting in Germany*, 8⅞ × 12⅛", corresponding to this in all details except colouring, is in the Albert H Wiggin Collection in the Boston Public Library (rep. Heinzelmann 1947 p. 45).

These travelling scenes were among Rowlandson's favourite subjects, and must have recalled his formative years spent in France as well as his numerous continental tours. To English eyes popery (the image on the wall) and beggary (the figure on the left) must have epitomised travelling on the continent. A somewhat related drawing, *Travelling in Holland*, 7⅞ × 12⅛", showing two carriages full of people on a road passing a country house, was exhibited at the Leger Galleries in November 1967 (20). Another drawing of a related subject, *A Party of Travellers*, 20.1 × 30.5 cms, is in the Print Room of the Rijksmuseum, Amsterdam (rep. Burlington Magazine Feb 1980 pl 64). Yet another showing a coachload of travellers departing from an inn, *Travelling in France*, 11¼ × 17½, in the Paul Mellon Collection, is more ambitious. Riely 1978 (42) suggests a date about 1790-95 for this drawing, on the grounds of the thin sharp line and the naturalistic treatment of the foliage, which would make it roughly contemporary with the Ulster Museum drawing.

Bibliography:
Redgrave, Graves RA, Graves S of A, Graves Loan, Binyon, Hughes, VAM, Williams, Cundall, Windsor, RA 1934, Roget, Nettlefold, Hardie, Mallalieu, Clarke, NGI.

D Grego: *Rowlandson the Caricaturist* 1880.

A P Oppé: *Thomas Rowlandson Drawings and Watercolours* 1923.

Osbert Sitwell: *Thomas Rowlandson* 1929.

V P Sabin: *Catalogue of Watercolours by Thomas Rowlandson* 1933, 1948.

F Gordon Roe: *Rowlandson* 1947.

Adrian Bury: *Rowlandson's Drawings* 1949.

Bernard Falk: *Thomas Rowlandson: his life and art, a documentary record* 1949.

John Hayes: *Catalogue of Watercolours in the London Museum* 1960.

Arthur W Heinzelmann: *The Watercolour Drawings of Thomas Rowlandson in the Albert H Wiggin Collection in the Boston Public Library* New York 1947.

Thomas Rowlandson and some contemporary comic draughtsmen Leeds Arts Calendar Summer 1955 p 5

John Hayes: *Rowlandson Watercolours and Drawings* 1972.

Ronald Paulson: *Rowlandson: a new interpretation* 1972.

Robert R Wark: *Drawings by Thomas Rowlandson in the Huntington Collection* 1972.

John Baskett and Dudley Snelgrove: *The Drawings of Thomas Rowlandson in the Paul Mellon Collection* 1977.

New Haven, Yale Center for British Art, and London, Royal Academy: *Rowlandson Drawings from the Paul Mellon Collection* catalogue by John Riely 1978.

John Barrell: *The Private Comedy of Thomas Rowlandson* Art History vol 6 no. 4, Dec 1983 p 423.

29

JOHN NIXON
Born London? c 1750; died Ryde, Isle of Wight 1818

Nixon was one of the best amateur draughtsmen and caricaturists of the late 18th century. He was a son of Robert Nixon of Uphall near Linlithgow and Tokenhouse Yard, London, a merchant who traded with Ireland, and whose business John inherited along with his brother Richard. John Nixon was living in Bow Church Yard in 1777, in Cateaton Street in 1792 and at 5 Basinghall Street, with his brother Richard, from 1798 until his death. There is a photograph of a lost watercolour of *Belfast from Friar's Bush Graveyard*, of about 1781, in the R J Welch collection in the Ulster Museum, and Nixon visited Ireland nearly every year between 1785 and 1798. In 1791 he accompanied the antiquarian Francis Grose. In 1792 he visited Bath with Rowlandson, under whose influence Nixon became a very competent draughtsman. Henry Angelo says "he could sketch a portrait, with a few scratches of his pencil, of a party whom he had not seen for twenty years, but with such marked traits of resemblance, as to be known at a glance". Nixon's travels elsewhere were wide: he went to St Omer in 1783, to the Netherlands in 1784, to Scotland in 1790 and perhaps 1791, and visited Paris during the break in the Napoleonic Wars in 1802-4. He also made annual tours in the south of England. He was a special juryman at the Guildhall and a Captain in the Guildhall Volunteers, was treasurer of the Sublime Society of Beefsteaks, and socialised with (and caricatured) actors and musicians. He was a member of the circle of the Margravine of Anspach (Lady Craven), and often acted in her amateur theatricals. He died on the Isle of Wight in the spring of 1818, and his death is recorded in the *Gentleman's Magazine* for May of that year.

His other brother, the Rev Robert Nixon (1759-1837) was rector of Foot's Cray, Kent, and an accomplished amateur watercolourist and etcher, the father of the Rev Francis Russell Nixon (1803-79), first Bishop of Tasmania and another able amateur watercolourist.

About 1973 Christie's in London obtained a very large collection of John Nixon drawings from the Huguenot Hospital of La Providence, now in Rochester, Kent, and they appeared in sales for some years.

---

15. *Magilligan Mountain, Co Londonderry*. 1791. (no. 2562).

Grey wash and watercolour on white paper
19.7 × 28.6 cms / 7⅞ × 11¼".
Inscribed in ink, b. "JN 1791 / Magilligan Mountain with the Town of Newtown Limavady. Co.Antrim [sic], from Mr Domenick McCausland's garden".
Inscribed on verso, on false margin "45".

Bought: London, Hartley Fine Art 1980.

What Nixon calls Magilligan Mountain is more generally known as Benevenagh, forming the north-western edge of the basalt plateau, and from the foot of which Magilligan Point extends towards the Donegal side of Lough Foyle. The hills of Inishowen can be seen in the distance across Lough Foyle, and the town of Limavady nestles at the foot of the mountain. This view must be looking due north from Roe Park. Two fashionably dressed ladies walk in the garden. Roe Park, originally called Daisy Hill, a house built early in the 18th century by William Connolly, Speaker of the Irish House of Commons, was acquired later in the century by the local landowning family of McCausland. Marcus McCausland made additions to the house, and his son Dominick, whose name appears on this watercolour, added a dining room after 1782. The house is now an old peoples' home. See Mark Bence-Jones: *Burke's Guide to Country Houses: volume 1, Ireland* 1978 p. 245. The McCauslands also owned nearby Drenagh.

The Ulster Museum has another Roe Valley view painted by Nixon in the same year, 1791, *The Glin, near Newtown-Limavady* (no. 2581).

The Ulster Museum's Department of Art has seven watercolours by Nixon, and the Department of Local History has thirteen more. Nixon does not appear to have visited Ireland after 1798, when possibly the United Irishmen's Rebellion deterred him from coming again.

Bibliography:
Redgrave, DNB, Graves RA, Cundall, Strickland, VAM, Elmes, Binyon, Williams, Hardie, Mallalieu, Hewitt, P of I.
Thomas Pennant: *Journey from London to the Isle of Wight* 1801 (illustrations after Nixon).

maccillisan. Mountain with the Town of Newton Limwady. C. antrim, from Mr Dominick McCausland's garden.

Henry Angelo: *Reminiscences* 1830.
London, Christie's: *Original Drawings and Sketches by John Nixon (part 1) sold by order of the Governor and Directors of the French Hospital of La Providence* sale catalogue with introduction, Tues 6 Nov 1973.
Huon Mallalieu: *John Nixon and his Circle* Country Life 12 May 1977 p. 1260.

FRANCIS TOWNE
Born Exeter? c 1740; died London 1816

Celebrated during his lifetime, forgotten at his death, rediscovered by A P Oppé in the 20th century, Towne is now one of the most admired figures in English watercolour painting. Traditionally he is believed to have been born in Exeter, though there is no record of him or his parents in any of the church registers there. He appears to have gone to London early to study with the painter John Shackleton (according to Farington) and at Shipley's School, and he won a prize at the Society of Arts in 1757. He exhibited landscapes between 1752 and 1815 at the Incorporated Society of Artists, the Free Society of Artists, the Royal Academy and the British Institution. In 1780 he went to Italy, where he met with John "Warwick" Smith, whose work was then close to his in style. They returned to England via Switzerland in 1781, and in Switzerland Towne painted his most original watercolours, notably *The Source of the Arveiron* (VAM), in which mountain scenery is expressed through an idiosyncratic style of pen-lines and flat washes. Towne toured the lake district in 1786 with his Exeter friends John Merivale and John White (uncle of John White Abbott, Towne's most talented amateur pupil). Towne was also friendly with William Pars, Richard Cosway and Ozias Humphrey. He worked in Exeter on and off for about fifty years. In 1800, at the age of about 60, he married a young French dancer named Jeannette Hilligsberg, who died in 1808 and is buried in Heavitree Churchyard, Exeter. From 1807 Towne lived in London and died there. He was buried in Heavitree Churchyard.

---

16. Trees and Rocks, Ambleside. (no. 864).

Pen and ink and watercolour on white laid paper
26.9 × 37.9 cms / 10⅝ × 14⅞".
Inscribed on verso: (in ink, large letters) "Louisa"; (in pencil, much smaller neat hand, upside-down to the drawing) "Light from the Right Hand".

Bought: London, Fine Art Society 1936.

This appears to be from a series of about 40 drawings, mostly based on sketches in Towne's *Sketchbook of the Lakes*, which belonged to the Misses Merivale (see Oppé 1920 p. 120 n). The sketches were made on his tour of the Lake District in 1786. Towne sold few of the finished drawings in his lifetime, and most passed into the Buckingham, Merivale and Solly collections. "Louisa" may refer to Louisa Heath Drury, who in 1803 married Towne's pupil John Herman Merivale (1779-1844). His father John Merivale (1752-1831) was Towne's main patron and accompanied him on his tour of the Lake District in 1786.

Other drawings from the series include a double-page *View at Ambleside*, 6⅛ × 18⅝", dated 1786 (Tate Gallery T1019, Herbert Powell bequest 1967); an upright watercolour of a *Waterfall near Ambleside* 1786, belonging to D L T Oppé and Miss Armide Oppé (rep. Bury 1961 pl VIII); two drawings of views in Cumberland, numbered 33 and 34, sold at Sotheby's 10 Dec 1958 (77, 78); and *Ambleside*, 6⅛ × 9¼" (Bristol City Art Gallery). The Bristol drawing is also inscribed with light directions: "No. 22 / Evening light from the right hand 7 o'clock / Ambleside taken behind the Inn (?) head of the Lake of Windermere, Westmoreland / drawn on the spot by Francis Towne / August 14th 1786 / London / Leicester Square / July..."(information from Miquette Livingstone, Bristol City Art Gallery, letter 19 Aug 1971).

A number of the Lake District drawings are now in the Yale Center for British Art. These include *View in Borrowdale of Eagle Crag and Rosthwaite*, an extensive view in which the trees are close in style to the Ulster Museum drawing; *Ambleside*, a small upright drawing with a delicacy almost like John White Abbott; another small delicate drawing *Near Ambleside*, signed b.l. "F Towne delt 1786 no. 4"; a small *Windermere at Sunset 1786 no. 29*; two double-page landscapes of *Lake Windermere 1786* and *View of Lake Coniston 1786*; and some more small drawings, very blue in colour, *The Grange at the Head of Keswick Lake 1786* and *The Entrance into Borrowdale 1786*.

Bibliography:
Redgrave, Graves RA, Graves S of A, Graves BI, Cundall, Binyon, VAM, DNB, RA 1934, Hughes, Nettlefold, Williams, Hardie, Mallalieu, Clarke.
A P Oppé: *Francis Towne: landscape painter* Walpole Society VIII 1920.
London, Burlington Fine Arts Club: *Catalogue of paintings and drawings by Francis Towne* 1929-30 (typescript in VAM Library).
Martin Hardie: *Francis Towne* Collector XI 1930.
Leeds Arts Calendar: *Drawings by Francis Towne* Summer 1954 p. 8.
Adrian Bury: *Francis Towne c 1739-1816)* OWCS XXVI 1961 p. 11.

Adrian Bury: *Francis Towne: lone star of watercolour painting*
   Charles Skilton 1962.
Exeter, Royal Albert Memorial Museum and Art Gallery:
   Francis Towne and John White Abbott 1971.
London, Marble Hill House: *Francis Towne, John White
   Abbott: paintings and watercolours from the Exeter Museums
   and Art Gallery* 1973.

JOHN WHITE ABBOTT
Born Exeter 1763; died Exeter 1851

The best amateur pupil of Francis Towne, Abbott practiced as a surgeon in Exeter. He was taken to London by his uncle, James White, and was introduced to Reynolds, Sir George Beaumont, Benjamin West and others. He exhibited at the Royal Academy 1794–1821. His only recorded trip away from the south of England was a visit to Scotland and the Lake District in 1791. In 1831 he was appointed Deputy Lieutenant for the county of Devon. Abbott never travelled abroad and never sold his own pictures.

17. Peamore Park, near Exeter. 1793. (no. 735).

Pen and watercolour on white wove paper, two sheets joined vertically down centre.
18.1 × 22 cms / 7⅛ × 8¾"
Signed in pencil b.l. "Abbott" (according to L G Duke, "not in the artist's hand").
Inscribed on verso t.l., in Abbott's hand, "Peamore, Sepr. 9. 1793".
Circumscribing line in black ink around extreme edge. Viewed from the back, the verso of the left-hand sheet has a fragment of foliage from another drawing which has been cut off by joining to the other sheet.

Provenance Bernard Squire; bought L G Duke Oct 1922, £4.10.0.; Duke Collection (165); bought H C Green 1945, £10. ; Fine Art Society.

Bought: London, Fine Art Society 1955.

L G Duke's manuscript catalogue of his collection is now in the possession of Dudley Snelgrove and Mrs Judy Egerton; a photocopy is in the British Museum. Duke noted in March 1942 "I see that Agnew's are now asking 10 guineas for a similar drawing by Abbott" (Judy Egerton: letter 9 Sept 1971). See also Judy Egerton: *L G Duke and his collection of English drawings* OWCS XLIX 1974 p. 11.

Abbott made many drawings in Peamore Park. This is a good example of his use of economical means to create an effect of sunlight through a wood. Note the man carrying a scythe, approaching along the path in the middle distance.

The drawing attributed to James Forrester (5) also came from Duke's collection.

Bibliography:
Redgrave, Graves RA, Binyon, Williams, Hardie, VAM, Mallalieu, Clarke.
A P Oppé: *John White Abbott of Exeter* OWCS XIII 1925.
Exeter, Royal Albert Memorial Museum and Art Gallery: *Paintings and Drawings by Francis Towne and John White Abbott* 1971.
London, Marble Hill House: *Francis Towne, John White Abbott: paintings and watercolours from the Exeter Museums and Art Gallery* 1973.

FRANCIS WHEATLEY
Born London 1747; died London 1801

Wheatley studied at Shipley's School and first exhibited at the Incorporated Society of Artists, entering the Royal Academy Schools in 1769. He was friendly with the dissolute John Hamilton Mortimer and sometimes copied his work. In 1779 he caused a scandal by eloping to Dublin with the wife of the drawing master John Alexander Gresse. There he painted some large group portraits, notably *The Volunteers in College Green* (NGI), but by 1783 or 84 he was discovered and was made to return to England. He became a director of the Incorporated Society in 1772, and was elected ARA in 1790 and RA in 1791. His specialities were small full-length portraits and genre scenes in oil, which have a Morland-like prettiness. The series of engravings *The Cries of London*, often reprinted, are probably his best-known work. Wheatley married Clara Maria Leigh, later Mrs Pope, whom he used as a model. Engravings after Wheatley are found in Francis Grose's *Antiquities of Ireland* 1791-95, and in Thomas Milton's *Views of Irish Seats* 1794.

---

18. *The Belfry Tower, Furness Abbey, Lancashire.* 1798. (no. 2439).

Watercolour over pencil on white wove paper
38.3 × 48 cms / 15⅛ × 18⅞″.
Signed b.r. "Francis Wheatley delt. 1798".

Bought: London, Christie's 14 June 1977 (83).

Provenance Mrs I J Dunne 1950; with M Bernard 1969.

Rep (colour) Adrian Bury: *Two Centuries of British Water-Colour Painting* 1950, as *Lakeland Scene*. Also. OWCS XXVIII 1950 pl II (reproduced from Bury 1950). Webster 1970 p. 95 fig 135 (colour).

This was bought at Christie's entitled *Figures near a Ruined Abbey on the Banks of a River*. The distinctive red sandstone arch covered with ball-flowers and flanked by buttresses with niches evidently belongs to the 14th century detached bell-tower of Furness Abbey. A pencil and watercolour sketch by Henry Edridge, *The Belfry Tower, Furness Abbey*, 13 × 19⅛″, dated "Sepr.9 1814", which was in Spink's annual exhibition, April-May 1984 (72), shows the tower from much the same angle.

Wheatley's watercolour *A Travelling Potter with his Wares outside a Cottage* in the Yale Center for British Art, 15⅜ × 19¼″, is also signed and dated b.r. "F. Wheatley delt. 1798". (Rep. Scott Wilcox: *British Watercolors: Drawings of the 18th and 19th centuries from*

the Yale Center for British Art New York, Hudson Hills Press 1985, no. 25).

It is very close to the Ulster Museum picture in handling, composition, and in the group of figures, and may even depict the same river. A church tower in the distance resembles Huby's Tower at Fountains Abbey, Yorkshire. It is possible that the watercolours are pendants representing fancy views of ruined abbeys in composed settings.

Bibliography:
Redgrave Dict, Redgrave Cent, Roget, Graves RA, Strickland, DNB, Cundall, VAM, RA 1934, Binyon, Williams, Waterhouse, Hardie, Mallalieu, NGI.
The Connoisseur, extra number 1910.
W Roberts: *The Cries of London* 1924.
F Gordon Roe: *A Sketch Portrait of Francis Wheatley* 1938.
Ross Watson: *Francis Wheatley in Ireland* Irish Georgian Society vol IX no. 2 1966 p. 35.
Mary Webster: *Francis Wheatley* 1970.
Mary Webster: *Francis Wheatley's Review in Belan Park* Apollo Oct 1985 p. 275.

JOHN JAMES BARRALET
Born Dublin c 1747; died Philadelphia 1815

Barralet was of Dublin Huguenot stock, the elder brother of John Melchior Barralet (c 1750-c 1787). He was trained at the Dublin Society's School of Art and became a drawing master in Dublin, going to London about 1770. He set up a drawing school in James's Street, Golden Square, in 1773, and opened another in St Alban's Street, Pall Mall, in 1777. He exhibited at the Royal Academy and the Society of Artists between 1770 and 1780. Barralet returned to Dublin in 1779, and accompanied Gabriel Beranger on tours making antiquarian sketches for Francis Grose in Wicklow and Wexford in 1780. In 1782 he was a scene painter at the Crow Street Theatre in Dublin. Emigrating to America in 1795, he settled in Philadelphia, where Redgrave states "though at first a great beau, he is said to have fallen into slovenly habits". Iolo Williams's description of him as "an inept and heavy handed, if ambitious artist" seems to be challenged by the drawings in the Ulster Museum, which Williams did not know about.

---

19. *Glenarm River and Bridge, looking towards the sea.* (no. 2600).

Sepia wash on white laid paper
37.2 × 49.8 cms / 14½ × 19⅝".

Bought: Belfast, John Gamble 1982.

Glenarm is an attractive village on the coast of Co Antrim; its Castle being the principal seat of the McDonnels, Earls of Antrim. The Mull of Kintyre in Scotland can be dimly discerned on the horizon through the bridge. This is presumably the bridge carrying the road rather than the private bridge leading into the Castle grounds. This drawing would have been made thirty years before the baronialisation of Glenarm Castle and grounds by William Vitruvius Morrison in the 1820s.

This is from a group of eight very interesting drawings of Glenarm and its vicinity. One of them is inscribed "Marchioness of Antrim's Cottage / Glenarm Deer Park". The Marquessate of Antrim became extinct on the death of the 6th Earl and 2nd Marquess on 29 July 1791. His widow, the Marchioness, lived on until 1801. The drawings were in a paper folder inscribed "Views of - from - or near / Glenarm - in 1787-88-89 - / Mostly by Mr Barrales [sic] / artist and drawing master". Some appear to be by Barralet's pupils - perhaps the family of the Marquess of Antrim (two are dated 1796, a year after Barralet had emigrated to America), but four of them are of much higher quality, including this one. If the inscription on the folder can be trusted, and the drawings date from the late 1780s, they can be seen as a distinct improvement on earlier dated drawings by him. A *View of Lucan House, Co Dublin*, dated 1782 (Yale Center for British Art), is a small finicky drawing in blues and browns, similar in technique to Sampson Toogood Roche. Two views in pen and grey wash of *Ledbury Church and Village, Herefordshire* and *Landscape with Ledbury Church Spire* (also Yale Center for British Art) are much weaker than the Glenarm drawings and would seem to be much earlier, before 1779 when he returned to Ireland.

Bibliography:
Redgrave, Graves RA, Graves S of A, Cundall, Williams, Strickland, Elmes, VAM, Hardie, Mallalieu, P of I.
Francis Grose: *The Antiquities of Ireland* 1791-5.

HORACE HONE
Born London 1754/6; died London 1825

Horace Hone was the second son of the portrait painter Nathaniel Hone RA, and was taught by his father. At the age of 17 he was placed in the Royal Academy Schools. He exhibited at the Royal Academy 1772-1822 and was elected ARA in 1779. In 1782 he set up practice as a miniature painter in his father's native Dublin, and lived in Dorset Street. His practice there was successful and in 1795 he became Miniature Painter to the Prince of Wales. After the Act of Union of 1800 his Dublin practice declined, and in 1804 he returned to London and worked also in Bath the same year. From 1807 Hone suffered from mental illness. He died at 20 Dover Street and is buried at St George's Chapel, Bayswater Road. Most of his miniatures are in watercolour on ivory.

---

20. *Portrait of Major Holt Waring.* 1796. (no. 1885).

Watercolour and bodycolour, with gum arabic, over pencil on white paper
11.1 × 9 cms / 4⅜ × 3½″.
Inscribed on back of mount: "*Major Waring* / Drawn by HHone [2 Hs in monogram] ARA. Miniature / Painter to His Rl.Hs. The Prince of / Wales - 1796 / Dublin".
Bought: Waringstown House, Co Down, John Ross & Co. sale Sept 1973 (65).
Exh Belfast, Ulster Museum: *Recent Acquisitions and Loans* 1974 (6).
Rep Gazette des Beaux-Arts Feb 1974 p 177.

Half-length to left, eyes facing, wearing own hair, sandy-coloured, grey overcoat and black cocked hat, and holding stick in right hand. The neckband and shirt are highlighted with white bodycolour.

Another version, practically identical, but dated 1782, was also in the Waringstown House sale 1973 (43).

Major Holt Waring (c 1722-1806) of Waringstown was the third son of Samuel Waring and his wife Grace (née Holt), who were married in 1696. At the Battle of Dettingen (1743) he attracted the notice of George II by "his intrepidity in the execution of a very dangerous piece of service, during the action". He was married in 1746, and died at Waringstown on 15 Jan 1806 in his 84th year. His obituary (Belfast News Letter 24 Jan 1806) states: "With a rich stock of anecdote, he combined a considerable degree of taste and talent for polite literature. He was a sincere friend, a pleasant companion, and, it is almost needless to add, a zealous supporter of the constitution in church and state".

At the Royal Academy in 1804 (487) Horace Hone exhibited a "Portrait of Colonel Vereker, Major H Waring, Dr Lindsay, and Mrs Siddons, in the year 1785" (presumably four separate miniatures in the same frame). Again at the Royal Academy 1815 (421) Hone exhibited "Major H Warring [sic; a sketch in enamel".

Bibliography:
Redgrave Dict, Graves RA, Strickland, Irish Portraits, Long, Reynolds, Foskett, NGI.
Joseph Farington: *Diary.*
T J Mulvany and J Gandon: *The Life of James Gandon, Esq.* 1846 (facsimile edition, edited by Maurice Craig, Cornmarket Press 1969).
New Haven, Yale Center for British Art: *English Portrait Drawings and Miniatures* catalogue by Patrick J Noon 1979.

ADAM BUCK
Born Cork 1759; died London 1833

Buck was the son of a Cork silversmith, and commenced practice there as a miniature painter. According to Pasquin he was self-taught, and invented a special wax crayon for portrait drawing. Pasquin also says he worked for a time in Dublin, but in 1795 he moved permanently to London. Here he exhibited at the Royal Academy, the British Institution and the Society of British Artists, and taught portrait drawing. Buck designed plates illustrating Sterne's *Sentimental Journey*, and in 1811 attempted to publish a series of his own etchings from paintings on Greek vases, a work which never got beyond the first facsicule of ten prints (1812). Rowlandson satirised Buck's preoccupation with the antique in a caricature etching *Buck's Beauty*. Buck lived in Piccadilly 1795-98, then in Frith Street until 1813, then in Bentinck Street until 1820. After that he changed his address practically every year, until his death at 15 Upper Seymour Street. Buck's younger brother Frederick Buck (1771-1840) remained as a miniature painter in Cork. Adam Buck's son Sidney Buck carried on his father's practice in London.

---

21. *Annie Charlotte Hill.* 1832. (no. 1179).

Watercolour with white, over pencil, on hot-pressed white paper
35.7 × 27 cms / 14 × 10⅝″.
Signed b.l. "Adam Buck 1832".

Provenance Macdonell family of Keppoch.

Bought: London, Sotheby's 24 June 1971 (159) through Emerald Isle Books, Belfast.

Whole-length facing, head slightly to left, tightly curled auburn hair; wearing white dress with puff sleeves decorated with pale blue ribbons; matching pale blue belt with gold buckle. The little girl holds a skipping-rope.

A manuscript label removed from the back of the discarded frame reads: "My maternal grandmother, Annie Charlotte Hill aged 7 years. Younger daughter of Henry Hill of Bold Manor and [something illegible]. (The house and park have been swallowed up in Darlington and no trace remains) She married [name illegible] MacDonell of Keppoch and died in 1906 [or 1908] aged 86 years. This is by Adam Buck. Anne MacDonell 4.8.59."

If Annie Charlotte Hill died in 1906 or 1908 at the age of 86 she would have been born in 1820 or 1822, which would put her age in 1832 when this was painted as either 10 or 12. This seems plausible. Enquiries in Darlington (Co Durham) about Bold Manor and the Hill family have not been fruitful (S C Dean, Darlington Borough Librarian and Curator, letter 10 July 1972).

This is a good example of the full-length watercolour portraits which were a natural extention of Buck's trade as a miniature painter. It was painted in the last year of Buck's life, and is still neoclassical in spirit. The head and face are executed in typical miniaturist's hatching, while the background is painted in transparent watercolour. The yellow grass, which now makes an attractive discord against the leaden sky, is unfortunately not Buck's intention. Exposure to sunlight at some time in the past has bleached out the fugitive blues, leaving the yellow. The edges formerly covered by the old mount show the original colour of the grass to have been rather dark green.

Bibliography:
Pasquin, Binyon, Graves RA, Cundall, Williams, Windsor, DNB, Redgrave, Hardie, Strickland, Foskett, Arnold, Doran, Mallalieu, Irish Portraits, NGI, P of I.
Harold Malet: *Adam Buck* The Connoisseur vol 50 no. 199. 1918 p 136.
Mrs Willoughby Hodgson: *The Art of Adam Buck* Apollo XXXVIII 1943 p 34.
New Haven, Yale Center for British Art: *English Portrait Drawings and Miniatures* catalogue by Patrick J Noon 1979, pp 92-96.
Dublin, Cynthia O'Connor Gallery: *Adam Buck 1759-1833* Aug 1984.
Ian Jenkins: *Adam Buck and the vogue for Greek vases* Burlington Magazine, June 1988, p 448.

Hugh William "Grecian" Williams

Born at sea 1773; died Edinburgh 1829

The son of a sea captain, born on shipboard in the South Atlantic, Williams was orphaned early and was brought up by an aunt and uncle in Edinburgh. He was a founder member of the Artists' Association in 1808 and in 1811-12 published six large engravings of views in the Scottish Highlands. Soon afterwards he spent some years in Italy and Greece, returning to Edinburgh in 1818. The volumes of prints which subsequently appeared earned him the nickname of "Grecian" Williams. He married into a fortune. The Print Room of the National Gallery of Scotland has a substantial collection of his work, including 25 drawings of Scottish views, 12 of Greece, 8 of Italy and one of Heidelberg. Though his early drawings are ambitious, and can sometimes rival John Robert Cozens, his later work can be conventionally topographical.

22. *Lake of Avernus*. 1816. (no. 1649).

Sepia wash over pencil on white paper
18.5 × 27.8 cms / 7¼ × 10⅞".
Signed b.l. "H W Williams 1816".

Bought: London, R E Abbott 1952.

According to Rebecca Bodmer (letter 2 June 1972) this is Williams's only known dated drawing of 1816. It was probably done when he was in Italy from sketches made on the spot, and is a sober, neat topographical drawing.

The figures moving through the trees on the right evoke a religious procession in classical times. These crater-lakes in the volcanic area known as the Phlegraean Fields, north-west of Naples, have been regarded with superstitious awe since antiquity. The entrance to Hades was reputed to be here. The area was painted by Richard Wilson, Wright of Derby, and, later, Turner, among many other artists. Lake Avernus is Virgil's setting for Aenaeas's consultation with the Cumaean Sybil, who lived in a cave nearby, an episode which was painted by Turner in 1798, long before his first visit to Italy in 1819. British readers were introduced to the volcanology of this region by Sir William Hamilton's lavish book *Campi Phlegraeae* (1776, 1783) with illustrations by Peter Fabris. It is interesting to see Williams recording the spot in 1816 in a factual way, but including a suggestive allusion to antique religion.

Bibliography:
Redgrave Dict, Roget, Cundall, DNB, Caw, VAM, Binyon, Williams, Hardie, Mallalieu, Irwin.
Hugh William Williams: *Travels in Italy, Greece and the Ionian Islands* 1820; *Select Views in Greece* 1827-29.
Edinburgh, National Gallery of Scotland: *Catalogue of Scottish Drawings* 1960.
Rebecca Sue Bodmer: *Hugh William Williams* unpublished MLitt thesis, University of Edinburgh 1973.

Sir William Pilkington
Born c 1775; died Chevet Hall, Wakefield, Yorkshire 1850

Pilkington was an amateur artist and architect influenced by Richard Wilson. (An architect named William Pilkington exhibited four designs at the Royal Academy between 1780 and 1790, but this is unlikely to be the same man). He was no relation to the author of the *Dictionary of Painters*, but was a descendant of Sir Arthur Pilkington of Stanley near Wakefield, who in the 17th century received a Scottish Baronetcy of Nova Scotia and a grant of 6,000 acres there. Sir William became the 8th Baronet in 1811. His wife Mary was co-heiress of Thomas Swinnerton of Butterton Hall, Staffordshire. Pilkington is reported in his obituary to have designed Butterton Hall, near Newcastle-under-Lyme, but there is no mention of it in Pevsner's *Staffordshire*. He is described as "a polished, unobtrusive gentleman - one of the old school", a practical agriculturalist, a family man who largely avoided the great world. However, he travelled widely, studied the Bible in the original languages, and published a translation of Schiller's *Marie Stuart*. He had an "illustrated library of rare productions", but though he owned works by Wilson, Morland and Thompson, he denied being considered a collector. Nevertheless, he possessed a portfolio of Turner's drawings, "of unusual excellence", including views in Italy, Switzerland and Great Britain. One of his last works was a large view of the 15th century chapel on Wakefield Bridge. Pilkington died aged 75 at Chevet Hall, near Wakefield, on 30 Sept 1850, and was succeeded as 9th Baronet by his son Sir Thomas Edward Pilkington (born 1829). In 1856 Pilkington's youngest son Lionel took the surnames of Milborne-Swinnerton by Royal Licence but subsequently resumed the final name of Pilkington, probably on becoming the 11th Baronet. The present (14th) Baronet lives near Hitchin in Hertfordshire, and there are collateral branches of the family in Ireland.

---

23. *View on the Palatine Hill, Rome.* (no. 2109).

Watercolour over pencil on white laid paper
22.6 × 28.6 cms / 8¾ × 11⅜″.
Inscribed in ink, top: "St. Bonaventura. Convent of Franciscans upon Mt. Palatine / with part of the Aquaduct of Claudius".
On verso: "Convent near the Colloseum" "Palazzo Pitti" [?]

Bought: London, Walker's Galleries 1956.

It is not known when Pilkington was in Rome, but presumably it was early in his life, as this crisp and able sketch is still 18th century in style. The vertical pencil shading seems idiosyncratic. It was probably drawn on the spot. A fragment of the Claudian Aquaduct is shown in the foreground, with, on the hill beyond, the Franciscan monastery whose monks still perform the minor charitable task of feeding the stray cats in the Forum.

Bibliography:
Obituary: Art Journal 1850 p 377.
Dod's *Peerage, Baronetage and Knightage* 1851.
Debrett's *Peerage, Baronetage and Knightage* 1985.

St. Bonaventura   Convent of Franciscans upon Mt Palatine
with part of the Aquaduct of Claudius

JOSEPH MALLORD WILLIAM TURNER
Born Covent Garden 1775; died Chelsea 1851

The greatest English painter of his generation, Turner has his roots in the English topographical watercolour tradition. The son of a barber in Maiden Lane, Covent Garden, he studied under Thomas Malton junior and Thomas Hardwick. He was a close friend of Thomas Girtin, who died at the age of 28, and both were patronised by Dr Thomas Monro. Both established their pre-eminence in topographical watercolour when they were 20 years old, and for the rest of his life Turner was famous. Since his admission as a student to the Royal Academy Schools in 1789, the Academy became the hub of Turner's life. He was elected ARA in 1799, RA in 1802, and was Professor of Perspective to the Royal Academy 1807-37. He attracted a number of faithful British patrons - Fawkes of Farnley, Munro of Novar, Lord Egremont at Petworth - and toured much on the continent between 1803 and 1840, visiting Italy in 1819 and 1828. The engravings forming the *Liber Studiorum* appeared between 1807 and 1819, but the series was never completed. Turner's late works of the 1840s were scarcely understood by the public, being so daring in brilliant colour and free brushwork, but were still admired. He never married, but lived a furtive private life in Margate and Chelsea. He died in some considerable squalour in Chelsea and was buried in St Paul's Cathedral, but the terms of his will, when settled, left some 300 oil paintings and over 19,000 watercolours and drawings to the National Collections, and a sum of £20,000 to the Royal Academy.

---

24. Beachy Head looking towards Newhaven. (no. 866).

Grey and blue washes over pencil on white paper
29.4 × 43.9 cms / 11½ × 17¼".
Bequeathed by Sir David Reid, Crossgar, Co Down 1951.

Formerly called *Sandy Cove with Boats*, it seems fairly certain that this is a view of the chalk cliffs at Beachy Head in Sussex. These "blue drawings" are associated with Turner's early period in the drawing school kept by Dr Thomas Monro, c 1794-97. A drawing of this subject from slightly farther away, grey and blue washes over pencil 20.3 × 27.5 cms, is in the Vaughan Bequest of Turner watercolours in the National Gallery of Scotland, Edinburgh, D(NG)855. See Finberg 1910, and the National Gallery of Scotland publication *The Vaughan Bequest of Turner Watercolours* 1980 pp 8-9.

Bibliography:
Redgrave Dict, Redgrave Cent, Graves RA, DNB, VAM, Binyon, Cundall, Williams, Windsor, RA 1934, Roget, Nettlefold, Hardie, Cordingly, Mellon, Mallalieu, Clarke, NGI.
John Pye: collection of correspondence etc, relating to Turner 1813-84; London, VAM Library.
Manuscript *Catalogue of Works in the possession of F H Fawkes of Farnley Hall* 1850; London, VAM Library.
John Burnet: *Turner and his works* 1852.
T Miller: *Turner and Girtin's Picturesque Views, Sixty Years Since* 1854.
John Ruskin: *Catalogue of Drawings...exhibited at Marlborough House* 1857-8.
G W Thornbury: *Life of J M W Turner* 1862.
P G Hamerton: *Life of J M W Turner* 1879.
John Ruskin: *Catalogue of Drawings and Sketches by Turner in the National Gallery* 1881.
C F Bell: *List of Works contributed to Public Exhibitions* 1901 (the copy in the VAM Library has notes by Bell).
Sir Walter Armstrong: *Turner* 1902.
Studio Special Number 1903 (the copy in the VAM Library has notes by C F Bell).
T A Cooke: *Watercolour Drawings of Turner in the National Gallery* 1904.
London, National Gallery: *Complete Inventory of the Drawings of the Turner Bequest* 1909.
A J Finberg: *Turner's Sketches and Drawings* 1910.
A J Finberg: *Turner's Watercolours at Farnley Hall* 1912.
A J Finberg: Walpole Society I 1911-12; II 1912-13; III 1913-14; IV 1917-18.
H W Underdown: *Five Turner Watercolours* 1923.
London, Tate Gallery: *Catalogue of the Turner Collection* 1920.
A P Oppé: *Watercolours of Turner* 1925.
G S Sandilands: *J M W Turner* 1928.
A J Finberg: *In Venice with Turner* 1930 (the copy in the VAM Library has notes by C F Bell).
Laurence Binyon: *English Watercolours from the Work of J M W Turner etc* Manx Museum Journal, Sept 1936.
Bernard Falk: *Turner the Painter: his Hidden Life* 1938.
A J Finberg: *Life of J M W Turner* 1939 (the copy in the VAM Library has notes by C F Bell).
C Clare: *J M W Turner: his life and work* 1951.
N W Hanson: *Some Painting Materials of J M W Turner* Studies in Conservation vol 1 1952-4 p 162.
Sir John Rothenstein and Martin Butlin: *Turner* 1962.

Jack Lindsay: *J M W Turner: a critical biography* 1965.

Lawrence Gowing: *Turner: imagination and reality* New York, Museum of Modern Art 1966.

John Gage: *Colour in Turner: poetry and truth* 1969.

Graham Reynolds: *Turner* Thames and Hudson 1969.

G Wilkinson: *Turner's Early Sketchbooks* 1972.

Frederick A Whiting: *Art and Acrimony* Apollo July 1973 p. 43.

Gerald E Finley: *Two Kindred Spirits in Scotland: Turner and Scott* the Connoisseur Aug 1973 p 239.

A G Backrach: *Turner and Rotterdam* 1974.

G Wilkinson: *The Sketches of Turner* London, Royal Academy 1974.

London, Royal Academy of Arts: *Turner* 1974.

Andrew Wilton: *The Life and Work of J M W Turner* 1979.

Andrew Wilton: *Turner and the Sublime* British Museum Publications 1980.

Malcolm Cormack: *J M W Turner: a selection of paintings and watercolours in the Yale Center for British Art* Artist's Limited Edition 1983.

Martin Butlin and Evelyn Joll: *The Paintings of J M W Turner* revised edition, 2 vols 1984.

Cecilia Powell: *Turner in the South: Rome, Naples, Florence* 1987.

John Gage: *J M W Turner: a wonderful range of mind* Yale University Press 1987.

Andrew Wilton: *Turner in his Time* 1987.

25. Beeston Castle, Cheshire. (no. 865).

Watercolour over pencil, with surface scraping, on white paper
21 × 32.8 cms / 8¼ × 12⅞".

Prov A trust estate, sold Christie's 29 April 1869; John Heugh 1874; Earl of Effingham; John H Baring 1927; Nettlefold Collection.

Given by Frederick John Nettlefold, Nutley, Sussex 1948.

Refs Armstrong 1902 p 242.
Nettlefold 1938 vol 4 p 30, rep. in colour.
Adrian Bury: *Mr F J Nettlefold's Gift to the Nation: distribution to Public Galleries* the Connoisseur CXXI 1948 p 78; rep. in colour opposite p 96.

This is a watercolour of Turner's middle period, but its dating could be any time between c 1806 and the 1820s. Two views of *Hampton Court, Herefordshire* of c 1806, in the Yale Center for British Art B1975-4-1765-6, one with felled trees in the foreground, are close in style. Also comparable is a larger view *On the Washburn*, c 1815 or earlier, with a kingfisher and feathery trees, Yale Center for British Art B1975-4-1620. This view contains much scraping. Another watercolour *Lulworth Castle, Dorset*, Yale Center for British Art B1975-4-747, is close to the Ulster Museum *Beeston Castle* but dates from the 1820s.

In his middle period Turner's watercolour technique attains a complexity never before found. Every trick of rubbing, washing, scraping and gumming is used to gain unprecedentedly subtle effects. The Castle itself is relegated to insignificance by the felled trees in the foreground. The view must be taken from the top of the high sandstone bluff on which Beeston Castle stands, or possibly from the edge of the nearby Peckforton Hills. The flat Cheshire plain, far below, can be seen through the trees in the background.

51

CORNELIUS VARLEY
Born Hackney 1781; died Stoke Newington 1873

Cornelius Varley was the younger brother of John Varley (1778-1842). As he lost his father when he was ten years old, Cornelius was brought up by an uncle, Samuel Varley, a maker of watches and scientific instruments. About 1800 he began to study art with his brother, and was patronised by Dr Thomas Monro. In 1807 he was a student in the Royal Academy Schools. Both Varleys were founder members of the Old Water-Colour Society in 1804. Cornelius's interests lay as much in science and technology as they did in art. His uncle Samuel had taught him to grind lenses, and together they constructed the first soda-syphon. About 1809 Cornelius made the first version of his "graphic telescope", which he patented in 1811. This was an improvement on the camera lucida which had been invented by Dr Wollaston in 1807. It was a success, and was used by Cotman, Prout, Chantrey, Horner and many others. In 1814 Varley was elected a Fellow of the Society of Arts, which awarded him several medals for his improved microscopes. He resigned from the OWCS after its second reorganisation in 1820, and from this time concentrated much more on science, though he still occasionally exhibited at the Royal Academy. At the Great Exhibition of 1851 he and his sons showed air-pumps, a graphic telescope on a stand, and a photographic camera, for which they won a prize medal. Cornelius Varley died at the age of 92. He had ten children, one of whom, Cromwell Fleetwood Varley, made many improvements in telegraphy.

---

26. Kerry Castle, Lixnaw, Co Kerry. 1842. (no. 1648).

Watercolour on white paper
38 × 55.4 cms / 14⅞ × 21¾".
Signed and dated b.l. "Cornelius Varley 1842".
Bought: London, Fine Art Society 1943.

The date on this watercolour shows the amount of time which could elapse between a sketch made on a tour and a studio watercolour. A drawing in black lead, *Remains of Kerry House at Lixna [sic], Kerry, Ireland*, 19.2 × 49.5 cms, signed and dated 1808, was in the exhibition at Colnaghi's 1973 (114). A small sepia drawing of the same subject, 8.9 × 13.4 cms, which may have been done at the same time, is in a Belfast private collection. A watercolour *Ruins of Kerry Castle*, 14⅝ × 21⅜", signed and dated 1830, in the VAM, is stated in Long's catalogue to have been painted from a sketch made in 1808. Finally there is the Ulster Museum watercolour dated 1842.

Lixnaw Castle, the seat of the Fitzmaurices, Earls of Kerry, is one of the great vanished houses of Ireland. It was a mediaeval castle enlarged in the 18th century, and had fine gardens. At the beginning of the 19th century, when Varley drew it, the house was decayed, and by 1837 it was in ruins. It is now almost obliterated. The circular domed mausoleum of the Earls of Kerry, which stood nearby, was destroyed more recently by quarrying operations. See Mark Bence-Jones: *Burke's Guide to Country Houses: no. 1 (Ireland)* 1978 p 189.

Smith's *History of Kerry* (1756) states that in the house of the Earl of Kerry at Lixnaw the walls of the chapel were painted with grisaille copies of Raphael's Cartoons by a foreigner named John Souillard. Some twenty years afterwards the house was in ruins and the paintings defaced. See Strickland (1913) under *Souillard*.

A large unfinished watercolour by Varley, *Ardfert, Kerry, Ireland*, in the Yale Center for British Art B1977.14.4337, presumably has its origin on the same Irish tour. It shows the cathedral ruins from the south, with a small church in front, and some boys apparently playing handball on the right. There is another dated drawing of *Muckruss Abbey, Killarney* 1808 in the Yale Center for British Art, B1977.14.4668. This is a tightly executed pencil drawing, almost like a Lear drawing. It was formerly in the collection of Martin Hardie, who wrote a note inside the mount: "Farington made drawings at Muckruss. See his sketchbook, with his notes, in the VAM".

Armagh County Museum has an important series of 10 pencil drawings done by Cornelius Varley during his Irish tour in 1808, showing views of Armagh, Markethill and Gosford. Six of these were bought from the Colnaghi exhibition in 1973. There are more at the Ulster Folk and Transport Museum, Cultra, Co Down.

Bibliography:
Redgrave Dict, Redgrave Cent, Roget, Graves RA, DNB, Binyon, VAM, Cundall, Williams, Windsor, Hughes, Hardie, Mallalieu, Clarke, NGI.

Cornelius Varley: *Etchings of Shipping* 1809.

Cornelius Varley: *A Treatise on Optical Drawing Instruments* 1845.

Basil S Long: *Cornelius Varley* OWCS XIV 1937.

R Seddon: *Turner and Cotman: two portraits by Cornelius Varley* Burlington Magazine Aug 1945 p 202.

Michael Pidgley: *Cornelius Varley, Cotman and the Graphic Telescope* Burlington Magazine Nov 1972 p 781.

London, P & D Colnaghi & Co.: *Exhibition of Drawings by Cornelius Varley* catalogue introduction by Michael Pidgley, 21 Feb – 16 March 1973.

JAMES GEORGE OBEN or O'BRIEN
Active, Dublin and London, 1779-1819

This artist, whose real name was Brien or O'Brien, studied in the Dublin Society's Schools and won their medal for landscape in 1779. In 1780 he was living at 30 Bride Street, Dublin, and exhibited at the Society of Artists in William Street. From 1785 to 1798 he lived at 45 and 49 Marlborough Street. Some of his drawings were engraved in Francis Grose's *Antiquities of Ireland* 1791-95. He moved to London in 1798 (possibly because of the rebellion in Ireland), but was back in Dublin in 1801, by which time he had Germanised his name to Oben in accord with London fashions for foreign artists. This caused some consternation when he exhibited in the Dublin Parliament House in July 1801 (anonymous *Diary*, see below). In 1809 he exhibited 70 landscapes in watercolour at 49 Marlborough Street. He returned to London and exhibited views of Ireland, Wales and the north of England at the Royal Academy 1810-16 from an address at 86 Charlotte Street. He was still living in 1819. His widow, Mary Oben, died at Ballylinan, Queen's County, on 8 Jan 1849 aged 74.

---

27. The Rock of Fennor on the Boyne. (no. 833).

Watercolour with gum arabic on white card
49.8 × 64.5 cms / 19⅝ × 25⅜".
Signed b.c. "J G Oben pinxt."

Bought: London, Colnaghi's 1970.

Rep P of I (1978) p 149.

Oben exhibited a *View of Fenner Rock, on the River Boyne* at the Royal Academy in 1811 (726), which may have been this version or one of several others:

A smaller version, 14 × 19¾", *A Ferry Boat at Fennor Rock on the River Boyne, Co Meath*, inscribed "by J G O'Brien of Dublin 1796", in the National Gallery of Ireland, Dublin (6882), was bought from Fry, London, in 1968. This has a party of figures being ferried across the river in the left foreground. It is less finished than the Ulster Museum version and the blues have faded.

Another smaller version, 13¾ × 19½", *The Rock of Fennor on the Boyne, with a gardener and his roller on a path in the foreground*, was sold at Christie's, London, 24 March 1981 (8).

The Ulster Museum version is much larger than any of these, but has only two tiny figures at the foot of the Rock. An impression of meticulous detail in the foliage and ferns is created almost entirely by colour-lifting or the use of stopping-out fluid. There is no bodycolour but much use of gum arabic. It is quite likely that this larger version was the one exhibited at the Royal Academy in 1811.

Bibliography:
Redgrave, Graves RA, Strickland, Mallalieu, P of I.
Dublin, Royal Irish Academy: Anonymous *Diary*, MSS 24 K14 pp 258-9, quoted in P of I (1978) p 149.

John Sell Cotman
Born Norwich 1782; died London 1842

Cotman was the son of a Norwich silk-mercer, and went to London in 1800 where he was befriended by Dr Thomas Monro. He exhibited at the Royal Academy until 1806, when he returned to Norwich and became secretary of the Norwich Society of Artists, of which he was vice-president in 1810 and president in 1811. In 1812 he moved with his wife and family to Yarmouth, and taught drawing there. In 1817, 1818 and 1820 he made tours of Normandy to illustrate Dawson Turner's *Architectural Antiquities of Normandy*. Cotman exhibited with the Old Water-Colour Society until 1835, and was elected associate in 1825. In 1834 he was appointed Professor of Drawing at King's College, London, a post which he held for the rest of his life. He died at 42 Hunter Street. The watercolours Cotman painted on the Greta River in North Yorkshire in 1803-1805 are regarded as among the greatest achievements in English watercolour.

---

28. Harlech Castle. (no. 761).

Watercolour over pencil, with some penwork, on white wove paper
34.4 × 43.9 cms / 13⅝ × 17¼″.
Inscribed in pencil on back of mount: "Harlech Castle / J.Cotman".
On front of mount, in pencil, in a different hand: "Harlech Castle" "Cotman".

Bought: London, Walker's Galleries 1935.

This almost monochrome drawing belongs to Cotman's very early period, when he worked under the strong influence of Thomas Girtin (1775-1802). Cotman exhibited a *Harlech Castle, Wales* in the Royal Academy of 1800 (550), a few months *before* his first tour of Wales with Girtin in July-August 1800, when he passed from Aberystwyth through Barmouth and Harlech, reaching Beddgelert on 5th August. Rajnai 1980, writing about the Tate Gallery watercolour of *Harlech Castle* (no. 28 in the catalogue), says that the Ulster Museum drawing must be the one exhibited at the Royal Academy before Cotman set off for Wales, and therefore would have been done after a drawing by someone else. It seems likely that the composition is derived from Paul Sandby's aquatint *Harlech Castle in Meirionethshire with Snowdon at a Distance*, plate 7 from *Twelve Views in North Wales*, 1776. Turner and Girtin adopted similar devices with the same subject in the 1790s. See New Haven, Yale Center for British Art: *The Art of Paul Sandby*, catalogue by Bruce Robertson 1985 (96).

A close comparison suggested by Dr Rajnai (letter 8 July 1976) is the *Aberystwyth Castle* in the Paul Mellon Collection, which is undated but based on a drawing in the British Museum dated "July 18. 1800", evidently done on the Welsh tour. Another *Harlech Castle*, described as a "drawing in bistre and indian ink", was in Cotman's sale at Christie's, 17-18 May 1843 (179). He made two soft-ground etchings of the Castle, Popham nos. 318 and 319. Another Girtinesque Cotman watercolour of *Harlech Castle*, already mentioned above, 10½ × 16⅞″, dated 1801, formerly in the Herbert Powell Collection, is now in the Tate Gallery (T969). This postdates the Welsh tour with Girtin. The Castle is seen from the ridge with the Snowdon Range beyond, rather than from the low marsh of Morfa Harlech, the viewpoint of the Sandby aquatint and the Ulster Museum drawing.

Sidney Kitson (OWCS VII, 1929-30 p 3; *Life* 1937 p 14) suggested that it was on the Welsh tour of 1800 that Cotman first met Girtin, but he must already have known Girtin's work through Dr Monro. Monro's sale catalogue shows that he owned about 100 Girtin drawings, mostly pencils or "sketches". Cotman was a member of "the Brothers", or "Girtin's Sketching Club": see T Girtin and D Loshak: *The Art of Thomas Girtin* 1954, p 38 note 1. There is only one known Girtin watercolour of *Harlech Castle*, an unfinished monochrome wash drawing, 14⅜ × 21½″ (Girtin and Loshak 1954 no. 267, then belonging to the executors of Sir Edward Marsh), but the Ulster Museum drawing seems to owe nothing to it. (Mr Tom Girtin, son of Loshak's collaborator: letter 17 July 1976).

Following Girtin's practice, Cotman used vegetable pigments in his skies (indigo, madder and lake), and in this drawing chemical change has caused the sky to become a rusty brown instead of a cool blue. This blue colour remains intact in Cotman's *St Mary Redcliffe, Bristol*, in the British Museum. Similar changes are found in several of Girtin's drawings.

Bibliography:
Binyon, Graves Dict, Graves RA, Graves BI, Redgrave, Hughes, Roget, DNB, Nettlefold, Hardie, Williams, Cordingly, Mallalieu, Clarke, VAM, NGI.

Studio Special Number 1903.

F Wedmore: *The Norwich School: Cotman and Crome* Magazine of Fine Arts no. 1, 1906.

A P Oppé: *The Watercolours of J S Cotman* Studio Special Number 1923.

A P Oppé: *Cotman and the Sketching Society* The Connoisseur 1923.

A Batchelor: *Cotman's Diary* 1924.

S C Kaines Smith: *Cotman* 1926.

C F Bell: *John Sell Cotman* (Bulwer Collection) Walker's Quarterly V 1926. (There is an annotated copy in the VAM Library).

S D Kitson: *John Sell Cotman letters from Normandy* Walpole Society XIV, XV 1926-7.

S D Kitson: *John Sell Cotman* OWCS VII, 1930.

Frank Rutter: *Cotman Sketches pasted on the back of Cotman Watercolours* Illustrated London News CLXXXIX 1936.

S D Kitson: *Life of John Sell Cotman* 1937.

London, Royal Institute of British Architects: *Architectural Drawings by John Sell Cotman* 1939 (the copy in the VAM Library has notes by C F Bell).

Laurence Binyon: *English Watercolours from the works of Turner, Cotman etc.* 1939.

A P Oppé: *Struggles of a Painter: John Sell Cotman* The London Mercury 1937.

A P Oppé: *Cotman and his Public* Burlington Magazine 1942.

R J Cotman: *The Cotman Collection* 1942.

Norwich, Castle Museum: *Norwich School Pictures* 1951.

V G R Reinacker: *John Sell Cotman 1782-1842* 1953.

John Gage: *Documents of Crome and Cotman* Burlington Magazine CXI, Jan-June 1969.

Michael Pidgley: *Cornelius Varley, Cotman and the Graphic Telescope* Burlington Magazine Nov 1972 p 781.

Norfolk Museums Service: *The Norwich Society of Artists 1805-1833: a dictionary of contributors and their work* by Miklos Rajnai, 1976.

Andrew Hemingway: *Cotman's Architectural Antiquities of Normandy: some amendments to Kitson's account* Walpole Society XLVI, 1976-78, p 164.

Andrew Hemingway: *Meaning in Cotman's Norfolk Subjects* Art History vol 7 no. 1, March 1984 p 57.

Miklos Rajnai, ed. *John Sell Cotman 1782-1842* Touring Exhibition, Arts Council of Great Britain 1980; catalogue by Rajnai, containing essays by David Thompson, Michael Pidgley, Andrew Hemingway and Marjorie Allthorpe-Guyton.

SAMUEL PROUT
Born Plymouth 1783; died Denmark Hill, London 1852

Prout received his first instruction from a drawing master in Plymouth. As a child he suffered a severe attack of sunstroke, which left him incapacitated for at least one day each week for many years. Nevertheless, he made many trips on the continent and was one of the most prolific topographical watercolourists of the early 19th century. He was employed by John Britton in Cornwall, illustrating *The Beauties of England and Wales*, and though his work was found unsatisfactory, he resided with Britton in Clerkenwell for two years after 1802. After living in the country, Prout returned to London in 1811. He was elected a member of the Old Water-Colour Society in 1819. His early work is influenced by Girtin and John Varley, but after 1819 he formed his own style, which is parallelled by that of Henry Edridge. Later, under the influence of Ruskin, he tended to crowd his work with architectural detail. He was appointed Painter in Water-Colours to George IV and to Queen Victoria. In 1845 he went to live at De Crespigny Terrace, Denmark Hill, Camberwell (near Ruskin's home).

---

29. Chapel in the Chateau d'Amboise. (no. 841).

Watercolour with Chinese white and bodycolour on white paper
46 × 33.1 cms / 18⅛ × 13″.
Signed b.l. "Prout".

Bought: London, Fine Art Society 1948.

Formerly called *Chartres Cathedral*, this is clearly a view of the ruined apsidal chapel at Amboise. It corresponds not exactly but fairly closely with a lithograph of *Amboise* by Prout, printed by Sprague & Co (*Sketches in France, Switzerland and Italy* 1839). Another watercolour version, with figures before a statue of the Madonna, 13⅜ × 8¼, was exhibited at Spink's, London: *One Hundred English Watercolours*, Autumn 1975 (69).

Richard Lockett, Birmingham Museum and Art Gallery (letter 18 Feb 1985) commented: "Although Prout made numerous versions of the same scene he never copied the figures from an earlier production; he always varied his figure groups, although admittedly to a well-established formula". Chinese white and bodycolour are confined to the figures and the statues in the niches. Though much of Prout's work can be heavy and turgid, this is a good fresh example in excellent condition.

Bibliography:
Redgrave Dict, Redgrave Cent, Roget, DNB, Graves RA, Graves BI, Cundall, Binyon, VAM, Williams, RA 1934, Hughes, Nettlefold, Williams, Hardie, Mallalieu.
John Ruskin: *Notes on Samuel Prout and Hunt* 1879.
Studio Special Number: *Samuel Prout* 1914.
Jane Quigley: *Prout and Roberts* 1926.
A Neumeyer: *An unknown collection of English Watercolours at Mills College* 1941.
C E Hughes: *Samuel Prout* OWCS VI 1928-9 p 1.
F Gordon Roe: *Some Letters of Samuel Prout* OWCS XXIV 1946 p 41.
Richard Lockett: *Samuel Prout* Batsford and VAM 1985.

59

DAVID COX
Born Deritend, Birmingham 1783; died Harborne, Birmingham 1859

The son of a blacksmith, Cox worked first in his father's smithy, but was encouraged to paint by his cousin Henry Allport, and studied nightly in the drawing school of Joseph Barber. After painting scenes at the Birmingham Theatre Royal, he went to London in 1804, where he worked at Astley's Amphitheatre and received some lessons from John Varley. He first exhibited at the Royal Academy in 1805. In 1812 he became a member of the Old Water-Colour Society, continuing to exhibit there regularly until 1859. He settled with his wife and family in Dulwich, where he taught drawing. He was drawing master at the Military College in Farnham in 1814, then taught in Hereford 1815-27. One of his pupils there was Joseph Murray Ince. Cox made many tours in Britain and on the continent, but from 1844 onwards his favourite area was Bettws-y-Coed in North Wales. In 1841 he moved from London to Harborne, Birmingham, where he lived for the rest of his life. Cox's distinctive late style won him many followers and imitators, including Thomas Collier, James Orrock, Edmund Morison Wimperis and Claude Hayes (see no. 61), taking the tradition well into the 20th century. Even today there are many British watercolourists working in what is recognisably Cox's style.

---

30. *The Snow Storm.* (no. 762).

Watercolour over crayon on hot-pressed white paper
37.5 × 54.7 cms / 14¾ × 21⅞".
Signed b.l. "David Cox".

Bought: London, Fine Art Society 1954.

This is the best and most characteristic of the Ulster Museum's five Cox watercolours. It is a work of the artist's maturity, probably painted near Bettws-y-Coed, in sheep country. The smooth white paper is, however, totally unlike the thick, rough, flecked Dundee wrapping paper, made of old linen sailcloth, which Cox especially liked and which was later marketed as "David Cox Paper".

Cox had made regular tours in North Wales from as early as 1805 (see Roe 1924 p 141), but it was only in his late period, after staying at Bettws-y-Coed with the painter H J Johnston in 1844, that the Conway and Llugwy Valleys became his favourite area. He revisited Bettws, staying at the Royal Oak, every year between 1846 and 1856, except 1851, and there he was surrounded by other artists.

A watercolour by Cox, *Lancaster Sands, Low Tide,* in the Yale Center for British Art, B1977.14.4672, has figures similar to the shepherd and dog in this drawing.

Bibliography:
Redgrave, DNB, Graves RA, Roget, Hughes, Binyon, Windsor, RA 1934, Nettlefold, Cundall, Williams, VAM, Hardie, Mallalieu, Clarke, NGI.
David Cox: *A Treatise on Landscape Painting and Effect in Water Colours* 1814; reprinted by *The Studio* 1922.
David Cox: *Progressive Lessons on Landscape for Young Beginners* 1816.
David Cox: *The Young Artist's Companion* 1825.
N N Solly: *A Memoir of the Life of David Cox* 1873; reprinted by Rodart Reprints 1973.
W Hall: *Biography of David Cox* 1881.
G R Redgrave: *David Cox and Peter de Wint* 1891.
F Wedmore: *David Cox* the Gentleman's Magazine March 1878.
A J Finberg: *The Drawings of David Cox* 1909.
F Gordon Roe: *David Cox* 1924.
A P Oppé: *Watercolours of Turner, Cox, etc.* 1925.
Basil S Long: *David Cox* OWCS X 1933.
F Gordon Roe: *Cox the Master* 1946.
Trenchard Cox: *David Cox* Birmingham Museum and Art Gallery, no date.
Trenchard Cox: *David Cox* 1947, reprinted 1954.
C A E Bunt: *David Cox* 1949.
Thomas B Brumbaugh: *David Cox in American Collections* The Connoisseur Feb 1978 p 83.
Scott Barnes Wilcox: *David Cox: a study of his development as a watercolour painter* unpublished PhD thesis, Yale University 1984.

WILLIAM MULREADY
Born Ennis, Co Clare 1786; died Bayswater, London 1863

One of the most successful genre painters of London in the first half of the 19th century, Mulready left his native Ireland very early. After some instruction and encouragement from the sculptor Thomas Banks, he entered the Royal Academy Schools at the age of 14 in 1800. He then taught in the studio of John Varley, and in 1803 married Varley's sister. The marriage did not last long. Mulready was elected ARA in 1815 and RA in 1816. He designed numerous book illustrations, and in 1840 designed the first postage envelope issued by Rowland Hill. But Mulready was best known for his sentimental genre scenes, comparable with those of Sir David Wilkie. He also produced many beautifully-finished drawings of the nude, which were admired and bought by Queen Victoria. Mulready died at Linden Grove, Bayswater, and was buried in an elaborate tomb in Kensal Green Cemetery.

---

31. *Giving a Bite.* (no. 829).

Watercolour and bodycolour over pencil on white paper, mounted on card
41.5 × 33 cms / 16⅜ × 13".
Signed b.r. "W.M."

Bought: Belfast, sale of Dr James Moore, Merlyn, Malone Road 1943.

Ref Heleniak 1980 p 211 no. 139.

Exh London VAM, Dublin NGI and Belfast, Ulster Museum 1986-7 (Pointon 1986 no. 131, rep. in colour p 117).

Mulready painted a number of versions of this subject, the earliest of which appears to be *Lending a Bite* 1819, oil on panel 30 × 26", commissioned from Mulready by Earl Grey in 1818, and now in a private collection (signed with monogram and dated 1819, sold at Sotheby's Belgravia 29 June 1976 (63) as "property of a gentleman", and stated in the sale catalogue to have been exhibited in the Royal Academy of 1819 (143) and in the Royal Academy exhibition *Works of Old Masters* 1889 (15) as *Lending a Bite*; also to have been in the collection of Thomas Pitt Miller, Singleton Park, Blackpool.) (Pointon 1986 no. 130, rep. p 122). This shows two main figures in a sort of inn-yard.

Some fifteen years later, this is followed by the Ulster Museum watercolour, which Pointon (1986 no. 131) dates to 1834 and regards as a replica of or study for the painting *Giving a Bite*, oil on panel 20 × 15½", London, Victoria and Albert Museum (Pointon 1986 no. 132, rep. in colour p 120), which corresponds to it in all essentials. The VAM painting was commissioned from Mulready by John Sheepshanks as a repeat of Earl Grey's picture of 1819, but Mulready altered the setting to a rural situation, and introduced more figures, including a monkey. The feathery brushstrokes, absent in 1819, now have a delicacy that recalls Gainsborough. The Ulster Museum watercolour has a suggestion of a vignette composition in the bottom corners.

A watercolour copy after Mulready, 19½ × 15⅜" is in the VAM, Dixon bequest 1190-1886, corresponding closely with the VAM oil painting.

Bibliography:
Graves Dict, Graves RA, Graves BI, DNB, Redgrave Dict, Redgrave Cent, Strickland, Binyon, Cundall, Roget, Hughes, Hardie, Mallalieu, NGI.
London, VAM Library: various manuscript material 1804–63.
T Marcliffe: *The Looking Glass* 1805.
F G Stephens: *Memorials of William Mulready* 1867.
J Dafforne: *Pictures and Biographical Sketch of William Mulready* 1872.
Bristol, Museum and Art Gallery: *William Mulready* 1964.
London, Victoria and Albert Museum: *The Drawings of William Mulready* catalogue by Anne Rorimer 1972.
Marcia Pointon: *Pictorial Narrative in the Art of William Mulready* Burlington Magazine April 1980 p 229.
Kathryn Moore Heleniak: *William Mulready* 1980.
Marcia Pointon: *The Benefits of Patronage: a study of the relationship between William Mulready RA and two of his patrons* Gazette des Beaux-Arts Sept 1980 p 75.
Kathryn Moore Heleniak: *John Gibbons and William Mulready: the relationship between a patron and a painter* Burlington Magazine March 1982 p 136.
Marcia Pointon: *Mulready*; a book with catalogue published to accompany the bicentenary exhibition, London VAM 1986; Dublin NGI; Belfast, Ulster Museum 1986-87.

ANTHONY VANDYKE COPLEY FIELDING
Born Halifax, Yorkshire 1787; died Worthing, Sussex 1855

Copley Fielding was the second, and most famous, of at least five painter sons of Nathan Theodore Fielding, who gave him his first lessons. The family soon moved to London, then to the Lake District. In 1809, Copley Fielding settled in London, where he became a pupil of John Varley and worked in the studio of Dr Thomas Monro. He was elected an associate of the Old Water-Colour Society in 1810 and a member in 1811. He held the offices of treasurer in 1817 and secretary in 1818, and he was president of the Society from 1831 until his death. In 1824 he won the Gold Medal at the Paris Salon. He settled at Brighton in 1829, retaining a studio in London, and about 1849 moved to Worthing. Fielding was a very rapid and prolific painter, but his work lies open to the criticism of being repetitive. He was highly successful financially, amassing a large fortune. He is buried in Hove Churchyard. Fielding's watercolours had a profound effect on the style of the Belfast painter Andrew Nicholl.

---

32. Bay Scene, Sunset. 1819. (no. 775).

Watercolour on white paper
29.8 × 40.7 cms / 11¾ × 16″.
Signed b.r. "Copley Fielding 1819".

Bought: London, Fine Art Society 1948.

This is the best of the Ulster Museum's five watercolours by Copley Fielding. The location is unknown. It dates from ten years before Fielding's removal to the South Coast, and if it does depict the South of England it would be a sunrise rather than a sunset scene, as it would be looking eastward. Another possibility is the North Coast of Wales, with the Great Orme's Head in the distance. Fielding exhibited a *Sunrise near Sandgate* at the Old Water-Colour Society in 1819 (18), but his watercolours of this sort of subject are legion.

This is a fine middle-period Copley Fielding, showing much influence of Turner in the handling of the sky. The far distance and the atmosphere are beautifully handled, but the scraped-out waves are rather schematic. This trait can also be seen in the work of Andrew Nicholl, which owes a lot to Fielding.

Bibliography:
Redgrave, Roget, Graves Dict, Graves Loan, Cundall, Binyon, Williams, DNB, Hardie, Nettlefold, RA 1934, Mallalieu, Cordingly, Clarke, NGI.
S C K Smith: *Copley Fielding* OWCS III 1925.

George Petrie
Born Dublin 1790; died Dublin 1866

With Andrew Nicholl and Henry O'Neill, Petrie was one of the leading Irish topographical draughtsmen of the 19th century. He was the son of James Petrie, a miniature painter of Scottish origin who had settled in Dublin. In 1799 he was sent to Samuel Whyte's drawing school in Grafton Street, and then to the Dublin Society's School, where he won the silver medal for figure drawing in 1805. He made a sketching tour in Wicklow in 1808 and in Wales in 1810. With his friends Francis Danby and James Arthur O'Connor, Petrie visited London in 1813, but soon returned to Dublin, leaving Danby in Bristol. Petrie exhibited at the Royal Hibernian Academy from 1826 to 1868, and was elected ARHA in 1826 and RHA in 1828. The following year he was appointed Librarian to the RHA. In 1856 he was elected President of the RHA, but resigned after a schism in 1859 and was made an Honorary Member. As well as being a painter, Petrie wrote essays on Irish antiquities and traditional music. He was elected a member of the Royal Irish Academy in 1828, and by 1830 was on its Council. In 1833 he was connected with the Ordnance Survey of Ireland. He was awarded the degree of Doctor of Laws by Trinity College, Dublin, in 1847, and a Civil List Pension in 1849. He is buried in Mount Jerome Cemetery. His daughter Mary Anne Petrie painted in the same style as her father.

33. The Eagle's Nest, Killarney.

Watercolour over pencil on white paper
26.2 × 36.4 cms / 10¼ × 14⅜".

Bought: Mrs Mary Clarke, 52 Upper Gardiner Street, Dublin 1910.

The location was identified by Peter Murray, verbally 1979. This is the most characteristic of the Ulster Museum's three Petrie watercolours, but is undated. The use of crimson lake for the heather is typical of Petrie. Some of his watercolours of similar terrain can be very large (e.g. *The Home of the Heron* in the National Gallery of Ireland, Dublin) but this is a small example.

After the "Wicklow Tour" (see under Forrester, no. 5 in this catalogue), the "Killarney Tour" was the most popular among travellers in search of the picturesque in 18th and early 19th century Ireland. Cornelius Varley (see no. 26) went there in 1808. The Ulster Museum has an oil painting of the *Eagle's Nest* by William Sadler (1782-1839), which shows a party of travellers with a guide firing a cannon to demonstrate the echo.

Bibliography:
Graves RA, Strickland, VAM, Elmes, Arnold, Mallalieu, P of I, Boylan, NGI.
Dublin, National Library of Ireland: George Petrie correspondence; this contains a series of letters from Petrie's friend the Belfast Pre-Raphaelite collector Francis McCracken (1802-63).
William Stokes: *The Life and Labours in Art and Archaeology of George Petrie* 1868.
Peter Murray: *George Petrie* unpublished MLitt thesis, Trinity College, Dublin 1980.
Jeanne Sheehy: *The Rediscovery of Ireland's Past: the Celtic Revival 1830-1930* Thames and Hudson 1980.

FRANCIS DANBY
Born Wexford 1793; died Exmouth, Devon 1861

Danby received his early training in Dublin at the Dublin Society Schools and under James Arthur O'Connor. In 1813, he, O'Connor and George Petrie set off for London by way of Bristol. On the way back, having run out of money to return to Dublin, Danby decided to settle in Bristol as a drawing master. Here he became the leader of a regional school of painters, exhibiting at the Royal Academy from 1821 onwards. He was elected ARA in 1825, and became celebrated for his large, many-figured pictures of Biblical disasters, comparable to those of John Martin. In 1829 domestic problems forced him abroad where living was cheaper, and until 1841 he lived mainly in Switzerland, on Lake Geneva, where he practiced boat-building and yachting. He returned to England in 1841, lived for a short time at Lewisham, and then settled for the rest of his life at Exmouth.

---

34. *Ringsend from Beggar's Bush, Co Dublin.* (no. 2095).

Watercolour on white wove paper
Overall 20.8 × 30.5 cms / 8⅜ × 12″;
painted area 14.7 × 20.4 cms / 5¾ × 8⅛″.
Signed b.r. "F. Danby".
Inscribed on recto in pencil, on bottom margin: "Rings end from Beggar's bush".
On verso, in pencil: "A.C-"; in ink: "Rings' End - from Beggar's bush" "Coote Carroll 19".

Source unknown. (Day Book 48/1974).

Rep Anglesea 1975.

Exh Bristol City Art Gallery and London, Tate Gallery: *Francis Danby* 1988-9 (63).

Ringsend and Beggar's Bush are suburbs to the south east of Dublin, south of where the River Liffey enters Dublin Bay, and where it is joined by the River Dodder. This watercolour is topographically interesting as it shows a glass factory on the right (the conical kiln), as well as some shipping.

This is one of a set of four early watercolours by Danby which pre-date his leaving of Ireland in 1813. For further details see the note on no. 35, below.

Bibliography:
Redgrave Dict, Redgrave Cent, Roget, Graves Dict, Graves RA, Graves BI, Binyon, VAM, Cundall, Strickland, Hardie, Arnold, Mallalieu, NGI.
Art Journal 1855.
William Stokes: *Life of George Petrie* 1868.
Geoffrey Grigson: *Some notes on Francis Danby* Cornhill Magazine 1946; The Harp of Aeolus 1948.
Eric Adams: *Francis Danby: varieties of poetic landscape* 1973.
Bristol, City Museum and Art Gallery: *The Bristol School of Artists: Francis Danby and Painting in Bristol 1810-1840* catalogue by Francis Greenacre 1973.
E Malins and M Bishop: *James Smetham and Francis Danby* 1974.
Martyn Anglesea: *Five unpublished drawings by Francis Danby* Burlington Magazine Jan 1975 p 47.
Bristol City Art Gallery and London, Tate Gallery: *Francis Danby 1793–1861* catalogue by Francis Greenacre, 1988.

35. *Castle Archdale on Lough Erne, Co Fermanagh.* (no. 2097).

Watercolour on white wove paper
Overall 22.2 × 30.5 cms / 8¾ × 12″;
painted area 17.2 × 24.8 cms / 6¾ × 9¾″.
Signed b.c. "F. Danby".
Inscribed on recto, in pencil, on bottom margin: "Castle
Archdale on Lough Erin" [sic].
On verso, in ink: "Castle Archdale on Lough Erin" [sic]
"Coote Carroll 17".

Source unknown (Day Book 48/1974).

Rep Anglesea 1975.

Exh Bristol City Art Gallery and London, Tate Gallery:
Francis Danby 1988-9 (62), reproduced in colour, pl 21.

This is the only one of the four early Danby
watercolours which represents a view in the north of
Ireland. The house built by Colonel Mervyn
Archdale in 1773 is seen at an angle from near the lake. Since
1959 this house has been derelict. See Mark Bence-
Jones: *Burke's Guide to Country Houses: no. 1 (Ireland)*
1978 p 61.

Like no. 34, this is one of four Irish views by
Danby which were discovered unrecorded in one of
the Ulster Museum's stores in 1974, and absorbed
into the collection. The remaining two are *Mill near
Beggar's Bush* (no. 2096, watermarked WHATMAN
1805) and *Dunleary from the South* (no. 2098,
watermarked WHATMAN 1811). Francis Greenacre,
Bristol City Art Gallery (letter 20 Jan 1975) pointed
out that as the latter is watermarked 1811 and Danby
left Ireland for good in 1813, this is the tightest
certain date bracket for any of his drawings before
1820.

The four little watercolours were in a paper folder
along with six small watercolours by John Henry
Campbell (1757-1828), all of which also have the
name "Coote Carroll" on the back, with a number.
Coote Carroll, who presumably commissioned, or at
least owned, the watercolours, was the second son of
Alexander Carroll of Dublin whose will was dated
and proved in 1768. Alexander's eldest son George
inherited an estate at Ashford, Co Wicklow. (See
Burke's *Landed Gentry of Great Britain* 7th ed. 1886,
vol 1 p 305, and the 1894 ed. vol 1 p 296). Possibly

the same Coote Carroll occurs in J J Howard and F A
Crisp: *The Visitation of Ireland* 1897-1918, vol 4 p 84,
as "of Ballymote, Co Sligo".

These four watercolours are important in the
Danby chronology as they are at present the earliest
known signed drawings by Danby, with the
exception of a watercolour *View in Co Wexford* in the
National Gallery of Ireland, Dublin (6881, possibly a
view of Clonmines and Bannow Bay), which is not of
the same quality. These, dating from before Danby
left Ireland in 1813, constitute his only known Irish
topographical work.

Greenacre (letter 20 Jan 1975) states that the quality
of the four Ulster Museum watercolours makes it
hard now to accept as by him a panel *Lake Scene* in a
private collection (exh. Bristol 1973 (1)). This was
provisionally accepted by Adams as a Danby of about
1813-16, and later identified by the Knight of Glin as
a view in Co Wicklow, with figures possibly by
O'Connor. Either this panel is much earlier, which
seems unlikely from the style of the figures, or else it
is not good enough to be ascribed to either Danby or
O'Connor.

Another early Danby watercolour of *Cader Idris*
(London, Courtauld Institute of Art, Witt Collection),
dated about 1813 by Adams, now appears to be
slightly later and is comparable with two drawings of
Bristol of about 1815-16 (Bristol exhibition 1973, nos
30 and 31). Three other drawings placeable in this
period have been discovered since the 1973 *Bristol
School* exhibition.

F Danby

71

DAVID ROBERTS
Born Stockbridge, Edinburgh 1796; died London 1864

With Samuel Prout, David Roberts was probably the most productive British draughtsman of foreign topography and architecture in the first half of the 19th century. The son of a shoemaker, he was apprenticed for seven years to a housepainter before working as a theatrical scene painter in Carlisle, Glasgow and Edinburgh. In 1822 he went to London and worked at Drury Lane Theatre with his friend Clarkson Stanfield. He was first Vice-President of the Society of British Artists 1823-4, and President in 1830. In the 1820s Roberts made several trips to Normandy, and in 1832-3, on Sir David Wilkie's advice, he visited Spain and Tangier. In 1838 he visited Egypt and Palestine, and in 1851 and 1853 he went to Italy and Austria. These tours provided him with much of his material, and he made a fortune from the volumes of lithographs published after his drawings. He was elected ARA in 1838, RA in 1841, and was one of the Commissioners for the Great Exhibition of 1851.

---

36. Church of San Jago, Jerez. (no. 1323).

Watercolour with white over pencil on buff paper
41.2 × 28.8 cms / 16¼ × 11⅜".
Inscribed b.r. "Church of San Jago Xerez".

Bought: London, Palser Gallery 1937.

This was conserved at the British Museum in 1973, when a 4 inch tear running down from the top edge was repaired.

This drawing must have been made in Jerez de la Frontiera about May or June 1833. Another version of it is in the Fitzwilliam Museum, Cambridge (Helen Guiterman: letter 18 Feb 1986). Katharine Sim 1984 p 90 refers to it as "a pleasing study of the exterior of the church of San Iago, lively with crumbling little houses built on to the side, and dramatic-looking Spaniards wearing large hats". Roberts himself wrote: "...I soon tired of [Cadiz] and at the end of two days took my departure for *Xerez* or as we call it *Sherry's*. At Xerez I stopt some days having letters to some Scottish friends from whom I received much kindness".

Roberts's Spanish tour was his most important European venture. He entered Spain from France in October 1832, travelling via Burgos, Vittoria and Madrid, which he reached on 16 December, staying three weeks. He went on to Cordoba and Granada, and reached Malaga in early March 1833, when he crossed from Gibraltar to Tangier and Tetuan. By this time he had accumulated 206 finished drawings, as well as small sketches. He returned through Gibraltar, via Ronda, Cadiz and *Jerez* (where, as may be expected, he enjoyed the sherry), reaching Seville where he spent four months. Here he was caught by an outbreak of cholera, which forced him to leave Spain. In five weeks journey he arrived in Cornwall on 22 October 1833, after twelve months abroad. See Guiterman 1984 p 59.

This view was lithographed by Thomas Shotter Boys, for *Picturesque Sketches in Spain taken during the years 1832 and 1833 by David Roberts* Hodgson & Graves 1837, plate VI, in a volume of 26 lithographs dedicated to the Marquis of Lansdowne. Roberts wrote in his *Journal* about these 26 prints "...nearly all of which I have worked less or more on the Stones themselves. Many of the figures are entirely my own drawing upon the Stone with the exception of one or two by Hague". Two of the prints are credited on the plates to Roberts, while others are by Boys, Thomas Allom and Louis Hague. The preparation of this book took Roberts seven months instead of the two months he had expected, and so in 1838 he was unable to exhibit. In 1857 it had a longer print run than any other lithographic work, and was "still selling although a mere shadow". See Guiterman 1984 pp 59-61.

Bibliography:
Redgrave Dict, Redgrave Cent, Bryan, Caw, Cundall, Graves Dict, Graves RA, Graves BI, Graves Loan, Binyon, VAM, DNB, RA 1934, Hughes, Nettlefold, Hardie, Mallalieu, Irwin.
London, VAM Library: David Roberts letter to W H Dixon, etc.
David Roberts: *Thumbnail Sketch Journal* Private Collection.
David Roberts: *Eastern Journal* MSS Edinburgh, National Library of Scotland.
David Roberts: *Christine Bicknell's Journal* MSS Edinburgh, National Library of Scotland.
James Ballantine: *The Life of David Roberts* Edinburgh, A & C Black 1866.
Jane Quigley: *David Roberts as a Watercolour Painter* Walker's Quarterly X, 1922.
Jane Quigley: *Prout and Roberts* 1926.
Martin Hardie: *David Roberts* OWCS XXV, 1947 p 10.
A G Reynolds: *British Artists Abroad: V. Roberts in Spain etc.* Geographical Magazine XXI, 1949.

Helen Guiterman: *David Roberts RA 1796-1864* (pamphlet)
  Dramrite Printers, Southwark 1978; revised edition 1981.

Edinburgh, Scottish Arts Council: *David Roberts: Artist*
  Adventurer touring exhibition, catalogue by Patsy
  Campbell, 1981.

Katharine Sim: *David Roberts RA: 1796-1864: a biography*
  Quartet Books 1984.

Helen Guiterman: *David Roberts RA: part 1* OWCS LIX,
  1984 p 53.

Helen Guiterman: *David Roberts RA: part 2* OWCS LX,
  1985 p 87.

London, Barbican Art Gallery: *David Roberts* catalogue by
  Bryony Llewellyn and Helen Guiterman, Phaidon 1986.

JAMES HOLLAND
Born Burslem, Staffordshire 1800; died London 1870

Holland worked as a boy decorating pottery in the Davenport factory, and his earliest works are floral designs. In 1819 he went to London, where he worked in potteries in Deptford and Southwark while teaching himself landscape and architectural painting. He visited Paris for the first time in 1831 and came under the influence of Bonington. In 1835 he was elected associate of the Old Water-Colour Society, and paid the first of many visits to Venice. His Venetian views are his best-known works. Other documented visits were to Portugal 1837, Paris 1841, Verona 1844, Holland 1845, Normandy and North Wales 1850, Genoa 1851 and Innsbruck 1857. Holland resigned from the Old Water-Colour Society in 1842, intending to concentrate on oil painting, but he failed to get elected to the Royal Academy and returned to the Old Water-Colour Society in 1856. He was elected a full member in 1857. The works remaining in his studio were sold at Christie's on 26 May 1870.

---

37. *A Venetian Canal.* (no. 804).

Watercolour over pencil on white paper
33.8 × 49.1 cms / 13⅜ × 19¾".

Bought: London, Fine Art Society 1939.

Provenance Collection of Edmund Wimperis FRIBA, son of the watercolour painter Edmund Morison Wimperis, a follower of David Cox: the sketch is reproduced in Stokes's article in Walker's Quarterly 1927 p 28 as "by permission of E Wimperis Esq."

This is a broadly-handled sketch, completely in transparent watercolour, of a narrow Rio looking towards the Grand Canal. It could well be imaginary, though the Post Office is indicated on the right. The Venetian Post Office is in the Fondaco dei Tedeschi, which does not look like this. Holland's Venetian views are not usually as large as this and often contain a certain amount of bodycolour, and, like Bonington's romantic scenes, are sometimes purely imaginary. It may be one of the numerous lots entitled "A Canal Scene, Venice", in the sale of Holland's remaining works at Christie's on 26 May 1870. This sale contained 50 oils and about 400 drawings and sketches in watercolour and pencil; they are listed in Davies 1930 pp 51-54.

Bibliography:
Redgrave Dict, Redgrave Cent, DNB, Roget, Graves Dict, Graves RA, Graves Loan, Binyon, VAM, Cundall, RA 1934, Nettlefold, Hardie, Mallalieu.
Studio Special Number 1915.
Hugh Stokes: *James Holland* Walker's Quarterly XXIII, 1927.
Randall Davies: *James Holland* OWCS VII 1930.
Morley Tonkin: *The Life of James Holland* OWCS XLII, 1967.

THOMAS SHOTTER BOYS
Born Pentonville, London 1803; died St John's Wood, London 1874

Boys was articled to the engraver George Cooke in 1817, then in 1823 went to Paris where he worked as an engraver and lithographer, principally with Richard Parkes Bonington, who introduced him to painting. In Paris, Boys taught William Callow and Ambrose Poynter. Returning to London in 1837, Boys exhibited at the New Water-Colour Society between 1824 and 1876, and was elected an associate in 1840 and a member in 1841. He published lithographs after David Roberts (see no. 36), and etched some plates for Ruskin's *The Stones of Venice*. He is buried at Finchley.

---

38. The King's Palace, Brussels. (no. 742).

Watercolour with bodycolour on white paper
16.8 × 26.1 cms / 6⅝ × 10¼".
Signed b.r. "T.Boys".

Bought: London, Palser Gallery 1937.

Exh Nottingham 1974 (10) rep. in colour in the catalogue, pl VI.

This is probably the watercolour *The King's Palace, Brussels* which Boys exhibited at the New Water-Colour Society in 1832 (270). The Nottingham catalogue states that it may have been painted before the Belgian Revolution of August 1830, which led to the fall of the House of Orange and the independence of Belgium from the United Kingdom of the Netherlands, set up in 1815.

Roundell 1974 p 26 quotes a letter from Boys to Henry Mogford, written from Paris on 17 Aug 1831: "...Damn the Belgians God Damn and blast the bloody Belgians". In spite of this outburst, Boys married a Belgian girl, Célestine Marie Barbe.

A date of 1830 would place this watercolour among the earliest examples of Boys's assured use of the medium. The technique involves many elements derived from Bonington - dragged washes of dry colour, scraped-out highlights, gumming, superimposition of transparent washes in the trees, and flat touches of bodycolour in the figures. The effect obtained is of an animated scene arrested for a second, whereas much of Boys's later work takes on the static qualities of architectural draughtsmanship.

Bibliography:
Graves RA, Binyon, DNB, VAM, Hughes, Cundall, Hardie, Mallalieu, Clarke.
Hugh Stokes: *Thomas Shotter Boys* Walker's Quarterly XVIII, 1926.
Architectural Review LX, 1926.
E Beresford Chancellor: *Original Views of London* 1926; re-issued 1954.
Nottingham University Art Gallery, and London, Agnew's: *Thomas Shotter Boys Centenary Exhibition* catalogue by Alistair Smart 1974.
James Roundell: *Thomas Shotter Boys* Octopus Books 1974.

ANDREW NICHOLL
Born Belfast 1804; died London 1886

The most successful Belfast landscape painter of the mid 19th century, Andrew Nicholl was born in Church Lane, the second son of a boot and shoe maker whose name is variously given as Andrew or Henry Nicholl. His elder brother William Nicholl was an amateur painter and gave him encouragement. At about the age of eighteen Andrew Nicholl was apprenticed as a compositor with the Belfast printer Francis Dalzell Finlay, who in 1824 started the newspaper *The Northern Whig*, and who spotted Nicholl's talent as a draughtsman. He was given many puffs by this newspaper, but was described as "a delicate young man" (see Adams 1984). In 1828 he made a series of 101 watercolour views of the Antrim Coast, and in 1829 was commissioned by Robert Thomson of Jennymount to sketch in his grounds. Other early patrons included James Lawson Drummond and Dr James MacDonnell. In 1830 Nicholl went to London, probably taken there by his main patron James Emerson (after marriage, Sir James Emerson Tennent) who was elected Whig MP for Belfast in 1832, but who turned Tory in 1834. In London, Nicholl studied in the Dulwich College Gallery, then the only collection of Old Master paintings open to the public. His style changed under the influence of Aelbert Cuyp, Copley Fielding, Peter de Wint and Turner. After a brief return to Belfast, Nicholl was again in London in 1832 when he exhibited at the Royal Academy for the first time, and was commissioned by Ackermann to make drawings in the Western Highlands of Scotland. Between then and 1834, Nicholl shuttled between London and Belfast, and made teaching excursions to Coleraine and Ballycastle. Of his many Belfast pupils, the most distinguished were Dr James Moore and the Rev Narcissus Batt. In October 1834 *Five Views of the Dublin and Kingstown Railway* appeared, and Nicholl began his association with the *Dublin Penny Journal*. He was elected ARHA in 1837, but did not become a full RHA until the constitution was revised in 1860. Between about 1834 and 1840 he was one of the team of artists illustrating *Hall's Ireland*, employed by Samuel Carter Hall (later editor of the *Art Journal*) and Mrs Hall. Nicholl supplied the Halls with archaeological information as well as sketches (see Anglesea: Studies 1982). About 1840, Nicholl moved again to London, and in 1842 illustrated John Fisher Murray's *The Environs of London*. In December 1844 his seven year old son Robert Andrew Nicholl died of a chest infection. Nicholl kept up the production of Northern Irish scenes for sale in Belfast, and by 1845 his work was being forged in Belfast (see Adams 1984). In July 1845, Emerson Tennent was appointed Colonial Secretary for Ceylon, and in August 1846 Nicholl followed him there as "teacher of landscape painting, scientific drawing and design" at the Colombo Academy. It seems likely that Nicholl was taken there by Tennent for the purpose of illustrating Tennent's authoritative book *Ceylon*, which is still admired by the Sri Lankans, although they regard Tennent's administration as disastrously insensitive (Tennent introduced a verandah tax and a dog tax). Both Tennent and Nicholl were on an exploratory expedition in the central province of Kandy during the Kandyan Rebellion of 1848 (did Tennent cause it?) and had to flee for their lives. Nicholl described his experiences in a long article in the *Dublin University Magazine* in 1852. Many of Nicholl's sketches still remain in the National Museum in Colombo, and among his pupils at the Academy was the father of the Sinhalese art-historian Ananda K Coomaraswamy (information from Mr Ismeth Raheem, Colombo). Nicholl seems to have returned to London by 1849, as he exhibited views of Ceylon in the Royal Academy that year. For many years Nicholl wrote light pastoral verse, a quantity of which was published in the *Dublin University Magazine*. From the 1850s Nicholl's chronology is hard to establish, as he rarely dated his work, but he continued to shuttle between London and Belfast. In 1870 he submitted twelve watercolours of Ceylon scenes to Queen Victoria, who bought two of them, and he presented a volume of sketches of Ceylon to the British Museum Print Room in 1883. He died at his London house, 7 Camberwell Grove, aged 83, on 16 April 1886, and a memorial exhibition was held in Belfast the following month. Nicholl's daughter Mary Anne presented fifty-six of her father's studies of plants of Ceylon to the Royal Hibernian Academy. The Ulster Museum has portraits of Nicholl by Felice Piccioni and Charles Grey.

39. McArt's Fort from the Mountain to between the Fort and the Caves. 1828. (no. 250).

Watercolour on white paper
24 × 35.5 cms / 9⅜ × 14″.
Signed b.l. "A Nicholl".

Bought: Belfast, Anthony Thomson (dealer) 1957.

Exh Belfast, Ulster Museum: *Andrew Nicholl* 1973 (3).

Rep Hewitt 1977 p 28 (in colour); Anglesea: *Antrim Coast* 1982.

"McArt's Fort" stands on the summit of Cave Hill, the basalt cliff that overlooks Belfast from the north. This is one of the series of 113 views of the Antrim Coast which are Nicholl's earliest datable work, two of them being dated 1828. He would then have been about 24, and was still an apprentice compositor under Finlay in Belfast. His early style is one of clean, crisp washes, rather like John Varley, and was probably derived from looking at aquatint illustrations in travel books. These early watercolours show a striking sense of linear design, but Nicholl's drawing of animals was later to improve.

Bibliography:
Graves RA, Strickland, Cundall, VAM, Binyon, Elmes, Hardie, Arnold, Mallalieu, Hewitt, P of I, NGI.

Andrew Nicholl et al.: *Picturesque Sketches of some of the finest Landscape and Coast Scenery of Ireland from drawings by G Petrie RHA, A Nicholl and H O'Neill* 6 parts, published by W K Wakeman, Dublin 1835.

Andrew Nicholl et al.: *Fourteen Views in the County of Wicklow, from original drawings by H O'Neill and A Nicholl* published by W F Wakeman, Dublin 1835.

Mr and Mrs S C Hall: *Ireland: its Scenery, Character, etc.* ("Hall's Ireland") 3 vols, London, Virtue and Co. 1841-43. This contains over 100 wood-engravings after drawings by Nicholl.

Andrew Nicholl: *A Sketching Tour of five weeks in the Forests of Ceylon. Its ruined temples, collossal statues, tanks, dagobahs etc.* Dublin University Magazine 40, 1852, part 1 p 527; part 2 p 691.

Sir James Emerson Tennent: *Ceylon: an Account of the Island, physical, historical and topographical, with Notices of its Natural History, Antiquities and Productions* 5th edition, thoroughly revised, 2 vols, Longmans 1860. This contains 31 engravings after Nicholl.

Belfast, Ulster Museum: *Scrapbook* belonging to Nicholl's daughter, Mary Anne Nicholl, containing letters, newspaper cuttings and proofs of engravings. ("Nicholl Scrapbook").

Belfast, Ulster Museum: MSS *Account of Nicholl's Life*, probably written by James F Johnston (for details of whom see under FUSELI, no. 10).

Catalogue of Watercolour Drawings by the late Andrew Nicholl, RHA, on exhibition at 55 Donegall Place, Belfast, 26th May 1886 ("Belfast Exhibition 1886").

Belfast Museum and Art Gallery: Quarterly Notes LX, March 1939.

Cork, Crawford Municipal Art Gallery: *Irish Art in the 19th Century* catalogue by Cyril Barrett, Rosc 1971.

Belfast, Ulster Museum: *Andrew Nicholl 1804-1886* catalogue by Martyn Anglesea 1973.

London, Spink and Son: *Andrew Nicholl and the Plants of Ceylon* 4–28 Aug 1981.

Martyn Anglesea: *Andrew Nicholl and his Patrons in Ireland and Ceylon* Studies, summer 1982 p 130.

Martyn Anglesea, introd.: *Andrew Nicholl's Views of the Antrim Coast in 1828* with notes on the places by members of the Society; Belfast, Glens of Antrim Historical Society 1982.

Ronald Adams: *Andrew Nicholl* Irish Arts Review, vol 1 no. 4, winter 1984 p 29.

40. West View of the Giant's Causeway from the Stookans. 1828. (no. 1421).

Watercolour on white paper
25 × 34.8 cms / 9⅞ × 13⅝″.
Signed b.r. "A Nicholl".

Bought: Belfast, Anthony Thomson (dealer) 1957.

Exh Belfast, Ulster Museum: *Andrew Nicholl* 1973 (31).

Rep Anglesea: *Antrim Coast* 1982 (in colour).

Like no. 39, this is another of the long series of early views of the Antrim Coast. The Causeway is presented literally and soberly, with no hint of the romantic exaggeration in style that Nicholl was later to acquire (see no. 42). The three strange little fashionably-dressed figures, placed dead centre in the foreground with their backs to the spectator, recall the work that Caspar David Friedrich was producing in Dresden at the same date, but this is, of course, purely coincidental. After his first visit to London in 1830, Nicholl lost this charming naive style and came under the influence of De Wint, Copley Fielding and Turner.

41. *A Bank of Flowers, with a View of Bray, Co Wicklow.* (no. 916).

Watercolour on white paper
35.1 × 52.1 cms / 13¾ × 20½″.
Signed b.r. "A Nicholl RHA".

Inscribed on verso: "Bray and the Valley of the Dargle from Killiney Hill, Co Dublin".

Bought: Belfast, Anthony Thomson (dealer) 1957.

Exh Belfast, Ulster Museum: *Andrew Nicholl* 1973 (50).

These views with flowers in the foreground make Nicholl's most original and attractive productions. They probably all date from the 1830s when Nicholl was living in Dublin. Little attention should be paid to the signature with its "RHA", as these letters appear on many of Nicholl's watercolours and were probably added later, not necessarily by Nicholl himself. Nicholl was not elected a full RHA until 1860.

Other examples of this type of Nicholl watercolour include one with *Carrickfergus Castle*, which was with the Leicester Galleries, London, in 1968; one with a view of *The White Rocks at Portrush*, belonging to the Knight of Glin; and one with a view of *Downhill, Co Londonderry*, in a private collection (reproduced on the cover of the Rosc exhibition catalogue *Irish Art of the 19th Century*, Cork, Crawford Municipal Art Gallery Oct-Dec 1971).

42. *The Giant's Causeway from the West.* (no. 1256).

Watercolour over pencil on white paper
45.8 × 69.8 cms / 18 × 27½"
Signed b.r. "A Nicholl RHA".

Bought: Belfast, Lady Musgrave 1954.

Exh Belfast, Ulster Museum: *Andrew Nicholl* 1973 (61).

The first trustworthy views of the Giant's Causeway were painted on the spot by Susanna Drury about 1739, and engraved by Francois Vivarès in London in 1743/4. Two pairs of Susanna Drury's gouaches on vellum exist, one in the Ulster Museum and the other belonging to the Knight of Glin. See Martyn Anglesea and John Preston: *A Philosophical Landscape: Susanna Drury and the Giant's Causeway* Art History, vol 3 no. 3, Sept 1980 p 252.

This is a watercolour of Nicholl's maturity, and makes an interesting contrast with his 1828 view of the same subject (no. 40). In this view the height of the cliffs and of the Grand Causeway itself is greatly exaggerated, but Nicholl has acquired an impressive repertoire of atmospheric effects. The old woman selling whiskey by the fresh water spring ("The Giant's Well"), on the right, was a local character around the 1840s. Many tourists, including Thackeray, bought whiskey from her. Presumably the whiskey came from the Bushmills Distillery nearby, which claims to be the oldest distillery in existence.

A smaller watercolour similar to this is in the British Museum, presented by Nicholl's daughter (1886-10-20-2).

WILLIAM JAMES MÜLLER
Born Bristol 1812; died Bristol 1845

Though he died at the early age of 33, Müller was the most celebrated artist of the Bristol School. The son of J S Müller, a native of Danzig who was curator of the Bristol Institution, Müller started as an engineer, then studied painting under J B Pyne. In 1831, after seeing Bulwer's collection of Cotman drawings, he toured Norfolk and Suffolk, and in 1833 he toured North Wales. He was one of the founders of the Bristol Sketching Club. Müller exhibited at the Royal Academy from 1833 to 1845, also at the British Institution and Suffolk Street. In 1834 he toured Germany, Switzerland and Italy with George Arthur Fripp, and in 1838 visited Greece and Egypt. He settled in London in 1839. In 1840 he visited France, and about that time he attempted to teach oil painting to the ageing David Cox. He accompanied the Government Expedition to Lycia (in present-day Turkey) in 1841-44. On his return his health failed, and he retired to Bristol, where he died of a heart attack. Müller was a prolific sketcher and was ambidextrous.

---

43. *Xanthus from the Theatre.* (no. 827).

Watercolour over pencil on rough white wove paper
37.3 × 56.7 cms / 14⅝ × 22⅜″.
Bought: Olaf H Barnett, Hassocks, Sussex 1951.

Müller went to Asia Minor in 1841 with the government-sponsored expedition to Lycia, which resulted in several monuments, including the Nereid Monument from Xanthus, being dismantled and transported to the British Museum, where they still remain. In a letter written at "Xanthus, Asia Minor, Nov 29 1843" (published in the Art Union in February 1844, and republished in the OWCS XXV, 1947, p 34), Müller describes the place:

"....Xanthus, the seat of the operations, is about 100 or 150 feet above the plain, and, on the left and right, is closed in by mountains of considerable height, backed by the Taurus, which is now capped with snow....But I would say a word or two previously on the antiquities and ruins of this place: they principally consist, then, of tombs - either in the rock or standing as they have existed for centuries past - shaken by earthquake, or pillaged by man. Their forms are most classical, and when covered with sculpture, as in the case of the two grand ones now in the process of removing, little inferior to the finest and purest Greek period of Art. Of these two tombs, I must say, if the expedition removed nothing else, they will add to our country two of the most beautiful and splendid remains in existence....The city was formerly very large, as its ruins now cover a vast extent of soil. There is little, unfortunately, in the remains of the buildings and temples that may be termed *sketchable*, - being principally piles of stones of enormous size. Cyclopean walls, with Roman ones built upon them, do not exactly suit the artist's folio...."

Some of Müller's best drawings were made on this expedition, when he was reduced to a restricted palette because he had run out of many of his watercolours, and his white had become unusable. The quantity of sketches made on this expedition occupied Müller for the last four years of his life. The two standing tombs seen above the seating of the Theatre still remain, and apart from the undergrowth having been partly cleared, Müller's view is still extant today.

Another watercolour in the same idiom and from the same expedition is *Ilos, Lycia* in the Yale Center for British Art, B1975.4.1567. This shows a range of snowcapped mountains in the distance.

Bibliography:
Redgrave Dict, Redgrave Cent, Graves Dict, Graves RA, Graves BI, DNB, Bryan, Cundall, Binyon, VAM, RA 1934, Roget, Hughes, Nettlefold, Hardie, Mallalieu.
William James Müller: *Sketches Illustrative of the Age of Francis I* 1841.
N N Solly: *Memoirs of the Life of William James Müller* 1875.
A Letter from William James Müller OWCS XXV, 1947.
C G E Bunt: *The Art and Life of William James Müller of Bristol* Leigh-on-Sea 1948.
Bristol, City Museum and Art Gallery: *The Bristol School of Artists 1810-40* catalogue by Francis Greenacre 1973.
Denis Thomas: *William James Müller and the Norwich connection* The Connoisseur, Feb 1978 p 792.
H J E Carter: *A Sketcher from Bristol* Country Life, 8 June 1978 p 1642.

JAMES HOWARD BURGESS
Born Belfast? c 1817; died Belfast 1890

It is not known where Burgess was born nor where he received his training. He first exhibited at the Royal Hibernian Academy in 1830, from an address at 11 Digges Street, Dublin. Strickland states that he painted miniatures as well as watercolour landscapes. "Hall's Ireland", published in 1841 (see under Andrew Nicholl), contains twenty-five illustrations engraved from Burgess's drawings. By this time he was a drawing master in Belfast. Martin's *Belfast Directory* of 1841-2 shows him as "professor of drawing, 90 Donegall Street". In 1843-4 the *Belfast Post Office Directory* has him entered as "landscape and animal painter, 4 Linenhall Street". He was living in Carrickfergus in 1846, when he was awarded £10 by the Royal Irish Art Union for a lithograph after *The Great Britain on Shore in Dundrum Bay*, painted by

Matthew Kendrick RHA (c 1797-1874). Kendrick's picture was bought by the Royal Irish Art Union in 1847 for £60. Burgess seems to have been the leading drawing master in Belfast during the absences of Andrew Nicholl (q.v.) in Dublin, London and Ceylon. In 1850 "J Howard Burgess's Drawing Academy, 16 Donegall Place" appears in *Henderson's Belfast Directory*, at the same address as Thomas Jackson, the architect. Burgess was no longer there in 1858-9. The premises later became the Imperial Hotel. Watercolours and drawings by Burgess in the Ulster Museum and the National Gallery of Ireland show that he travelled in Scotland, Wales and Yorkshire as well as Ireland. Burgess died in the Royal Hospital, Belfast, on 9 November 1890.

---

44. *"Cahan Abbey", with the O'Cahan Tomb, Dungiven, Co Londonderry.* (no. 1001).

Watercolour with Chinese white over pencil on buff paper 35.5 × 26.3 cms / 14 × 10⅜".
Signed on ledger-stone, b.c. "J H Burgess".
Given by W T Braithwaite, 1906.

The Augustinian Church at Dungiven was founded by the local O'Cahan chieftains in the 12th century. The flamboyant canopied tomb on the south side of the chancel, with its traceried arch of a distinctive Irish type, has been traditionally identified as that of Cooey na nGall O'Cahan who died in 1385. Stylistic evidence, however, places the tomb approximately in the last quarter of the 15th century. See John Hunt: *Irish Mediaeval Figure Sculpture 1200-1600* Irish University Press / Sotheby Parke Bernet, Dublin and London 1974, vol 1 pp 131-2.

The tomb was ignorantly "restored" about 1875, when the recumbent effigy and the figures of gallowglass warriors around the tomb-chest were given "Phrygian caps". Burgess shows the tomb in its dilapidated state before restoration, as it also appears in a drawing of 1840 by George du Noyer in the National Library of Ireland, Dublin.

The ruined church is now in state care of the Department of the Environment (Northern Ireland).

Bibliography:
Strickland, Hewitt, Mallalieu, NGI.

EDWARD DUNCAN
Born Hampstead, London 1803; died London 1882

Duncan was best known as a marine painter. He was apprenticed to the Havell family of aquatint engravers, and started his career by engraving marine and coaching prints. He engraved some of the marine pictures of William Huggins, and married his daughter Bertha. Duncan exhibited at both the Old and New Water-Colour Societies from 1830 to 1882. He was elected NWCS in 1833 but resigned in 1847. In 1848 he was elected an associate of the Old Water-Colour Society, and a member in 1849. He made regular sketching tours in the south of England and the Bristol Channel area, and visited Holland in 1840, the Channel Islands in the 1850s and Italy in 1865. He also visited Scotland and Wales several times. For many years, Duncan was an illustrator for the *Illustrated London News*, and in particular he provided illustrations of agricultural workers. As well as marine views, Duncan painted peaceful rural scenes in the Thames Valley. He died at 36 Upper Park Road, Haverstock Hill, and his remaining works were sold at Christie's on 11 March 1885.

45. *Two studies of a French peasant woman, (1) carrying a container, (2) bending.*
(no. 1509).

Watercolour over pencil on white paper
20 × 27 cms / 7⅞ × 10⅝″.
Signed in pencil, b.r. "E. Duncan".
Studio stamp b.l. "ED".

Given by James F Johnston 1896.

This is a beautiful and delicate study of a figure in two positions. It is one of a series of 52 sketches by Edward Duncan, which came from two sketchbooks or albums, of which manuscript lists of contents are in the Ulster Museum files, on notepaper headed "36, Upper Park Road, Haverstock Hill. [London] N.W." - the address at which Duncan died. They all have Duncan's studio monogram stamp, which according to Lack (1985 p 16) shows that they were in the Christie's sale after Duncan's death (Lugt 842).

They were given by Johnston, the first curator of the Belfast Art Gallery, who also gave the ten drawings by Fuseli (see under Fuseli, no. 10, for further details). Many of them, though undated, indicate as yet undocumented travels by Duncan in France in 1835 and 1839, and one shows that he was apparently in Scotland in 1876. It is not known how Johnston came by the drawings, but the sale of Duncan's remaining works at Christie's, 11 March 1885, included some 300 watercolours, sketches and paintings, another 80 sepia drawings, 34 pencil drawings, 34 pen and ink drawings, and 54 albums containing a further 1,551 sketches. It is fairly certain that this was their ultimate source.

Bibliography:
Bryan, Roget, Graves RA, Graves BI, Binyon, VAM, Cundall, Nettlefold, DNB, Redgrave Cent, Hardie, Cordingly, Mallalieu,
Randall Davies: *Edward Duncan* OWCS VI, 1928-9 p 31.
Frank Emanuel: *Edward Duncan* Walker's Quarterly 13, Oct 1923.
London, National Maritime Museum: *Two Victorian Marine Painters: E Duncan and T S Robins* 1971.
Christofer Lack: *Edward Duncan RWS 1803-1882: his membership of societies and exhibited works* OWCS LX, 1985 p 1.

EDWARD LEAR
Born Highgate, London 1812; died San Remo, Italy 1888

Lear was of Danish descent, and was a lifelong victim of epilepsy. He was both an artistic and musical prodigy, and at the age of fifteen was earning his living by drawing animals and birds. In 1831, he was appointed draughtsman to the Zoological Society, and in 1832 he published the coloured lithographic plates of *Illustrations of the Family of the Psittacidae or Parrots*. John Gould published a number of Lear's lithographic illustrations in his many bird books. From 1832 to 1836 the Earl of Derby employed Lear to draw his private collection of animals and birds at Knowsley Hall near Liverpool. Here he wrote and illustrated *A Book of Nonsense* to amuse the Earl's children. It was not published until

1846, when it instantly became a best-seller. From 1836, Lear turned his attention to landscape, and spent several years teaching drawing to the British community in Rome. In 1845 he gave drawing lessons to Queen Victoria. His travels in Europe, the Balkans, North Africa and India were extensive, and he spent his last years in San Remo on the Italian Riviera. Lear was a prolific draughtsman, leaving over 10,000 sheets of sketches at his death. Though he had ambitions as a landscape painter in oil, he never approached the unmistakable quality of his drawings, and in his lifetime his fame as a writer of nonsense verse eclipsed his achievement as an artist.

---

46. Corfu: the Citadel from near the Village of Ascension. 1856. (no. 808).

Watercolour with white over pencil on buff paper
17.6 × 25.4 cms / 6⅞ × 9⅞".
Signed and dated b.r. "Corfu. 1856. Edward Lear".
Bought: London, Fine Art Society 1953.

From 1855 to 1864 Lear lived on Corfu during the winters, while touring Greece, Albania and the Holy Land at other times of the year, returning occasionally to England. This is an early version of Lear's much-repeated view looking towards the mountains of Albania from above or below Ascension (now called Analipsis). Lear wrote to his sister Ann on 29 June 1856: "....I have some idea of devoting a good bit of time to illustrating this small promontory for it is...full of interest, as the old city of Ascension (Coreyra) was built on it, ancient coins and marbles are still found".

Another drawing, *Corfu*, dated 1856, is in the Witt Collection, Courtauld Institute of Art, University of London. An oil painting, *Corfu from below Ascension*, 13 × 21", about 1857, is in the Yale Center for British Art (exh. Royal Academy 1985 (54)). Lear painted at least 15 oils of this view, saying in another letter to Ann (3 Dec 1857): "...the whole scene, in general, and in detail, was so perfectly lovely". The view became one of Lear's "tyrants" - his term for finished watercolours which he had frequently to repeat to order, for the sake of the money rather than through inclination. A "tyrant" watercolour, 7 × 14¾", dated 1862, of the Citadel taken from above the village of Ascension, much higher up, is in the VAM (exh. Royal Academy 1985 (39 b), and a similar

watercolour, 6¾ × 14¼", was sold at Sotheby's, London, 16 Oct 1981 (38).

Lear also published a lithograph of a view similar to this, but with a different foreground, in *Views of the Seven Ionian Islands*, 1863.

Bibliography:
The literature on Lear is now enormous; a full bibliography is given in the Royal Academy catalogue 1985 pp 207-211.

Bryan, DNB, Graves RA, Graves BI, Binyon, VAM, Hardie, Mellon, Mallalieu.

Edward Lear: *The Letters of Edward Lear* 1907.

Edward Lear: *Later Letters* 1911.

A Davidson: *Edward Lear: Landscape Painter and Nonsense Poet* John Murray 1938, 2nd ed. 1978.

London, Adams Gallery: *Watercolour Drawings of the Ionian Islands by Edward Lear* Nov-Dec 1946.

Ray Murphy, ed. : *Edward Lear's Indian Journal* Jarrold 1953.

Philip Hofer: *Edward Lear* Oxford and New York 1962.

Lawrence Durrell, introd. and ed.: *Edward Lear's Corfu: an Anthology drawn from the Painter's Letters* Corfu Travel 1965.

Philip Hofer: *Edward Lear Drawings at Harvard* the Connoisseur CLXIV, 1967 p 31.

Philip Hofer: *Edward Lear as a Landscape Draftsman* Cambridge, Massachusetts 1967; Oxford 1968.

Worcester, Massachusetts, Art Museum: *Edward Lear: Painter, Poet and Draftsman* 1968.

Vivian Noakes: *Edward Lear: the Life of a Wanderer* Collins 1968; revised ed. Fontana 1979; revised ed. BBC Publications 1985.

London, Royal Academy: *Edward Lear 1812-1888* catalogue by Vivian Noakes 1985.

47. *Malta*. 1866. (no. 809).

Pen and watercolour with white over pencil on buff paper 24.8 × 35.5 cms / 9¾ × 13⅞″.
Dated b.r. "Malta 30 January 1866. 4 pm. Near S.Angelo. Hal Far".
Inscribed: centre: "gray rox" (twice) "wall" "cactus" "white";
b.r. "light side of tower" "light of sky" "white divisions of oker stones" "sparkle light cactus leaf here & there" "43"; on tower: "white wall" "dark oker".

Given by Mr R P Smyth, 24 Osborne Gardens, Belfast 9, 1969.

The eccentric spelling of "rox" and "oker" is quite typical of Lear's whimsical sense of humour. A drawing of *A Temple by the Nile*, 1867, in the Yale Center for British Art, is inscribed "rox" and "mud brix".

Lear visited Malta on his way back to England from Corfu in May 1862, and returned in December 1865. Noakes writes: "...He was...to spend a sad and lonely winter in Malta in 1865-66, and the island ceased to have any charm for him". (Royal Academy 1985 (30), on a watercolour view of *Valletta*, dated 1862, Liverpool, Walker Art Gallery). He left Malta in April 1866 for Corfu and Dalmatia. Later in the same year he visited Trieste, en route for England, and in December went to Egypt. It was in this year that Lear contemplated marriage to Gussie Bethell, a daughter of Lord Westbury, but this idea came to nothing.

A Lear drawing of *Gozo near Malta*, dated "March 21 2 pm 1866", is in the Yale Center for British Art.

Dr James Moore
Born Belfast 1819; died Belfast 1883

An outstanding amateur painter, Moore was described by Vinycomb (1907) as "certainly the most thoroughly realistic and truthful portrayer of Nature that Belfast has produced, professional or otherwise". The son of a naval surgeon, Dr David Moore, and his Greek wife Margarita Medin (daughter of the Governor of the Adriatic island of Corzula), Moore appears to have taken lessons from Andrew Nicholl (q.v.) in Belfast. He was enrolled as a medical student at Edinburgh University about 1837, and graduated MD in 1842. The title of his MD thesis was *Can acquired habits and physical configuration of the body descend to the offspring?* At Edinburgh he was engaged by James Syme, Professor of Clinical Surgery, to illustrate his textbook *Principles of Surgery* (1842). Also he established contact with several Scottish painters, including John Thomson of Duddingston (died 1840), Erskine Nicol (1825-1904, q.v.), who was later to paint figures in some of Moore's watercolours, and Sam Bough (1822-78), with whom Moore kept up lifelong contact (Moore's sketch of Bough, done at Jordanbank, Edinburgh, in 1878, is in the Ulster Museum's Moore albums). About 1843 Moore spent the customary year "walking the hospitals", which took him to Dublin and Paris. On returning to Belfast he became a consultant surgeon at the Royal Hospital (now the Royal Victoria Hospital). He travelled frequently on professional business in Ireland, Britain, and sometimes on the continent, and always carried a sketchbook and his watercolour box. He was a much more facile spontaneous sketcher than his master Nicholl ever was. Moore's standing as a surgeon is confirmed by the fact that Sir Charles Bell, Professor Goodsir of Edinburgh, and Dr Thomas Reade of Belfast all bequeathed him their cases of operating instruments. He was Medical Inspector of Emigration and Quarantine to the Port of Belfast. He was also a member of the College of Surgeons of England, the Royal Irish Academy, the Wernerian Society of Edinburgh, the Society for the Prevention of Cruelty to Animals, and the Poor-Law Board. He frequently exhibited large gallery-watercolours at the Royal Hibernian Academy in Dublin, and was elected Honorary Academician in 1868. He took a leading part in the cultural life of Belfast, was interested in music and was one of the promoters for the building of the Ulster Hall, he gave hospitality to visiting actors, and was a friend of Charles Dickens who gave readings in Belfast. Moore's personal manner was rough and brusque. Esler (1886) writes: "...Dr Moore was a genius, and, like most men of genius, had certain peculiarities, but we who were his pupils would remember those only which leaned to the side of virtue". He married Thomasine, daughter of Alexander McDonnell, and had four daughters and one son, who at the time of his father's death was serving as an army officer in India. Moore died aged 64, of congestion of the lungs, at his house, 7 Chichester Street, and was buried in Knockbreda Churchyard. Very few of his works were in private hands, most remaining with the family. The Ulster Museum has 14 albums containing 409 watercolour sketches, as well as a few large exhibition watercolours. A charcoal portrait of Moore as a young medical student, by Felice Piccioni, is in a Belfast private collection (rep. Strickland 1913, vol II pl xlii), and a photograph of him later in life as President of the Ulster Medical Society (1865-6) shows an unkempt, formidable bearded man very like Karl Marx.

---

48. Glenarm, Co Antrim. 1856. (no. 2942).

Watercolour on white paper
11.9 × 18.5 cms / 4¾ × 7¼".
Inscribed b. "Glenarm July 9th 1856".

Provenance unknown.

Exh Belfast, Ulster Museum, and Dublin, National Gallery of Ireland: *James Moore* 1973 (68).

The Ulster Museum collection contains work by Moore dating from 1836 until 1882. This, painted when he was about 37, shows him at the height of his powers. The sense of recession and the damp atmosphere are conveyed with an effortless assurance never matched by his master Andrew Nicholl.

For an earlier view of Glenarm, see J J Barralet (no. 19).

Glenarm July 9th 1856.

Bibliography:

Strickland, Hewitt, Mallalieu, Anglesea RUA.

Obituaries:-Belfast News-Letter, Mon 29 Oct 1883: *Death of James Moore Esq, MD, Hon RHA.*

Belfast Evening Telegraph, Mon 29 Oct 1883: *Death of Dr James Moore RHA MRIA.*

The Northern Whig, Mon 29 Oct 1883: *Death of Dr James Moore.*

Belfast News-Letter, Thurs 1 Nov 1883: *Funeral of the late Dr James Moore.*

British Medical Journal, 3 Nov 1883, p 890.

James Syme: *Principles of Surgery* Edinburgh and London 1842. Illustrated with 14 lithographic plates and 64 text woodcuts after drawings by James Moore. The lithographic process used had recently been invented by S Leith of Edinburgh, and lent itself particularly well to scientific illustration. The woodcuts were done by Bastin of London.

List of Graduates in Medicine of the University of Edinburgh from 1705 to 1866 Edinburgh 1867. Moore is listed as "Jacobus Moore, Hibernus".

Robert Esler: *Sketch of the Ulster Medical Society* Quarterly Journal of Medical Science 1886.

Transactions of the Ulster Medical Society, 1885-6 pp 28-29.

Richard H Hunter: *A History of the Ulster Medical Society* Ulster Medical Journal vol V pp 107 ff.

John Vinycomb: *Paintings by the Late James Moore, MD, Hon RHA* Belfast Museum and Art Gallery Quarterly Notes VII, Sept 1907 p 3.

Belfast, Ulster Museum: *James Moore 1819-1883* catalogue by Martyn Anglesea 1973.

DR JAMES MOORE

49. The Sham Fight at Scarva, Co Down. (no. 2977).

Watercolour and bodycolour on white paper
18 × 26 cms / 7¼ × 10″.
Inscribed b. "The Orange Gathering 'Sham Fight' July 13th
Scarva. Painted from the window of T O'Reiley Esq Scarva
House".

Provenance unknown.

Exh Belfast, Ulster Museum, and Dublin, National Gallery
of Ireland: *James Moore* 1973 (102).

Rep Hewitt 1977 p 35.

Moore usually carefully dated his sketches, but in this
remarkable example he has unfortunately left out the
year. There are in the collection comparable sketches
of *Coleraine Regatta*, dated "Augt 27th 1847", and of
the Maze Race-Course, dated "Augt 3rd 1852" and
"14th July 1868". So this can reasonably be dated any
time between 1848 and 1868. This is all the more
remarkable as the vivid suggestion of movement
anticipates the "moving crowd" pictures painted by
Monet and Renoir in the mid–1870s. Hewitt (1977)
p 34 points out similarities with the work of Jack B
Yeats (q.v.). Moore certainly visited Paris on his
travels, but whether he ever saw the work of Boudin
or the impressionists is a tantalising thought.

"T O'Reiley Esq" was actually John Temple Reilly
of Scarva House, who was Lord Lieutenant of Co
Down. The "Sham Fight", a bizarre re-enactment of
the Battle of the Boyne by local Orangemen, still
takes place at Scarva House on 13 July each year.

JOHN SHERRIN
Born London 1819; died Ramsgate, Kent 1896

Sherrin, along with Anna Maria Fitzjames of Bath, was one of the few pupils of William Henry Hunt (1790-1864). He was initially apprenticed as a jeweller with Samuel Smith, and later worked for the designers Howell and James, and for the diamond merchants Matthews and Peake. Matthews left him a large legacy. Sherrin's still-lifes of fruit and flowers etc. were exhibited from 1859 at the Royal Academy, the New Water-Colour Society and Suffolk Street. He was elected an associate of the New Society (later the Royal Institute of Painters in Water-Colour) in 1866, and a member in 1879. Some of his works were reproduced as chromolithographs. Sherrin was one of the many converts of the Baptist preacher Charles Hannan Spurgeon.

---

50. *Bird's nest and hawthorn.* 1869. (no. 1133).

Watercolour and bodycolour on white paper
20 × 25.6 cms / 7⅞ × 10⅛″.
Signed b.c. "JSherrin"; dated b.l. "1869".

Bought: Belfast, Rodman's 1938.

This appears to be a blackbird's nest (i.e. the European blackbird, *Turdus merula*, which is a thrush, unlike the American blackbird family which are icterids). The painting is so close to the late work of Sherrin's master William Henry ("Bird's Nest") Hunt, that if it were not signed and dated it could be mistaken for one of his. Though somewhat akin to Holman Hunt and Millais's early Pre-Raphaelite methods of 1848-9, this technique does not involve a wet ground. Areas of smooth zinc white ("Chinese" white) bodycolour would be laid on the paper and left to harden, so as to provide a luminous base for the hatchings of bright watercolour built up on top. A pearly, glowing effect is the result.

A similar *Still Life of a Bird's Nest* by Sherrin, 10 × 8″, and a whimsical subject attributed to him, *Fairies Raiding a Bird's Nest*, 7½ × 9¾″, were sold at Sotheby's, London, 27 April 1978 (385, 386).

Bibliography:
Graves RA, Graves Dict, VAM, Hardie, Mallalieu.

HERCULES BRABAZON BRABAZON

Born Hercules Brabazon Sharpe, Paris 1821; died Oaklands, Sussex 1906).

Hercules Brabazon Sharpe was a younger son of Hercules Sharpe of Blackhalls, Co Durham, and Oaklands, Battle, Sussex. He was educated at Harrow and Trinity College, Cambridge, where he read mathematics. He then studied art in Rome, and was taught by J H d'Egville and Alfred Downing Fripp. He also travelled with Ruskin and Arthur Severn. He inherited the Brabazon estates in Ireland on the death of his elder brother, and took the surname of Brabazon in 1847. On his father's death in 1858, he inherited the family estates in England. He was an absentee landlord, spending his summers in England and his winters in France, Spain, Italy, Germany, North Africa and Egypt. All his life, Brabazon was an amateur painter, but his status and fame were radically altered in 1891, when he was elected to the New English Art Club, and then, in 1892, when he was persuaded to hold his first one-man-show at the Goupil Gallery, at the age of 71. This was one of the most successful one-man-shows ever held, and Brabazon suddenly found himself the centre of attention among the modernists, from whom he received extravagant praise. On his death in 1906, George Moore described him as "the father of the New English Art Club" (Saturday Review 23 June 1906). Until about 1926 Brabazon's work continued to command high prices, but then it suffered the inevitable reversal. Gertrude Jekyll, the garden designer, was his pupil.

---

51. View of Sousse, Tunisia. (no. 743).

Watercolour with bodycolour, over pencil and red chalk, on white paper
24.9 × 34.8 cms / 9¾ × 13⅝ ".
Signed b.r. "H.B.B."

Exh Dublin, Waddington Galleries 1936 (8).
Given by the Friends of the National Collections of Ireland (Dr R I Best bequest) 1959.

Al Weil (letter 28 Dec 1972) dated this between 1870 and 1873, and wrote: "...All the dark area (doorway and shadowy figure on left, railing, doorway on right) seem to have been done in Brabazon's characteristic 'one-stroke' application. By this is meant that he loaded his brush first with watercolour and then with Chinese white on the tip. It was his mastery that he could exactly judge the right proportions, and then apply the brushload in a single stroke to get the effect he wanted, without mixing the two ingredients. In this way, he did not depend on the white of the paper as lighting agent".

Bibliography:
Cundall, VAM, Hardie, Mallalieu, NGI.
T M Wood: *The Watercolour Art of Hercules Brabazon Brabazon* The Studio XXXV, 1905.
Sir F Wedmore: *Hercules Brabazon Brabazon* 1910 (?).
Mrs H B Combe: *Notes on the Life of Hercules Brabazon* 1910 (?).
D S Maccoll: *The Study of Brabazon* 1910 (?).
C Lewis Hind: *Hercules Brabazon Brabazon* 1912.
Al Weil: unpublished typescript, copy in Ulster Museum files.
London, Leighton House: *Hercules Brabazon Brabazon 1821-1906* catalogue by Al Weil 1971.
Flushing, New York, Queen's College: *Hercules Brabazon Brabazon* Godwin-Ternbach Museum, April-June 1985; catalogue by Hilarie Faberman.

RICHARD DOYLE
Born London 1824; died London 1883

R ichard (or "Dicky") Doyle was the second son of an Irish-born caricaturist, John Doyle (1797-1868). He was a youthful prodigy and was taught by his father. From 1843 to 1850 he was a regular draughtsman for *Punch*, but he afterwards turned more to book-illustration and watercolour painting. Allegedly he left *Punch* because of attacks made by his rival John Leech and others on Cardinal Wiseman and the newly-restored Roman Catholic hierarchy in England. Doyle illustrated many of Thackeray's works, as well as books and stories by Dickens, Ruskin and others. His fantastic imagination revelled in elves, gnomes and fairies. Doyle suffered an apoplectic stroke when leaving the Athenaeum Club, and died the following morning at his house, 7 Finborough Road. An exhibition of his work was held at the Grosvenor Gallery in 1881. His brothers James William Edmund (1822-92), Henry Edward (1827-92) and Charles Altimont Doyle (1832-93) were also painters and illustrators. Sir Arthur Conan Doyle was the son of Charles Doyle.

---

52. A girl reading (portrait of Christina Rossetti?). (no. 1024).

Pen and watercolour on hot-pressed white paper
22.7 × 16.5 cms / 8⅞ × 6½".
Signed b.l. "D".

Bought: London, R E Abbott 1952.

This shows a Rossetti-like girl sitting reading in a landscape inhabited by fanciful creatures. A huge dragon uncoils itself in the right background, and two small birds appear to be having a conversation at the bottom right.

Simon Cooke (letter 30 June 1986) dates this fantasy to the early or mid 1850s, partly on grounds of style, but also because the girl may possibly be a portrait of Dante Gabriel Rossetti's sister, the poet Christina Georgina Rossetti. Doyle was a favourite in the Rossetti household during the early 1850s. He drew Elizabeth Siddall about the same time. This picture may be compared with Rossetti's own portrayal of his sister in *Ecce Ancilla Domini* 1850 (London, Tate Gallery).

This does not appear to be a book illustration, but rather a typical piece of Doyleiana, suggesting myth and fable, and presenting an image of an idealised beauty within her bower, threatened, perhaps sexually, by supernatural creatures outside.

According to Simon Cooke (letter 2 June 1986), the letter "D" is a rare form of Doyle's signature. Before 1840 Doyle used the monogram "R Doyle"; after 1840 he signed himself "Dick", then in 1842-43 "Dick Kitkat", and he finally replaced his signature by a tiny "Dicky" bird. Cooke suggests that the two small birds at the bottom right are Doyle's true signature.

Bibliography:
Binyon, Cundall, DNB, Redgrave Cent, Strickland, VAM, Hardie, Mallalieu, NGI.
Frederic G Kitton: *Dickens and his Illustrators* 1899.
Daria Hambourg: *Richard Doyle* 1948.
Simon G Cooke: uncompleted PhD thesis on Richard Doyle, St David's College, Lampeter (University of Wales). Due for completion in late 1987 or early 1988.

107

MYLES BIRKET FOSTER

Born North Shields, Northumberland 1825; died Weybridge, Surrey 1899

Birket Foster is perhaps the most appealing of the "Victorian Picturesque" watercolour painters. The roots of his style (like that of G J Pinwell, q.v.) lie in wood-engraving. His father and grandfather, living on Tyneside, knew Thomas Bewick (1753-1828), and were familiar with his engraved work. Foster's family moved to London when he was five years old, and he was sent to Quaker schools in London and Hitchin. Apprenticed to the wood-engraver Peter Landells at the age of 16, Foster worked as an engraver and black-and-white illustrator from 1846 through the 1850s, principally for the *Illustrated London News* and *Punch*. In his spare time he taught himself to paint in watercolour, and began to concentrate exclusively on painting from about 1859. He exhibited regularly with the Old Water-Colour Society, of which he was elected associate in 1860 and member in 1862. Between 1869 and 1877 he exhibited at the Royal Academy. He lived at Witley, near Godalming, Surrey, where his house "the Hill" became a rendezvous for artists, and was decorated by Burne-Jones, Stacy Marks and other painters. After 1852 Foster travelled a lot on the continent. In 1893 he moved to Weybridge because of ill-health. He was buried at Witley.

53. *Bringing Daddy's Dinner.* (no. 782).

Watercolour and bodycolour on white paper
18.1 × 13.2 cms / 7⅛ × 5¼".
Signed b.l. monogram "BF".

Given by Lady Cleaver, in memory of her husband Sir James Frederick Cleaver 1936.

Ref Reynolds 1984 p 207.

All except one of the Ulster Museum's fine group of ten Birket Foster watercolours belonged to Sir Frederick Cleaver, founder of the large Belfast department store, Robinson and Cleaver. They tell us something about the taste of a big Belfast store-owner in the late Victorian and Edwardian period.

This small composition shows perhaps better than any other example the way in which Birket Foster's distinctive hatching technique in watercolour and bodycolour relates to the pecking methods of mid-19th century reproductive wood-engraving.

Birket Foster's saccharine subject-matter, his way of dealing with the rural poor without any suggestion of the hardships they suffered, endeared him to bourgeois patrons. Over the years his work has occasioned criticism, but it has never been without admirers.

Bibliography:
Graves Dict, DNB, Cundall, VAM, Nettlefold, Hughes, Hardie, Mallalieu.
H M Cundall: *Birket Foster* 1906.
Forrest Reid: *Illustrators of the Sixties* 1928.
L Glasson: *Birket Foster* OWCS XI 1933.
Pauline Flick: *A Victorian Artistic Haven: the Foster Family at Witley* Country Life 4 Dec 1975 p 1548.
Jan Reynolds: *Birket Foster* Batsford 1984.

54. *A Pedlar.* (no. 1191).

Watercolour and bodycolour on white paper
44.4 × 76.8 cms / 17½ × 26¾".
Signed b.r. monogram "BF".

Exh Royal Academy 1873 (973) (or this may have been an oil version of the same subject: see Jan Reynolds, letter 12 July 1982).

Given by Lady Cleaver 1936 (see note on no. 53).

Ref Reynolds 1984 p 207.

Rep ibid p 156 pl 92.

This is a fine example of Birket Foster's large-scale watercolours. The female pedlar, who seems to have carried her huge basket of crockery down an interminable country lane, holds out a mug inscribed "A Present from Godalming", which is presumably an allusion to Foster's home, "the Hill", near Godalming. The brick houses with red tiled roofs are typical of Surrey.

Though Birket Foster is most celebrated for his highly finished watercolours like this one, some of his less-finished sketches can be charming, as for example *The Balloon* in the Yale Center for British Art, B1981.25.2587. Like William Henry Hunt, John Frederick Lewis and John Sherrin (q.v.), Foster began by making a careful pencil drawing which he would then fill in with washes of watercolour. Next he would lay on patches of Chinese white, which he left to harden, and upon which he built up his intricate meshes of hatching strokes. The Chinese white of his skies was left sufficiently tacky for his tiny brushstrokes to be clearly visible.

ERSKINE NICOL
Born Leith, Scotland 1825; died Feltham, Middlesex 1904

Apprenticed to a house-painter, Erskine Nicol studied in his spare time at the Edinburgh Trustees' Academy from the age of twelve. He became a drawing master at Leith High School, and in 1846, at the age of twenty, went to Dublin where he spent four years with the Department of Science and Art. After his return to Edinburgh, he continued to pay annual visits to Ireland, where he found many of his humorous genre subjects, though he also painted Scottish peasant subjects. He was elected associate of the Royal Scottish Academy in 1855, and RSA in 1859. In 1862 he moved to London, and in 1868 was elected ARA. He was made an Honorary Retired Associate in 1885, but was still exhibiting at the Royal Academy as late as 1893. Nicol retired to Scotland, but later moved south to Feltham. His sons, Erskine E Nicol (died 1926) and John Watson Nicol (died 1926), were both landscape painters, the former in a style reminiscent of late Turner. Erskine E Nicol's daughter Mary married Louis Leakey, the distinguished African anthropologist. She was an anthropologist in her own right, and illustrated her own books.

---

55. *Paddy at Versailles*. 1856. (no. 1111).

Watercolour and bodycolour over pencil on buff paper
36.2 × 26.4 cms / 14½ × 10⅜".
Signed b.l. "E Nicol ARSA 1856".
The composition has been extended upwards by adding a 1¼" strip to the top edge (see the Paul Sandby watercolour, no. 2, for a similar addition. Sometimes this was done simply by painting on the mount).

Bought: Belfast, Rodman's 1930.

Scenes featuring the comic stage-Irishman were Nicol's stock-in-trade, and this picture of a bewildered Paddy in incongruous surroundings is an excellent example. The following example (no. 56) shows that in this genre Nicol could also be serious and compassionate. Liberal use of bodycolour and impasted white is very characteristic.

Bibliography:
Graves RA, Graves BI, Strickland, VAM, Caw, Irwin, Mallalieu, NGI.
Art Journal, March 1870.
A M Hall: *Tales of Irish Life and Character* 1909 (Nicol illustrations).
W Harvey: *Irish Life and Humour* 1909 (Nicol illustrations).
Esme Gordon: *The Royal Scottish Academy 1826-1976* Edinburgh, Charles Skilton 1976.

113

56. *The 'merican difficulty*. 1862. (no. 2453).

Watercolour and bodycolour over pencil on buff paper
30.7 × 23.2 cms / 12⅛ × 9⅛″.
Signed on edge of table, b.r. "E [reversed] Nicol RSA /
1862".
Inscribed b.r. "The 'Merican difficulty".

Bought: London, Abbott and Holder 1977.

Abbott and Holder's list 175, Nov 1977 no. 77,
describes this as "a nice intelligent old Irish lady
seated at a table avidly reading her newspaper, 1862
(presumably about the 'Alabama incident'). An
absolutely splendid watercolour."

It is unlikely that an old Irish lady should be
particularly concerned about an international incident
resulting from the boarding of an American battleship
(the Alabama) by the British navy. What is much
more likely is that she is anxiously following the
course of the American Civil War, in which many
Irish Americans, including presumably her children,
were in the front lines on both the Union and
Confederate sides.

This was painted in the year that Nicol moved to
London. The white bodycolour is thickly impasted on
the bonnet, the wall and the newspaper.

The Ulster Museum's one oil painting by Erskine
Nicol, *Rejected* 1865, also expresses pathos rather than
comedy.

ANTHONY FREDERICK AUGUSTUS SANDYS
Born Norwich 1829; died Kensington, London 1904

Frederick Sandys was one of the later adherents of the Pre-Raphaelite movement. The son of a Norwich portrait painter, he exhibited a portrait at the Royal Academy before he was twenty. He then moved to London, where he studied in the Royal Academy Schools under George Richmond. He was living with Rossetti in 1860, and illustrated poems by Christina Rossetti (see no. 52) and Swinburne. Illustrations by Sandys were published in *Once a Week*, *Good Words* and the *Cornhill Magazine*. The rich Norfolk banking family, the Gurneys, commissioned Sandys to make animal and bird studies, and he also produced landscape and architectural watercolours which compare favourably with those of William Callow. He is best known, however, for his ideal female figures which link Pre-Raphaelitism with Art Nouveau.

---

57. *Head of a red-haired girl.* 1890. (no. 852).

Pencil and coloured chalks on white paper
35.8 × 26.4 cms / 14⅛ × 10⅜″.
Signed t.r. "F.Sandys 1890".

Bought: Belfast, Rodman's 1931.

Exh Brighton and Sheffield 1974 (127).

The model was one of Sandys's daughters. After 1868 Sandys almost ceased to paint in oils, but concentrated throughout the 1870s, 80s and 90s on a long series of coloured chalk drawings of symbolic, ideal female figures much influenced by the late work of Rossetti. See Crombie 1965.

This drawing was badly foxed before being sterilised and cleaned as far as was possible by G Morrow at the British Museum in 1973-4.

The Ulster Museum also has an oil on panel by Sandys, *Cassandra*, before 1865, exhibited at Brighton and Sheffield 1974 (65).

Bibliography:
Graves RA, DNB, Waters, VAM, Mallalieu.
J M Gray: *Frederick Sandys and the Woodcut Designers of Thirty Years Ago* Art Journal, new series vol IV, March 1884, p 73.
Esther Wood: *A Consideration of the Art of Frederick Sandys* The Artist, special winter number, Nov 1896.
A L Baldry: *Drawings by Frederick Sandys* Art Journal vol LXXI, May 1909, p 149.
Arthur B Chamberlain: *Works by Frederick Sandys in the Birmingham Art Gallery* Apollo, Nov 1925.
Forrest Reid: *Illustrators of the Sixties* 1928.
T Earle Welby: *The Victorian Romantics* 1929 (quotes Swinburne on Sandys's *Medea*).
William S A Dale: *A Portrait by Frederick Sandys* Burlington Magazine May 1965 p 250.
Theodore Crombie: *Some Portraits by Frederick Sandys* Apollo Nov 1965 p 398.
Richard L Ormond: *Another Bulwer Portrait by Frederick Sandys* Burlington Magazine April 1966 p 194.
Brighton Art Gallery and Sheffield, Mappin Art Gallery: *Frederick Sandys* catalogue by Betty O'Looney 1974.
London, Tate Gallery: *The Pre-Raphaelites* 1984.
Douglas E Schoenherr: *Frederick Sandys's Amor Mundi* Apollo, May 1988, p 311.

117

George John Pinwell
Born High Wycombe 1842; died Haverstock Hill, London 1875

The son of a builder, Pinwell studied at the St Martin's Lane School and Heatherley's School of Art. He became a designer and illustrator, and worked for *Once a Week* and other periodicals. In 1864 he joined the engraving firm of the Dalziel Brothers. Like Birket Foster (q.v.), his style was formed by the techniques of wood-engraving. In the 1860s he was particularly associated, both in style and in subject-matter, with Fred Walker and J W North. He was elected an associate of the Old Water-Colour Society in 1869, and a member in 1870. He spent several winters in Tangier for health reasons, but died of consumption in London after returning from one such stay. He is buried in Highgate Cemetery.

---

58. The Last Load. 1869. (no. 1121).

Watercolour and bodycolour on white paper
41.7 × 61.1 cms / 16⅜ × 24″.
Signed b.l. "G J Pinwell '69".

Bought: London, Leger Galleries 1952.

Exh London, Old Water-Colour Society, Winter 1869-70. Williamson (1900) reproduces between pp 40 and 41 a plate taken from Pinwell's own photograph of his work. The definition is not very good but it is almost certainly the Ulster Museum watercolour. Williamson was unable to trace the owner. It is not in the catalogue of Pinwell's remaining works sold at Christie's on 16 March 1876.
London, Deschamps Gallery Feb-March 1876: *The Last Load* (16 × 23½″), lent by Edward Dalziel.
Belfast, Ulster Museum: *Peasantries* (Belfast only) May-June 1982. This was a travelling exhibition organised by Newcastle Polytechnic, and previously toured to Sheffield, Paisley and Aberdeen. In Belfast an extra section of related works from the Ulster Museum collection was added, including *The Last Load,* which complemented the only Pinwell watercolour in the catalogue, *The Princess and the Ploughman* (41), lent by Aberdeen Art Gallery.

A monochrome sketch for this composition, *First Sketch in Water-Colour for "the Last Load"*, 5½ × 8½″, was exhibited at the Deschamps Gallery in 1876, also lent by Edward Dalziel. Williamson (1900) reproduces Pinwell's photograph of it and states that its current owner was H T Hartley.

While Pinwell frequently took his subject-matter from literature or folklore, this is an unidealised contemporary scene of haymakers finishing their work in the evening, and connects Pinwell with slightly later painters like Clausen (q.v.) and La Thangue.

The debt of Pinwell's technique to the hatching methods of contemporary wood-engraving is very obvious, and this elegiac idyll may be compared and contrasted with Birket Foster's treatment of a related subject, *Haymakers*, also in the Ulster Museum collection. Pinwell's peasants look much more work-weary. The bodycolour is applied quite thickly in places, and there are small paint losses at the top centre and along the top edge.

Molly Whelan (a child) was Pinwell's favourite model, and possibly appears in this composition. His favourite adult model was his wife's sister, Mrs Walker.

Bibliography:
Redgrave Cent, Bryan, Cundall, DNB, Roget, Graves Dict, Graves Loan, VAM, Binyon, Hardie, Mallalieu.
Art Journal 1875.
London, Deschamps Gallery, Old Bond Street: *Works of the late G J Pinwell* Feb-March 1876.
Birmingham, Royal Birmingham Society of Artists: *Works by George Mason and George J Pinwell ARWS* introduction by Harry Quilter, March 1895.
George C Williamson: *George J Pinwell and his Works* 1900.
Forrest Reid: *Illustrators of the Sixties* 1928.
Arts Council of Great Britain: *English Influences on Vincent van Gogh* catalogue by Ronald Pickvance 1974.
Newcastle-upon-Tyne, Polytechnic Art Gallery: *Peasantries: 19th century French and British pictures of peasants and field workers* catalogue by Kenneth McConkey 1981 (the entry on Pinwell was written by Ysanne Holt).

119

SIR GEORGE CLAUSEN
Born London 1852; died Newbury, Berkshire 1944

The son of a decorative painter of Danish extraction, Clausen studied at the South Kensington Museum in 1867, then worked in a drawing office before entering the South Kensington School of Design in 1873-75. For several years he served as assistant to Edward Long RA. In 1875-76 he visited Belgium and Holland, and was greatly influenced by Bastien-Lepage and the French plein-air painters. He became their foremost English disciple. In 1883 he went to Paris to study at the Académie Julian under Bouguéreau. He was elected ARI in 1876, ARWS in 1879, RI in 1886, RWS in 1898, ARA in 1895 and RA in 1908. In 1886 he was a founder member of the New English Art Club. Clausen was Professor of Painting to the Royal Academy in 1904-6, and was head of the Royal Academy Schools. He was an Official War Artist during the First World War. In 1927 he was knighted. He died at Cold Ash, Newbury.

---

59. *Twilight.* (no. 755).

Watercolour and bodycolour on white paper
24.3 × 29.4 cms / 9½ × 11⅝″.
Signed in ink, b.r. "G Clausen".

Given by the Contemporary Art Society 1943.

Clausen exhibited watercolours called *Twilight* at the RWS in Autumn 1936 (44), Winter 1936 (1), Autumn 1937 (8), Autumn 1938 (25) and 1943 (44). This may be one of these. It was given to the Museum by the Contemporary Art Society the year before Clausen's death, so would not have been among the remaining works in his studio. One of Clausen's brush-hairs remains embedded in the paint, centre left, and his finger or thumb print may be seen, centre right.

Clausen's watercolours are extremely numerous, and include many colour studies like this. Roe (1945) p 16, writes: "...They represent all his periods and his every mood. In them, one notices, over and over again, how he 'found' the subject and then made what he wanted of it. At his home at Widdington, Essex, or his home on Carlton Hill, or wherever up and down the country he might be, Clausen looked out of window, or paused in a lane to note what he saw...He set down what he saw, or what he chose to see, directly and left it as soon as he had stated all he needed. Whether that satisfied him or whether he carried the idea further on another day or in the studio, depended entirely on himself thus".

The Ulster Museum also has an oil painting by Clausen, *Sunrise on the Road*, which was bought in 1947.

Bibliography:
Graves Dict, Graves RA, RA Exhibitors 1905-75, Tate Mod Brit, Who's Who 1912, Hardie, Huish, Mallalieu, Waters, Farr.
George Clausen: *Lectures on Painting* 1904.
George Clausen: *Aims and Ideals in Art* 1906.
Dyneley Hussey: *George Clausen* Benn's Contemporary British Artists Series 1923.
George Clausen: *Autobiographical Notes* Artwork no. 25, Spring 1931.
F Gordon Roe: *Sir George Clausen RA RWS (1852-1944)* OWCS XXIII, 1945 p 13.
Bradford Art Gallery and Tyne and Wear Art Galleries: *Sir George Clausen RA 1852-1944* catalogue by Kenneth McConkey 1980.
Newcastle-upon-Tyne, Polytechnic Art Gallery: *Peasantries: 19th century French and British pictures of peasants and field workers* catalogue by Kenneth McConkey 1981.

ROSE BARTON
Born Dublin 1856; died London 1929

She is sometimes known as Rose Maynard Barton, but there seems to be no foundation for the middle name. Rose Barton was the daughter of a solicitor, Augustine Hugh Barton, of Rochestown, Co Tipperary, and was a cousin of Edith Somerville. In 1872 she was presented at Dublin Castle. After her father's death in 1874, the family moved to Brussels, where living was cheaper, and where Rose and her sister received drawing lessons. Then they travelled up the Rhine and stayed for a time in Geneva. On deciding in the early 1880s to take up painting professionally, Rose studied in Paris under Henri Gervex. Mildred Anne Butler of Kilmurry, Co Kilkenny, studied in the same studio, and they became lifelong friends. Rose Barton exhibited at the Royal Hibernian Academy for the first time in 1878, at the Royal Academy from 1884–89, and at the RWS, of which she was elected an associate in 1893, and became the first woman member in 1911. She illustrated Francis Gerard's *Picturesque Dublin* (1898), and published her own book *Familiar London* in 1904. From this time she lived permanently in London, where she had a flat in Knightsbridge. She was fond of betting and horse-racing, and according to the RWS Members' Book she backed two winners on the day of her death from asthma.

---

60. St Patrick's Close, Dublin. 1881. (no. 1570).

Watercolour on white paper
52.1 × 34.9 cms / 20½ × 13⅞".
Signed b.l. "Rose Barton / 1881".

Bequeathed: McCleery estate, Antrim Road, Belfast, through l'Estrange and Brett, solicitors, 1968.

This is the earliest datable Dublin street scene by Rose Barton. The tower in the distance is that of Christ Church Cathedral, not St Patrick's. The view is more likely to be looking north up Bride Street and Werburgh Street (both now demolished), than to be from St Patrick's Close.

Rebecca Rowe (Cork catalogue 1987) devotes a section to Rose Barton's Dublin views, and makes the point that she seldom included detailed foreground figures in her later work, which becomes softer in handling and at times very close in style to that of her friend Mildred Butler. Another watercolour, *Market in St Patrick's Close*, signed and dated 1885, 28 × 16¼", belongs to Major Victor McCalmont (exh. Cork 1987 (21)).

The concept of this early watercolour resembles the work of Louise Rayner (1832-1924), a prolific painter of street scenes in Chester, York, Edinburgh and other British cities.

Bibliography:
Huish, Rosc '75, NGI, Mallalieu, P of I.
Dublin, Trinity College, Department of History of Art: Correspondence between Rose Barton and Mildred Butler.
Obituary: OWCS VII, 1930.
Raymond F Brooke (the artist's nephew): *The Brimming River* Dublin 1961.
Cork, Crawford Municipal Art Gallery: *Rose Barton RWS. Exhibition of Watercolours and Drawings* 1987, introduction by Anne Crookshank and the Knight of Glin, essays by Charles Nugent and Rebecca Rowe, catalogue by Orla Walsh (shown also at the Fine Art Society, London, Ulster Museum, Belfast, and the Butler Gallery, Kilkenny).

123

CLAUDE HAYES

Born Dublin 1852; died Brockenhurst, Hampshire 1922

Claude Hayes's life bears an uncanny resemblance to that of his father, the marine painter Edwin Hayes (1820–1904). He escaped his father's intention of putting him in commerce by running away to sea. After serving in the Abyssinian Expedition in 1867–8, and then spending a year farming in America, he went to London to study art at Heatherley's and the Royal Academy Schools. He then studied in Antwerp under Verlat. Though he first practiced as a portrait painter, Hayes soon turned to landscape, where he continued the tradition of David Cox (q.v.) and Tom Collier, with whom he often painted. Along with his associates James Aumonier, Edmund Morison Wimperis, and his brother-in-law William Charles Estall, Hayes spread the influence of Cox and Collier well into the twentieth century. He was elected RI in 1886. In his successful years Hayes claimed that he never made less than £700 a year from his painting, but his life ended in failing health and financial disaster.

---

61. *A Windmill in Sussex.* (no. 1561).

Watercolour over pencil on white paper
49.4 × 74.9 cms / 19⅜ × 29½".
Signed b.r. "Claude Hayes".

Bought: Belfast, J Douglas, 13 Lombard Street, 1930.

After his marriage in 1888, Hayes lived mainly in Surrey. This breezy view of a post mill, presumably on the Sussex Downs, is a good example of his mature style, which he learned from Tom Collier (1840-1891). Hayes's technique is described in detail by Reynolds (1922), who had received lessons from him. These large watercolours, intended for exhibition, were painted in the studio, based on many small sketches made out of doors. Hayes did not approve of the widespread practice of soaking and straining the paper, as he felt that this destroyed the brilliance and "bloom" of the surface. The paper was held loosely in the sketching frame, which was placed nearly vertically on the easel. The whole composition would be worked out carefully before commencing. The large washes of colour would run rapidly down the paper. When they were laid in, Hayes would build up the details in firm, decisive strokes, never losing the whiteness of the paper. His control of distance and skies, and the beautiful simplicity of his best work, were greatly admired.

The Ulster Museum has another large, typical watercolour by Claude Hayes, *Across the Common*, which he exhibited at the Belfast Art Society in 1911. Another good example of a moorland scene with sheep and shepherd is in the Yale Center for British Art, B1975.3.174.

Bibliography:
Graves Dict, Graves RA, VAM, Hardie, Mallalieu.
The Studio XXXIII.
Edward P Reynolds: *Claude Hayes* Walker's Quarterly no. 7, April 1922.

HENRY TONKS
Born Solihull, Warwickshire 1862; died London 1937

Though he became one of the most influential art teachers of the early 20th century, Tonks's original career was as a surgeon. He was elected Fellow of the Royal College of Surgeons in 1888. In the meantime he was attending evening classes under Fred Brown at the Westminster School of Art, and in 1893 he gave up surgery to join the staff of the Slade School of Art. Tonks was Slade Professor from 1918 to 1930, during which time he taught many of the major figures in British art. The practice he advocated for producing a matt finish, by using rags and paper to draw the oil from paintings, was called by the students "tonking". From 1895 Tonks was a member of the New English Art Club. During the First World War he fell back on his surgical experience and on the technique of pastel to produce an extraordinary series of studies of *Facial Wounds*, illustrating the stages of plastic surgery. In 1919 he was an official war artist with the White Army in Archangel, Russia. A retrospective exhibition of his work was held at the Tate Gallery in 1936.

62. *Girl in a Green Dress.* (no. 863).

Pastel, black crayon and some black ink on white paper
24.8 × 16.4 cms / 9¾ × 7¼".

Bought: London, Sotheby's: *Modern British Drawings, Paintings and Sculpture*, 9 Dec 1970 (32).

This pastel sketch of an auburn-haired girl in a low-cut green dress and a large red hat is difficult to date. As in many modern pastels, the influence of Degas is very apparent. Tonks's fellow-members of the New English Art Club, particularly Sickert, regarded Degas with great reverence. The medium of pastel was used by Tonks with singular effect in his *Facial Wounds* studies, made during the First World War (see Freeman 1985).

Bibliography:
Tate Mod Brit, VAM, Waters, Farr.
Joseph Hone: *The Life of Henry Tonks* 1939.
Meirion and Susie Harries: *The War Artists* 1983.
Norwich School of Art: *Henry Tonks and the Art of Pure Drawing* 1985.
Julian Freeman: *Professor Tonks: War Artist* Burlington Magazine May 1985 p 285.

ROBERT POLHILL BEVAN
Born Hove, Sussex 1865; died London 1925

Robert Bevan attended the Westminster School of Art and the Académie Julian in Paris. He was in Tangier with Joseph Crawhall in 1892, and met Gauguin at Pont-Aven in 1894. In 1897 he married the Polish painter Stanislawa de Karlowska, and visited Poland with her many times. He was living in Brighton in 1898, but in 1900 he settled in Hampstead, and had a one-man-show at the Baillie Gallery in 1905. In 1908 Bevan joined the circle of painters who met in Sickert's studio in Fitzroy Street, and was a founder member of the Camden Town Group in 1911, the London Group in 1913, and the Cumberland Market Group in 1914. He was elected a member of the New English Art Club in 1922. Bevan's specialities were scenes of markets and horse-sales, as well as Devon landscapes.

---

63. *Tapster Water.* (no. 739).

Black crayon and watercolour on white laid paper
34.6 × 43.3 cms / 13⅝ × 17″.
Signed b.l. "Robert Bevan".

Bought: London, R E Abbott 1954.

At the time of acquisition, this was entitled *Yard Gate, Devon* (John Hewitt to R E Abbott, letter 17 Sept 1954). However, a black crayon drawing by Bevan entitled *Tapster Water*, 8½ × 10¾″, evidently showing the same farm from almost the same viewpoint, was in the Arts Council of Great Britain exhibition *Drawings of the Camden Town Group* (16), and was with the Hamet Gallery, London, in 1971 (Malcolm Rodway, Hamet Gallery, letter 11 Aug 1971).

Bevan did much work in Devon. "Tapster Water" presumably refers to the stream, crossed by the wooden footbridge on the left and the ford on the right. Judging from the Cézanne-like handling of the trees on the right, it may postdate the Grafton Galleries exhibition *Manet and the Post-Impressionists* of 1911, which was selected by Roger Fry.

The Ulster Museum also has an oil painting by Bevan, *Yard Gate, Mydlow*, painted about 1907 on one of his many visits to Poland.

Bibliography:
Tate Mod Brit, Waters, Mallalieu, Farr.
R A Bevan: *Robert Bevan 1865-1925: a memoir by his son* 1965.
Wendy Baron: *The Camden Town Group* Scolar Press 1979.
Jonathan Benington: *Robert Bevan, Dunn's Cottage and Applehayes* Leeds Arts Calendar 94, 1984 p 15.
Maureen Connett: *The Sketchbooks of Robert Bevan* Apollo, March 1988, p 168.

Robert Beran.

JACK BUTLER YEATS
Born London 1871; died Dublin 1957

The most distinguished Irish painter of this century, Jack Yeats was the youngest of five children of the painter John Butler Yeats (1839-1922), and brother of the poet William Butler Yeats (1865-1939). He was taken to Sligo at the age of eight to live with his mother's parents, the Anglo-Irish Pollexfen family, and much of his imagery was formed there. When he was seventeen he returned to London to study at the South Kensington School of Design under Sir Thomas Armstrong, and at the Westminster School of Art under Fred Brown. Between 1888 and 1910, he worked as a professional illustrator for many papers, including *The Vegetarian, Lika Joko, Paddock Life, The Boy's Own Paper*, and *Punch*. He married in 1894 and went to live in Devon. After 1910 he worked as an illustrator exclusively for *Punch*, under the name of "W. Bird". It was in this year that he re-settled in Ireland, first at Greystones, Co Wicklow, and later in Dublin. He did not work regularly in oils until after 1905, but was influenced by Sir Hugh Lane's collection of French Impressionist paintings, and in 1913 he was among the European artists featured in the Armory Show in New York. His mature work is an idiosyncratic form of expressionism, having some similarity to the late work of Lovis Corinth, but with a strong literary dependency. He was elected ARHA in 1914, RHA in 1915, and was made an Officer of the Légion d'Honneur in 1949. Yeats produced a quantity of articles and a number of books, novels and plays, including *Life in the West of Ireland* 1912, *Sligo* 1930, *The Amaranthers* 1936, *The Careless Flower* 1947 and *In Sand* 1949. He died in Dublin and is buried in Mount Jerome Cemetery.

---

64. The End of the World. 1909. (no. 1329).

Pen and ink and watercolour on buff paper
20.5 × 30.5 cms / 8⅛ × 12".
Signed b.l. "Jack B Yeats".
Inscribed: "The End of the World".

Provenance unknown.

Published in *A Broadside* no. 5, 1909.

Yeats had published an illustration entitled *The World's End* in the magazine *Judy*, vol 19, Oct 1892 p 188.

Much of the imagery of Jack Yeats's pictures comes from life in Sligo, particularly the world of the rural Irish race-meeting. These horse-races were often held on sandy beaches. Even such a foreboding subject as the end of the world is conceived in the holiday spirit of a country race-meeting, with shoeblacks and touts offering for sale "Souvenir Cards of the Day".

This 1909 illustration was seen in *A Broadside* by Yeats's friend, the poet John Masefield, who wrote to Yeats that year: "...Let me tell you how much I enjoyed your picture of 'the End of the World'. That was one of the best of all your drawings. I liked to think that the two gentlemen making for the tree were you and I". See Pyle (1970) p 96, and Eugene Mason: *Mr Jack B Yeats and the poets of 'A Broadside'*, Today, Oct 1917.

Bibliography:
Tate Mod Brit, Arnold, Waters, Rosc '75, Boylan, Farr, P of I.
E Marriott: *Jack B Yeats: being a true and impartial view of his pictorial and dramatic art* Elkin Matthews 1911.
Thomas McGreevy: *Jack B Yeats: an appreciation and an interpretation* Dublin, Waddington 1945.
T G Rosenthal: *Jack Yeats*, Knowledge Publications, "The Masters" series no. 40, 1966.
John Berger: *Jack Butler Yeats*; essay in *Permanent Red* 1960.
Hilary Pyle: *Jack Butler Yeats: a Biography* 1970 (contains exhaustive bibliography).
Dublin, National Gallery of Ireland, Belfast, Ulster Museum, and New York: *Jack Butler Yeats 1871-1957: a Centenary Exhibition* 1971-72.
Dublin, National Gallery of Ireland: *Jack B Yeats in the National Gallery of Ireland* catalogue by Hilary Pyle 1986.
Hilary Pyle: *There is no Night* Irish Arts Review vol 3 no. 2, Summer 1986 p 36.

A ROMILLY FEDDEN
Born Henbury, Gloucestershire 1875, died 1939

Romilly Fedden was the son of Henry Fedden of Henbury, and studied at Herkomer's art school at Bushey, then at the Académie Julian in Paris and also in Spain. He was strongly influenced by the Scottish painter Arthur Melville (1858-1904), and used a similar "wet method" of watercolour on primed white paper, working into a wash of water. The method is described by Hardie and by Fedden himself in his book *Modern Water-Colour*. Though superficially reckless, the method is fully controlled and demands great experience. Fedden lived mainly abroad, in France, Spain, North Africa and Egypt. He owned a house at Chantemerle, near Vetheuil, on the Seine, which was previously owned by Charles Conder. He died on 30 March 1939.

---

65. *The Fun of the Fair.* 1908. (no. 2575).

Watercolour on white paper
30 × 66 cms / 11¾ × 26¼".
Signed in ink, b.r. "A. Romilly Fedden / 08".
Inscribed in pencil on backboard: "Old Fair, Burford" / "The Fun of the Fair 20 gns".

Provenance unknown.

This is a lively night scene at a country fair, with bright lights and crowds of people, entirely painted in Fedden's difficult "wet method", which he learned from Arthur Melville. This kind of subject is rarely ventured in watercolour. A day scene, called *The Village Fair*, 12 × 16", apparently of the same period, is reproduced in Fedden's book *Modern Water-Colour* (1917), colourplate facing p 92. This possibly shows the same steam-driven roundabout.

The "wet method" involves working on heavy paper placed horizontally and thoroughly saturated with water. Washes must be laid on rapidly, and blobs of strong colour can be dropped onto the wet surface from a loaded brush. Much practice is necessary with this method, or the painter will risk colours running into each other and creating an appalling mess.

Burford, Oxfordshire, is just over the county boundary from Fedden's native county of Gloucestershire, but quite a distance from Henbury, which is near Bristol. A watercolour *The Lonely Road, scene near Burford*, dated 1910, is in the VAM, P1-1919, given by Martin Hardie.

Bibliography:
Hardie, VAM, Waters, RA Exhibitors 1905-1970.
A Romilly Fedden: *Modern Water-Colour* 1917.
A Romilly Fedden: *Golden Days from the Fishing Log of a Painter in Brittany* 1919.
A Romilly Fedden: *Arthur Melville RWS* OWCS I, 1923-4 p 41.

133

GWEN JOHN

Born Haverfordwest, Pembrokeshire 1876, died Dieppe 1939

Gwendoline Mary, the elder sister of Augustus John (1878-1961), studied at the Slade School of Art at the same time as her brother, 1894-97, and then went to Whistler's school in Paris. She exhibited with the New English Art Club. Most of her life was spent in France - in Paris and later in Meudon. She posed for Rodin, and became his mistress. Received into the Roman Catholic Church in 1913, she lived a reclusive life, devoted to painting and to her cats. All her life she eschewed fame, though her work was admired. Except for the pictures commissioned from her by the American collector John Quin, most of her work remained in her studio.

---

66. *Cat.* (no. 2075).

Watercolour with Chinese white over pencil on buff laid paper
Sight 21 × 16.7 cms / 8⅜ × 6⅝".
Exh London, Leicester Galleries: *Artists of Fame and Promise* part 1, July 1948 (40), bought by Major M Forbes.
Given by S A Forbes, 1974.

This sketch is almost in monochrome except for a touch of yellow watercolour about the cat's eyes. Gwen John kept many cats and constantly drew them. A favourite cat of the period 1905-8 was a white-fronted tortoiseshell with a white face, which is obviously not this cat (see Langdale and Jenkins 1985, nos 59-62). The simplified quality of this drawing, with its use of white bodycolour and pencil outline, seems to call for comparison more with Gwen John's work of about 1915-20.

Bibliography:
Tate Mod Brit, Waters, Farr.
Mary Chamot: *An Undiscovered Artist: Gwen John* Country Life, 19 June 1926 pp 884-85.
The John Quin Collection of Paintings, Water Colors, Drawings and Sculpture New York 1926.
Augustus John: *Gwendolen John* Burlington Magazine 1942 pp 236-37.
Wyndham Lewis: *The Art of Gwen John* The Listener, 10 Oct 1946 p 484.
J Wood Palmer: *Gwen John* The Studio, Nov 1947 pp 138-9.
Augustus John: *Chiaroscuro: Fragments of Autobiography* First Series 1952.
John Rothenstein: *Gwen John* in *Modern English Painters* vol 1, 1952.
Annela Twitchin: *Gwen John: her art and her religion* unpublished MA report, University of London, Courtauld Institute of Art, May 1972.
Michael Holroyd: *Augustus John* vol 1 1974, vol 2 1975.
Susan Chitty: *Gwen John* 1981.
London, Barbican Art Gallery: *Gwen John: an interior life* catalogue by Cecily Langdale and David Fraser Jenkins 1985.
Cecily Langdale: *Gwen John: a Catalogue Raisonné of the Paintings and a Selection of the Drawings* Yale University Press 1986.

Isaac Charles Ginner
Born Cannes, France 1878; died London 1952

Born in France of Anglo-Scottish parents, Charles Ginner went to Paris in 1899 to study architecture. In 1904 he transferred to painting, working at the École des Beaux-Arts and the Académie Vitti under Anglada y Camarasa. He was influenced by the work of Van Gogh. In 1909 he travelled to Buenos Aires and held his first exhibition there. On settling in London in 1910, Ginner exhibited with the Allied Artists Association, frequented the Fitzroy Street studio of Sickert, and was a founder-member of the Camden Town Group in 1911, and the London Group in 1913. He exhibited with Harold Gilman at the Goupil Gallery in 1914. From 1916 to 1918 he served in the Intelligence Corps, and later worked as an artist for the Canadian War Records. Ginner exhibited jointly with Ethelbert White at the Everyman Theatre in 1931. He was elected a member of the New English Art Club in 1922, and in 1945 was elected both ARA and RWS. In 1950 he was awarded a CBE.

---

67. *Storm over Clearbury Ring.* (no. 798).

Pen and ink, watercolour and bodycolour on buff paper
28.2 × 38 cms / 11⅛ × 15″.
Signed b.r. "C.Ginner".

Given by the National Art Collections Fund 1946.

Exh London, Leger Galleries: *Charles Ginner* 1935.

Prov Mrs Dora Fulford.

Dr Wendy Baron (letter 11 Sept 1977, in Malcolm Drummond file) dated this drawing to 1935 and supplied the provenance.
Clearbury Ring is a Saxon camp on a hill above the River Avon in South Wiltshire, three and a half miles south of Salisbury. While only the perimeter pen-line appears to be ruled, this watercolour shows Ginner's original method of depicting rain by using straight parallel lines in both black ink and Chinese white. The buff paper provides the middle tones. A vivid green, used in small patches, is characteristic of Ginner's watercolours.

Ginner seems to have perfected this watercolour style in the early 1930s. A drawing in pencil and watercolour, *Woodlane Farm, Beasley*, 15½ × 12¼″, dated 1932 (with Spink, London: *English Watercolour Drawings* 1975 (96)), is rather looser in handling, but this may be simply because Ginner was using pencil rather than pen for the line work. Another drawing in pen and watercolour, *Boscastle Landscape, Cornwall*, 9 × 13″ (with Agnew's, London, accession no. 2151; photograph in Yale Center for British Art, Newbury negative A3467), is very close to the Ulster Museum watercolour, but is a fine-weather view.

The Ulster Museum has an oil painting by Ginner, *Clarendon Dock, Belfast*, c 1922, and a squared-up watercolour sketch *Hampstead Study*.

Bibliography:
Tate Mod Brit, Waters, Farr.
Charles Ginner: *Neo-Realism* (Manifesto): The New Age, 1 Jan 1914.
Charles Ginner: *Notebooks* (unpublished).
John Rothenstein: chapter on Ginner in *Modern English Painters*, vol 1 *(Sickert to Smith)* 1952.
B Fairfax Hall: *Paintings and Drawings by Harold Gilman and Charles Ginner in the Collection of Edward le Bas* 1965.
Malcolm Easton: *Charles Ginner: Viewing and Finding* Apollo, March 1970.
Wendy Baron: *The Camden Town Group* Scolar Press 1979.

WILLIAM CONOR
Born Belfast 1881; died Belfast 1968

Probably the most popular and representative Belfast painter of his generation, Conor was the son of a tinsmith and gas fitter. He attended the Government School of Design, and worked as a poster designer (or "black man", as he worked in black and white) for the Belfast lithographic printers David Allen and Sons. In 1912 he visited Paris. He produced war art work in both World Wars, but was never commissioned as an Official War Artist. Conor spent a short time in London after the First World War, when he made the acquaintance of Sir John Lavery, Augustus John, the Café Royal circle and the Chelsea Arts Club. In 1921 he was commissioned to paint the opening of the Stormont Parliament by King George V and Queen Mary. Though in 1926 he paid a brief visit to New York, the remainder of Conor's life was spent exclusively in Belfast. His mural *Ulster Past and Present* was unveiled in the Ulster Museum in 1932. Conor was the first Irish member of the Royal Institute of Oil-Painters (ROI). He exhibited at the Royal Academy, the Royal Portrait Society and the Society of Portrait Painters. He was elected ARHA in 1938 and RHA in 1946. From 1957 to 1964 he was president of the Royal Ulster Academy. He received an honorary MA from the Queen's University of Belfast in 1957, and was awarded a Civil List Pension in 1959. Conor never married. He died at his house in Salisbury Avenue and was buried in Carnmoney churchyard.

---

68. Men of the Home Front (Shipyard Workers Crossing Queen's Bridge). (no. 1239).

Coloured crayons with scraping, on white paper
37.5 × 46.8 cms / 14⅞ × 21¼".
Signed b.r. "Conor".

Bought from the artist 1941.

Exh (probably) Belfast, Brand's Arcade, War Weapons Week, 2 Dec 1940.
Cultra, Co Down, Ulster Folk and Transport Museum: *Conor Centenary Exhibition* 1981 (74).

The Ulster Museum has a series of 28 drawings made by Conor in Belfast during the Second World War, which includes a crayon study for the group of men on the right, 15 × 10⅞" (881), and a slightly smaller version of the complete composition, 13⅝ × 18⅜" (1248). The smaller version passed through the War Artists' Advisory Committee and was given to the Belfast Museum in 1947.

Only five of this group of World War II drawings by Conor were handled by the War Artists' Advisory Committee through the Imperial War Museum. The remaining twenty-three, including this one, were bought directly from Conor by the Belfast Museum in 1941. A series of six or eight drawings illustrating Ulster's War effort was commissioned from Conor by the Ministry of Information in April 1940, for a fee of £50 plus £1 per day travelling expenses and maintenance allowance for time away from home (see Wilson 1981 p 65). These drawings were exhibited in Brand's Arcade, Belfast, during War Weapons Week, opening on 2 December 1940. A photograph of the exhibition is reproduced in Wilson 1981, pl 49. This shows that at least some of the additional drawings acquired by the Museum in 1941 were also in this exhibition. Later efforts by Conor to obtain further commissions for Official War Artist's work met with negative response (see Wilson 1981, p 68).

Conor perfected his distinctive drawing style using wax crayons scraped with a razor blade in the early 1930s. By the War period he was using this method almost exclusively. Most of his War drawings show military, police and Territorial Army activities, but there are also a number of illustrations of civilian contributions to the War effort, such as collecting scrap metal, building air-raid shelters, working in munition factories. This view of the shift-workers leaving Harland and Wolff's famous shipyard is one of the best drawings in the latter group, and has a fine sense of rhythm and movement. Much of Conor's work depicts the Belfast working classes, but as John Hewitt points out (afterword to Wilson 1981), Conor was "a proletarian artist without protest".

The Ulster Museum has 15 oil paintings and 47 drawings and watercolours by William Conor. Another large collection of Conor's work formerly belonged to the Linen Hall Library, Belfast, and is now in the Ulster Folk and Transport Museum at Cultra, Co Down.

Bibliography:
Rosc '75, Hewitt, Anglesea RUA, Boylan.
Obituary: Irish Times, 7 Feb 1968.
Cultra, Co Down, Ulster Folk and Transport Museum:
    William Conor Centenary Exhibition Summer 1981.
Brian Fallon: *The People's Painter* Irish Times, 1 Aug 1981.
Judith C Wilson: *Conor 1881-1968: the Life and Work of an
    Ulster Artist* (with afterword by John Hewitt) Belfast,
    Blackstaff Press 1981.
Martyn Anglesea: review of Wilson 1981, Museums Journal,
    March 1982 p 248.

PERCY WYNDHAM LEWIS
Born Amherst, Nova Scotia 1882; died London 1957

Lewis was the principal figure in the English vorticist movement. The son of an American father and a British mother, he was born on his father's yacht. He won a scholarship to the Slade School in 1898-1901, and then travelled in Germany, spending six months at the Akademie Heimann in Munich. Between 1902 and 1909 he visited Paris, Holland and Spain. In 1911 he was a member of the Camden Town Group, and exhibited in the second Post-Impressionist Exhibition at the Grafton Galleries in 1912. In 1913 he was a founder-member of the London Group, and spent a brief and uncomfortable period in Roger Fry's Omega Workshops. In 1914, along with Edward Wadsworth, Frederick Etchells, C F Hamilton and (later) William Roberts (q.v.), Lewis founded the Rebel Art Centre. This developed into the vorticist movement in 1914, and Lewis edited its polemical magazine *Blast!* He served in the Artillery from 1915 to 1917. In 1920 he exhibited with Group X at the Mansard Gallery. He spent the Second World War in Canada and the USA. In 1951 he became blind. The Tate Gallery gave him a retrospective exhibition in 1956. Lewis was a prolific writer of criticism (anti-Bloomsbury), political pamphlets (right-wing extremist) and novels.

---

69. *Seated Woman*. 1922. (no. 814).

Pencil with watercolour on white paper
46 × 34.1 cms / 18⅛ × 13⅜".
Signed and dated b.r. "Wyndham Lewis 1922".

Bought: Mrs Allan Williams, 5 Cleaver Park, Belfast, 1959, along with a life drawing by Epstein (no. 948).

This drawing is not included in the catalogue in Michel 1971. It is a mainly monochrome line-drawing in which the only touch of colour is the dark emerald green of the kerchief on the head. Walter Michel (letter 27 June 1971) replied to an enquiry from Ailsa Kelly (27 May 1971) as to whether it might be Michel 550, *Seated Lady 1922* (exh London, Redfern Gallery: *Wyndham Lewis* 1949 (37)), as it comes close in dimensions: "...it's definitely not 550, as is quite clear from Mr Handley-Read's sketch of that picture". Michel was unable to identify the sitter.

The headgear seems similar to that in Lewis's drawing of *Edith Sitwell*, 1921 (London, National Portrait Gallery, ex coll Sir Osbert Sitwell, Michel 485 and pl 52). Another drawing of *Edith Sitwell* of about the same time (Adelaide, National Gallery of South Australia, ex coll L G Duke, Michel 487 and pl 52), is similar in composition, but reversed. Lewis's oil painting *Praxitella*, 1921-2, 56 × 40", (Leeds City Art Gallery, Michel P 30 and pl 67), is very similar in composition to the Ulster Museum drawing. This drawing has at some time been badly mounted and may have been trimmed.

Bibliography:
Tate Mod Brit, Waters, Johnston & Greutzner, Farr.
Charles Handley-Read (ed.): *The Art of Wyndham Lewis* 1951.
London, Tate Gallery: *Wyndham Lewis Retrospective* 1956.
W K Rose (ed.): *The Letters of Wyndham Lewis* 1963.
Quentin Bell and Stephen Chaplin: *The Ideal Home Rumpus* Apollo, Oct 1964 p 284.
Walter Michel: *Wyndham Lewis: Tyros and Portraits* Apollo LXXXII, 1965 p 128.
Walter Michel: *Wyndham Lewis* Thames and Hudson 1971; contains extensive bibliography.
Walter Michel and C J Fox (eds.): *Wyndham Lewis on Art* New York 1970, London 1971.
Wendy Baron: *The Camden Town Group* Scolar Press 1979.
Jeffrey Meyers: *The Enemy: A Biography of Wyndham Lewis* Boston 1980.

KENNETH DENTON SHOESMITH
Born Halifax, Yorkshire 1890; died Hampstead, London 1939

One of the unique acquisitions of the Ulster Museum in the last decade has been the bequest by this artist's widow of the entire contents of her husband's studio, practically untouched since his death in 1939. Born in Yorkshire, Shoesmith was brought up in Blackpool, where as a boy he followed a correspondence course organised by T R Ablett of the Royal Drawing Society from 1902 to 1908. From 1906 to 1909 Shoesmith was a cadet on HMS Conway, then based at Rock Ferry near Birkenhead. In 1909 he joined the Royal Mail Company as a junior officer. Already he was an able and prolific marine watercolour painter in a style related to W L Wyllie, Norman Wilkinson and Charles Dixon, and his years at sea provided him with quantities of material. Having been promoted to Chief Officer in the Mercantile Marine during the First World War, Shoesmith had to curb his hobby, but when the War ended he wanted to paint full-time, so gave up the sea. He became a professional commercial artist, working with the publicity department of his old company, Royal Mail, for nearly twenty years. He was also an easel painter, sometimes in oil, and was elected a member of the Royal Institute of Painters in Water-Colour in 1926. In 1936 he was commissioned by Cunard to paint murals, including the two Roman Catholic altarpieces, for the *Queen Mary*. He had no time for art school practice, or for modern critics, and when Duncan Grant's murals were rejected by Cunard, Shoesmith wrote a letter attacking "Clive Bell and the little world of incompetence for whom, apparently, he speaks", published in *The Listener* on 6 May 1936. Until about 1936 Shoesmith and his wife lived at 16 Alyth Gardens, Golders Green. They then moved to a studio house, 4 Willifield Way, Hampstead Garden Suburb, which was where he died. His ashes were scattered from the Royal Mail steamship *Asturias* in the English Channel. Shoesmith's widow returned to her native Belfast (she was the daughter of a wealthy shipowner), and a memorial exhibition was held at John Magee's Gallery, Donegall Square, in 1941. In 1975 Mrs Shoesmith died, bequeathing 312 paintings and drawings, with a large selection of graphic material, to the Ulster Museum.

---

70. *Cranes, Baker Street.* (no. 2285).

Watercolour and bodycolour over pencil on white laminated board
75.9 × 50.8 cms / 29⅞ × 20″.
Signed b.l. "Kenneth D Shoesmith".

Exh Old label from discarded frame: "Royal Institute of Painters in Watercolours 195 Piccadilly (3)" [no year given, but it was presumably after 1936 as Shoesmith's address is given as 4 Willifield Way, London NW11].

Bequeathed by the artist's widow, Mrs Sarah Shoesmith, Cultra, Co Down 1975.

Exh Belfast, Ulster Museum 1977 (51), then Liverpool, Hull, Southampton and Scottish Arts Council 1977-8.

Rep Wirth and Timmington 1978 p 9.

This late work showing hoardings, timber scaffolding and cranes on a site in Baker Street, London, is a rare example of a non-maritime subject by Shoesmith. Influences from Fred Taylor and possibly Frank Brangwyn are detectable, and it shows how impressive on a large scale this poster-artist could be. There is no attempt to glamorise a workaday subject. Shoesmith often painted in watercolour on the artists' laminated boards then available, which could be as much as half an inch thick, and obviously eliminated the tendency for paper to cockle when wet.

Bibliography:
Waters, RA Exhibitors 1905-70.
Sidney R Jones: *Posters and Publicity* The Studio 1926 (Shoesmith's *Asturias* poster is reproduced in pl 23 and a Royal Mail Line *Bermuda* booklet in pl 25.
Obituary: Hampstead and Highgate Express, 14 April 1939.
Belfast, Ulster Museum: large collection of photographs, newspaper cuttings, printed matter and memorabilia bequeathed by Mrs Shoesmith.
Belfast, Ulster Museum: *Kenneth Shoesmith 1890-1939: Paintings and Graphics* catalogue by Martyn Anglesea, Jan 1977. In 1977-8 this exhibition was toured to Liverpool (Merseyside County Museums), Hull (Ferens Art Gallery), Southampton Art Gallery, and was circulated to a number of Scottish venues by the Scottish Arts Council.
William Feaver: *Ship-Shape Shoesmith* The Observer Colour Magazine, 17 April 1977 p 12.
Gunther Wirth (text), Tony Timmington (photos): *Kenneth Shoesmith: Maler zur See* Illustrierte Wochenzeitung (Stuttgart) 1/78, 7 Januar 1978 pp 6-10.

Southampton Art Gallery: *Art on the Liners: a celebration of elegance at sea* catalogue by Alastair Forsyth, May-June 1986.

Alastair Forsyth: *Ambassadors of Style: Art and Design on the greatest British Liners* Waterstone & Co, in preparation for Spring 1987.

GERALD LESLIE BROCKHURST
Born Birmingham 1890; died Franklin Lakes, New Jersey 1978

Brockhurst is known mainly as an etcher of outstanding technical ability. As a child he was an artistic prodigy, but apart from that he was a very backward pupil and had difficulty with writing. At the age of twelve he was sent to the Birmingham School of Art, where the teaching was still Burne-Jonesian in character. In 1907 he went on to the Royal Academy Schools, where he won the Landseer Scholarship and other awards which took him to Paris and Milan. In Italy he carefully copied pictures by Piero della Francesca and Botticelli. He published his earliest etchings in 1920. He was friendly with Oliver St John Gogarty, and visited Ireland several times. In 1921 he was elected ARE and RE, ARA in 1928 and RA in 1937. For a time he lived in Chelsea, but in 1939 he moved to New York. From 1941 Brockhurst lived at Franklin Lakes, New Jersey, where he died in 1978.

---

71. *Portrait of an Unknown Man.* (no. 2584).

Pencil, grey wash and watercolour on rough white wove paper
45.7 × 32.4 cms / 22 × 15".
Signed b.r. "G L Brockhurst".

Aquired from the Leicester Galleries, London, in 1930, along with three other works, in exchange for a *Nude* by Wilson Steer which had been bought the previous year. See the Lloyd Patterson catalogue, Ulster Museum 1982, p 17, for the circumstances of this exchange.

Exh Belfast, Ulster Museum: *Lloyd Patterson Collection* 1982. Sheffield, Birmingham, National Portrait Gallery: *Gerald Leslie Brockhurst RA 1890-1978* 1986-87.

Almost full-face, slightly to right, wearing coat, waistcoat and floppy bow-tie, sandy hair curling at back. The face and head are drawn with very fine pencil hatching, while the clothes are sketched in with a full brush of liquid watercolour. Brockhurst's models were usually seductive young females, and male portraits occur comparatively rarely in his work. This portrait appears to date from the late 1920s, but why would what is apparently a commissioned portrait be with a commercial gallery so early? This, and the distinguished-looking but so-far unidentified sitter, are two mysteries attached to this impressive drawing.

Bibliography:
Waters, Guichard.
H Stokes: *Etchings of G L Brockhurst* Print Collectors' Quarterly XI, 1924, p 409.
H J L Wright: *A Catalogue of Etchings by G L Brockhurst* Print Collectors' Quarterly XI, 1924, p 424.
M C Salaman: *G L Brockhurst* 1928.
H J L Wright: *The Later Etchings of G L Brockhurst ARA* Print Collector's Quarterly XXI, 1934, p 317, and XXII, 1935, p 63.
Belfast, Ulster Museum: *British Etchings and Engravings 1870-1940* catalogue by Martyn Anglesea 1978.
London, Maclean Gallery: *Gerald Leslie Brockhurst 1890-1978: a Classicist of the '20s and '30s* 1980.
Belfast, Ulster Museum: *British Art 1900-1937: The Robert Lloyd Patterson Collection* catalogue by Brian Kennedy 1982 pp 16-17.
Sheffield, Graves Art Gallery; Birmingham, Museum and Art Gallery; and London, National Portrait Gallery: *Gerald Leslie Brockhurst RA 1890-1978* catalogue by Anne Goodchild 1986.

JOHN NORTHCOTE NASH
Born London 1893; died 1977

John Nash worked first for a local paper, but was encouraged to draw and paint by his more famous elder brother Paul Nash (1889-1946). He had no formal art training. The two brothers exhibited together at the Dorian Leigh Galleries in 1913, and John had his first one-man-show at the Goupil Gallery in 1921. He was admitted as a member of the Friday Group in 1913, the London Group in 1914, the Cumberland Market Group in 1915, and the New English Art Club and the Society of Wood Engravers in 1921. During 1916-1918 Nash served in the Artists' Rifles, and in 1918 was commissioned as an Official War Artist. From 1918 to 1921 he lived at Gerrard's Cross, and was art critic for the London Mercury in 1919. He moved to Prince's Risborough, Buckinghamshire, in 1921, and taught at the Ruskin School of Drawing, Oxford, 1922-27, and at the Royal College of Art 1934-40 and 1945-57. In 1939 Nash joined the Observer Corps, and again worked as an Official War Artist to the Admiralty in 1940. In 1944 he moved to Bottengoms Farm, Wormingford, Colchester, Essex. He was elected ARA in 1940 and RA in 1951.

---

72. *View of the Plain.* (no. 831).

Pen and watercolour, with Chinese white, over pencil on white paper
28.2 × 39.6 cms / 11⅛ × 15⅝″.
Signed b.r. "John Nash".
Inscribed with colour notes: "hay colour" "red".

Bought: Coventry, J Heritage-Peters 1951.

This watercolour contains a considerable amount of pen-hatching. John Nash (letters 17 Feb and 7 March 1975) described it as a view of the Aylesbury Plain in Buckinghamshire painted about 1924, and added: "...Thatched cottages in foreground were the clubhouse of the Little Whiteleaf Golf Course, near Princes Risborough. Chalk pit in distance just over dark tree marked the edge of the Chiltern escarpment, with the plain behind. Chequers Court [formerly the home of Lord Lee of Fareham, who willed it to the nation as a country residence for the British prime-minister] is back behind the top of the tree on the extreme right".

Nash lived on the edge of the Aylesbury Plain near Princes Risborough from 1921, while teaching at the Ruskin School of Drawing at Oxford.

The Ulster Museum has a contemporary watercolour by John Nash, *Farm at Kimble* (832), as well as an oil painting *The Garden Under Snow* 1924-30 (474), and two of his wood-engravings, *The Fisherman* (P5) and *The Sacred Grove* (P6).

Bibliography:
Tate Mod Brit, Waters, Farr, RA Exhibitors 1905-1970.
John Nash: *The Artist Plantsman* Anthony d'Offay 1976.
John Lewis: *John Nash the Painter as Illustrator* foreword by Wilfred Blunt, Pendomer Press 1978.
Albert Garret: *A History of British Wood-Engraving* Midas Books 1978.
Wendy Baron: *The Camden Town Group* Scolar Press 1979.
Andrew Causey: *Paul Nash* Oxford 1980.
Meirion and Susie Harries: *The War Artists* Michael Joseph 1983.
Sir John Rothenstein: *John Nash* Macdonald 1983.

EVIE HONE (EVA SYDNEY HONE)

Born Roebuck Grove, Dublin 1894; died Rathfarnham, Dublin 1955

Evie Hone was a descendant of Joseph Hone, a brother of Nathaniel Hone RA (1718-84: see entry under Horace Hone). Her father, also named Joseph Hone, was a maltster. By the age of eleven she was partially crippled by infant paralysis, and needed prolonged treatment, including visits to the continent. A visit to Assisi in 1911 made a profound impression. She went to London about 1913 to study at the Byam Shaw School of Art. After the War she studied under Sickert at the Westminster School of Art, and at the Central School under Bernard Meninsky, who advised her to go to Paris. She and her friend Mainie Jellett (1897-1944) went to Paris in 1920, working the first in the studio of André Lhôte. In 1921 they both became pupils of the cubist painter Albert Gleizes, who had turned increasingly to religion, and they worked with him each year until 1931. In 1925 Evie Hone joined an Anglican community in Truro, Cornwall, but left after about a year. She converted to Roman Catholicism. In 1933 she began working in stained glass, and her greatest achievement was in this medium. Her career culminated with the east window for Eton College Chapel, 1948-52. In 1943, again with Jellett, she was a founder-member of the Irish Exhibition of Living Art.

73. Composition. (no. 805).

Gouache on white laminated board
29.5 × 42 cms / 11⅝ × 16½".
Signed in pencil, b.l. "E.Hone".

Bought: Dublin, Dawson Gallery 1965.

This low-keyed composition of purples and blues, apparently based on a still-life, seems to date from the mid to late 1920s when Evie Hone and Mainie Jellett had come under the influence of Gleizes. In this period the work of the two Irish artists is so close stylistically that they can be difficult to distinguish.

The Ulster Museum also has an oil on panel by Evie Hone, *Ruin at Ardmore*, c 1946 (308).

Bibliography:
Tate Mod Brit, Rosc '75, Waters, P of I, NGI, Boylan.
C P Curran: *Evie Hone: Stained Glass Worker* Studies, Summer 1955 pp 129-42.
Stella Frost: *A Tribute to Evie Hone and Mainie Jellett* Dublin 1957.
Dublin, University College: *Evie Hone 1894-1955: An Exhibition* catalogue introduction by James White 1958.
James White and Michael Wynne: *Irish Stained Glass* Dublin 1963.
John Rothenstein: *An Ardent Spirit* Art and Artists, April 1985 p 16.
Dublin, National Gallery of Ireland and Douglas Hyde Gallery: *Irish Women Artists from the Eighteenth Century to the Present Day* (biography by Nicole Arnould, p 168) 1987.

WILLIAM PATRICK ROBERTS
Born London 1895; died London 1980

Originally apprenticed to a firm of commercial artists, William Roberts attended St Martin's School of Art and the Slade School between 1910 and 1913. He became interested in cubism, travelled in France and Italy, and in 1913 spent a brief period in Roger Fry's Omega Workshops. In 1914 he joined Wyndham Lewis (q.v.) at the Rebel Art Centre, and was one of the signatories of the Vorticist Manifesto in the first issue of the magazine *Blast!* He exhibited with the vorticists, and from 1915 was a member of the London Group. In 1916 Roberts joined the Royal Field Artillery, and was an Official War Artist in 1917-18. After 1920 he exhibited with Group X. Roberts had a one-man-show at the Chenil Galleries in 1923. After 1952 he exhibited at the Royal Academy. He was elected ARA in 1958 and RA in 1966. Like Edward Burra, Roberts became a recluse in his later years. He remained faithful to the simplified rounded forms he evolved in the 1920s. In his books of 1956 and 1957, Roberts denied the leadership of Wyndham Lewis, and proclaimed himself a "plain English cubist", in association with Bomberg, Nevinson, Wadsworth and Gaudier-Brzeska.

---

74. *Watching a Raid.* (no. 1324).

Watercolour over pencil on white paper
35.4 × 25.3 cms / 14 × 10".
Signed in pencil b.c. "Roberts".
Inscribed in pencil, t.r. "the O.P." [observation post].
Given by the Contemporary Art Society 1964.

This is a scene in the trenches during the First World War. The red armband of the soldier on the right is inscribed "RA" [Royal Artillery]. Roberts joined the Royal Field Artillery in April 1916, and in August of that year he was with the British Expeditionary Force in France. He then made "a twenty-two months' tour of the Flanders battle-field" (*Some Early Abstract and Cubist Work* 1957 p 8). He received a commission from the Canadian War Memorials Fund in 1918, which encouraged him away from the Bomberg-like abstraction which he had previously been practicing. The British Museum has a watercolour of a *Red Cross Dressing Station* 1918 (1983-7-23-1).

On his return to England in April 1918, Roberts produced his major war painting *The First German Gas Attack on Ypres* (Ottawa, National Gallery of Canada), and in 1919 he painted *A Shell Dump* (London, Imperial War Museum) for the Ministry of Information.

The angular figures in this drawing are similar to those in Roberts's drawing *The Travelling Cradle* of 1918 (Southampton Art Gallery, reproduced in *Some Early Abstract and Cubist Work* 1957 pl 8).

The Ulster Museum has two oil paintings by William Roberts: *Sawing Wood* c 1930 (496) and *Les Routiers* c 1931 (492).

Bibliography:
Tate Mod Brit, Waters, Farr, RA Exhibitors 1905-70.
William Roberts: *The Vortex Pamphlets* 1956-8.
William Roberts: *Some Early Abstract and Cubist Work 1913–20* 1957.
William Roberts: *Paintings 1917-1958* 1960.
John Rothenstein: *Modern English Painters: vol 2, Lewis to Moore* Macdonald 1956.
London, National Portrait Gallery: *William Roberts ARA: Paintings and Drawings 1909-1964* 1964.
London, Tate Gallery: *William Roberts* (Arts Council retrospective) 1965.
London, Tate Gallery: *Paintings and Drawings by William Roberts RA* 1976.
London, Tate Gallery: *William Roberts: Early Years* 1982.
Reading, Museum and Art Gallery: *William Roberts Retrospective* 1983.
Meirion and Susie Harries: *The War Artists* Michael Joseph 1983.
London, National Portrait Gallery: *William Roberts: An Artist and his Family* catalogue by Robin Gibson and Honor Clerk 1984.

Harry Aaron Kernoff

Born London 1900; died Dublin 1974

Harry Kernoff was the son of a Russian Jewish furniture maker and a Spanish mother, and was brought to Dublin when the family moved there in 1914. At first apprenticed to his father, he attended night classes at the Metropolitan School of Art and won a Taylor Scholarship in 1923. His greatest influences were the painters Patrick Tuohy and Séan Keating. Kernoff worked in Dublin all his life, and was a prolific artist and illustrator, painting portraits of many literary and theatrical figures, and producing woodcuts for the Gayfield Press and the Three Candles Press. He was elected RHA in 1936. Kernoff died in the Meath Hospital on Christmas Day 1974. The National Gallery of Ireland has a large collection of his drawings.

---

75. *Boon Companions*. 1934. (no. 1074).

Watercolour over pencil on white paper
25.5 × 32.4 cms / 10 × 12¾".
Signed and dated t.l. "Kernoff '34".
Inscribed with title.

Given by the Hon. Mr Justice Creed Meredith, Hopeton, Rathgar, Co Dublin, 1935.

In 1936 Kernoff painted an oil version of this, on board 59.6 × 72.5 cms (now in a private collection), exh. Dublin, Hugh Lane Municipal Gallery 1976-7 (55) as *Self Portrait with Davy Byrne and Martin Murphy (set maker at the Gate Theatre) in Davy's Parlour Snug 1936*. Another oil on board, 95.2 × 72.5 cms, *In Davy's Back Snug, Dublin 1936*, was in the same exhibition (56).

Davy Byrne's was, and still is, a well-known literary pub off Grafton Street, Dublin. This Joycean subject is an unusual one for watercolour, but the watercolour version has an immediacy and freshness which the later oil version lacks.

To celebrate his election as RHA, Kernoff presented the Belfast Museum with eight of his woodcuts, and wrote to the then curator, Arthur Deane (letter 8 Nov 1935): "...The last time I was in Belfast I noticed that Justice Meredith had presented you with a small water-colour of mine. The mount seemed to have been unneccessarily abbreviated, it should be at least 4 or 5 inches wide for that picture". Deane replied (11 Nov 1935) that the mount was just as it was received from Judge Meredith. The watercolour was remounted in the 1970s with a wide margin.

Bibliography:
Rosc '75, Waters, NGI, Boylan.
Obituaries: Irish Times 25, 26, 27 Dec 1974.
Dublin, Godolphin Gallery: *Harry Kernoff: a Selection of Dublin Paintings*, introduction by John Ryan, 1974.
Dublin, Hugh Lane Municipal Gallery of Modern Art: *Harry Kernoff Memorial Exhibition* catalogue by Ciaràn MacGonigal 1976-7.
Diarmuid Peavoy: *The Life and Times of Harry Kernoff* Hibernia, Fri 4 Feb 1977.

NORMAN MACK MORROW
Born Belfast 1879; died London 1917

Norman Morrow was the youngest of the eight sons of George Morrow, a Belfast painter and decorator. Five of the brothers studied art and became painters or illustrators: Albert (1863-1927), George (1869-1955), Jack (1872-1926), Edwin (born 1877) and finally Norman. George Morrow, the best-known, became art editor of *Punch* 1932-37. Norman was born at 18 North Queen Street, Belfast, on 21 Aug 1879, and attended the Government School of Design. He followed his brothers to London, becoming a popular illustrator and poster artist. He contributed a weekly theatrical sketch to *The Bystander*. The writer of his obituary in that magazine describes him as "the shyest genius I think I ever knew", and says that he only sent pictures to exhibitions "in weak moments". He died in London, aged 38, on 8 Sept 1917, apparently of an illness and not as a consequence of the War.

76. *Man and Woman.* (no. 1202).

Poster-paint over pencil on grey paper
29.9 × 25 cms / 11¾ × 10″.
Signed in pencil, b.r. "NM".

Bought: London, Sotheby's 23 Jan 1969 (93) with two other Norman Morrow drawings.

Rep Anglesea RUA p 47.

As his career was tragically cut short, Norman Morrow did not achieve the celebrity of his elder brother George. His drawings show him to have been an inventive and talented illustrator in the tradition of John Hassall (1868-1948). Much of his work is overtly comic in spirit. This broad sketch of a working class couple who might be at a race meeting is no caricature, but has sensitivity and panache. It is evidently the work of a commercially-trained artist.

Bibliography:
Hewitt, Anglesea RUA.
Obituary by "B.M.H.": The Bystander, 12 Sept 1917.
Information from Mr George Morrow (nephew), Lambeg, Co Antrim, 1974, including photographs and copies of pages from the Morrow family Bible with dates of births and deaths; Ulster Museum files.

JOHN PIPER
Born Epsom, Surrey 1903

The son of a solicitor, Piper visited Italy regularly as a child, and in 1924 published an illustrated edition of his own poems. He has remained a regular writer as well as an illustrator, landscape painter and designer of stained glass and stage decor. Until 1928 he worked in his father's office, then studied at Richmond and Kingston Schools of Art, and at the Royal College of Art 1928-9. After a visit to Paris in 1933 his work turned temporarily abstract. Piper married the writer Myfanwy Evans in 1935. He held his first one-man-show at the London Gallery in 1938. In the same year he began writing articles in the *Architectural Review*, which was then edited by John Betjeman. Also in 1938 he produced his first stage designs for Stephen Spender's *Trial of a Judge*. Piper was an Official War Artist 1940-42, a Trustee of the Tate Gallery 1946-52 and 1954-61, and a member of the Arts Council Panel 1952-57. In 1948 he designed the sets and costumes for Vaughan Williams's opera *Job*, and subsequently designed six operas by Benjamin Britten. Piper's stained glass may be seen at Oundle School Chapel (1954-6), Coventry Cathedral (1958) and the Metropolitan Cathedral, Liverpool (1965-6).

---

77. *Bladon*. 1945. (no. 2658).

Pen, black ink and watercolour on white paper
Sight 55.9 × 74.2 cms / 22 × 28½".
Signed in ink, b.l. "John Piper / Bladon / May 23 / 45".
Inscribed on verso: "Woodstock Park (Blenheim)".

Exh Dublin, Irish Exhibition of Living Art 1951 (label on back of frame).

Provenance The Derry-born painter Norah McGuinness (1903-1980), who bequeathed it to the Friends of the National Art Collections of Ireland, "with the hope that it be lent from time to time to Derry when a suitable gallery becomes available".
Given by the Friends of the National Art Collections of Ireland, in memory of Norah McGuinness 1982.

Bladon, Oxfordshire, is one of the estate villages on the edge of the park of Blenheim Palace, the great house designed by Sir John Vanbrugh for the Duke of Marlborough, and still lived in by the Duke's descendants. Sir Winston Churchill, who was born at the Palace, was buried in Bladon Churchyard in 1965. The church tower can be seen above the trees in this sombre rainy view, one of a large number of gloomy parkland scenes which Piper painted throughout the 1940s. From about 1938 he worked increasingly from his own photographs. Piper lived not too far away, at Fawley Bottom, near Henley-on-Thames.

Bibliography:
Tate Mod Brit, Waters, Farr.
John Piper: *English Romantic Artists* 1942.
John Piper: *Buildings and Prospects* 1948.
John Betjeman: *John Piper* Penguin Modern Painters 1944.
S John Woods: *John Piper: Paintings, Drawings and Theatre Designs 1932-54* 1955.
John Rothenstein: *British Art Since 1900* Phaidon 1962.
Belfast, Ulster Museum: *John Piper* March-April 1967.
London, Marlborough Fine Art: *John Piper* Sept-Oct 1975.
Dublin, Solomon Gallery: *An Exhibition of Paintings by John Piper* Jan-Feb 1982 (catalogue contains detailed biography).
London, Tate Gallery: *John Piper* catalogue by David Fraser Jenkins, with introduction by John Russell 1983.
Meirion and Susie Harries: *The War Artists* Michael Joseph 1983.

ANTHONY GROSS
Born Dulwich, London 1905; died Le Boulvé, Lot, France 1984

A son of the map publisher Alexander Gross, Anthony Gross was educated at Repton. He studied at the Slade School of Art in 1923, and later at the Central School of Arts and Crafts, the Académie Julian and the École des Beaux-Arts, where he specialised in etching. He held his first one-man-show in London in 1924, and went on to study etching in Madrid, exploring Spain on a donkey. In France he was friendly with Picabia, Zadkine, Léger and Balthus, as well as with the expatriate printmakers Stanley Hayter and Joseph Hecht. From making black and white etchings in the 1920s he progressed in the 1930s to animated films, including *La Joie de Vivre* (1934) and *Round the World in Eighty Days*, which was interrupted by the War in 1939. In 1937 he illustrated Cocteau's *Les Enfants Terribles*.

Gross served as an Official War Artist between 1941 and 1945 in Britain, the Middle East, India, Burma, North Africa, Germany and France, and the Imperial War Museum has over three hundred of his works. He taught at the Central School 1948-54, and at the Slade School 1955-71, and was one of the main revivers of printmaking in Britain in the 1950s and 1960s. He joined the London Group in 1946, and for many years worked during the summers in the Dordogne, settling at Le Boulvé in 1955. He worked extensively as an illustrator, and in 1980 published *The Very Rich Hours of Le Boulvé*, in which he described the village and its history. He was elected ARA in 1979, RA in 1980, and was awarded a CBE in 1982.

---

78. *Red cock and hen.* (no. 801).

Pen, watercolour and bodycolour on white paper
37.9 × 55.6 cms / 14⅞ × 22¼".
Signed b.r. "Anthony Gross".

Bought: London, Mayor Gallery, Brook Street 1954.

According to the artist (letter 19 Feb 1975), this farmyard scene was painted at Montgesty, Lot, France, in either 1947 or 1948, and was shown with some other watercolours at the Leicester Galleries, London, in Autumn 1948. The catalogue of Gross's retrospective exhibition of graphic work at the VAM (1968) stated that this show was in 1947, but Gross himself thought 1948 more likely.

Some other watercolours in the series were painted while staying on a farm at Jarcan (Lot et Garonne), and the rest, mostly park scenes, were painted in London. *Village Children, Montgesty*, watercolour 14⅛ × 22⅝", in the Victoria and Albert Museum (P.2-1948), a group of boys and girls sitting on a bench, belongs to this series.

The Ulster Museum also has a much earlier etching made in France by Gross, *Café Cambrils* 1933 (P643).

Bibliography:
Tate Mod Brit, Waters, Guichard.
James Laver: *The Etchings of Anthony Gross* The Bookman's Journal XI, 1924 p 28.
New York, Associated American Artists: *Anthony Gross: A Retrospective covering Thirty Years of Etching* 1964.
London, Victoria and Albert Museum: *The Etchings of Anthony Gross* 1968.
Anthony Gross: *Etching, Engraving and Intaglio Printing* 1970.
Meirion and Susie Harries: *The War Artists* Michael Joseph 1983.
Obituary: The Times 12 Sept 1984.
Graham Reynolds: *Anthony Gross: a Tribute* Apollo, Jan 1986 p 42.

John Luke
Born Belfast 1906; died Belfast 1975

Born in North Belfast, the son of a fireman, Luke studied at the Belfast School of Art under James Stoupe and Newton Penpraze, and in 1927 won a Dunville Scholarship to the Slade School in London. Here he studied under Henry Tonks (q.v.), and for a time shared a studio with F E McWilliam (q.v.). He took his Slade Diploma in 1931, and after spending some time at the Westminster School of Art under Walter Bayes, Luke returned to Belfast in 1931, where he became friendly with John Hewitt and William McClughin. Luke, who never married, lived with his parents in Lewis Street. He taught the life classes in the Belfast School of Art for many years (until 1973), and was renowned among the students for exceptional exactitude and strictness. He admired Eric Gill, and his drawings and sculpture certainly show this. On the other hand, his later paintings, usually executed in a slow, deliberate tempera technique which he developed himself, recall nothing more than the book-illustrations of Edmund Dulac writ large. In 1941 Luke and his mother went to live at Knappagh, Co Armagh. Always a solitary, Luke finally became torpid through lack of nourishment at his home in Duncairn Gardens, Belfast, and, after removal to the Mater Hospital, he died. Patric Coogan (born 1935), a student of Luke's in Belfast in the 1960s, was deeply influenced by his style and outlook.

79. *Self portrait.* (no. 2526).

Pencil on white paper
Sight 30.2 × 25 cms / 16⅜ × 11½".
Signed b.r. "J.Luke".

Provenance The artist's estate.

Bought: Belfast, Mrs S McKee (Luke's sister) 1979.

Exh Arts Councils of Ireland: *John Luke* 1978 (78). Limerick, National Institute for Higher Education: *National Self Portrait Collection* 1982.

Though undated, this drawing is so close in style to Luke's oil *Self Portrait* 1928 (Ulster Museum 2331) to make it certain that it was drawn during his period at the Slade School, 1927-30. Hewitt (1978 p 14) describes Luke at that time: "...six feet tall, dark, handsome, of an erect spare build...always tidy, his clothes brushed, his hair short, he was not at all close to the romantic stereotype of the artist".

Luke's pupil Pat Coogan, in an essay quoted by Hewitt 1978 p 101, recalled Luke's reminiscences of Henry Tonks: "Luke, as a young man, won his way to the Slade mainly on the strength of a tremendous capacity for literal description - such ability was highly rated in those days at the Belfast College of Art. It was of course misguided for the young man had been led to believe in the absurd concept of light and shade imitation. To such an extent that on reaching the Slade, he received a rather severe shock when Tonks said, 'To put it bluntly, John, you don't know the first thing about drawing. These things you have been doing are quite good, as far as they go - the trouble is that they don't go nearly far enough; there is absolutely no form-expression in any of them'. Many years later, after he had recalled something of this interview, I asked if that meant that one could expect to find this quality of form-expression in Tonks's work. 'Well, to put it bluntly', he smiled, 'I don't think that Tonks knew what he was talking about. What Tonks knew...was only the beginning; he didn't take it nearly far enough. Of course...I feel grateful to Tonks for directing my attention to it. I could have spent the rest of my life in ignorance of the possibility. Before that,...I had assumed, as most people seem to do, that old masters like Michelangelo and Da Vinci for example were simply light and shade painters..."

The Ulster Museum has 30 paintings, drawings and sculptures by John Luke, including a long series of drawings which document the evolvement of his tempera painting *The Rehearsal* (1950).

Bibliography:
Waters, Hewitt, Anglesea RUA, Johnson & Greutzner, Stewart.
John Hewitt: *John Luke (1906-1975)* Belfast, Arts Councils of Ireland, 1978.

THOMAS CARR
Born Belfast 1909

The son of a Belfast stockbroker, Tom Carr as a boy received some lessons from the Swiss painter Hans Iten (1874-1930), who settled in Belfast. Later, at Oundle School, Northamptonshire, he was taught by the art master, the Belfast-born E M O'Rorke Dickey (1894-1977). In 1927 Carr went to the Slade School of Art, where he studied under Henry Tonks (q.v.). After a brief period in Italy, Carr was associated first with the Objective Abstractionists, and then with the Euston Road School (William Coldstream, Victor Pasmore, Claude Rogers, Graham

Bell etc). By the outbreak of the Second World War he had returned to Ulster, and settled with his wife and family at Newcastle, Co Down. He was an Official War Artist. In 1957 he opened the Piccolo Gallery in Belfast, in partnership with the architect Robert McKinstry. Tom Carr still lives in Belfast. He is an academician of the Royal Ulster Academy, and the only Northern Ireland Member of the Royal Society of Painters in Water-Colour (RWS). His work has strongly influenced Terence P Flanagan (q.v.).

---

80. *Ormond Quay, Dublin.* (no. 2084).

Watercolour over pencil on white paper
Sight 21.6 × 27.4 cms / 8½ × 10¾".
Signed b.l. "T.Carr".

Bought: Belfast, Tom Caldwell Gallery 1974.

Exh Belfast, Tom Caldwell Gallery, March 1974 (20).
Arts Council of Northern Ireland: *Tom Carr Retrospective* 1983-4 (4).

This was probably painted on a visit to Dublin with Graham Bell in 1939. A larger oil version belongs to Mr Edwin Bryson, Comber, Co Down, and Graham Bell's work executed at the same time is very close in style.

During February and March 1939 Tom Carr visited Dublin with the South African painter Graham Bell (1910-43) who was one of the mainstays of the Euston Road School. They had already painted together at Dover in 1938. They made a contract to hold an exhibition in Dublin after painting pictures of the city. Bell at this time was deeply involved in anti-fascist propaganda, but the Dublin episode enabled him to concentrate for a short time on objective painting. He filled a sketchbook with drawings. Some of the paintings that Graham Bell produced at this time are reproduced in Laughton 1986 pp 198-99.

In October 1942 Graham Bell shared an exhibition at the Leicester Galleries, London, with three Euston Road pupils, Tom Carr, Anthony Devas, and Lawrence Gowing, who was some eight years younger than the rest. Carr was a much less intellectually analytic painter than the orthodox Euston Roaders, and less dogmatic than the Objective Abstractionists to whom he had previously been attached. Laughton 1986 pp 275-6 states that Carr, a gentle, natural painter, used his "objective

abstraction" paintings to roof his beehives, saying in a letter to Mrs Quentin Bell in 1980 that he "could not speak too highly of their weather resistant qualities".

Bibliography:
Rosc '75, Hewitt, Waters, Anglesea RUA.
Arts Council of Northern Ireland: *Tom Carr Retrospective* Belfast, Ulster Museum, and Dublin, Douglas Hyde Gallery, Trinity College, 1983-4; catalogue introduction by T P Flanagan.
Bruce Laughton: *The Euston Road School: a Study in Objective Painting* Scolar Press 1986.

T. Cass.

FREDERICK EDWARD McWILLIAM
Born Banbridge, Co Down 1909

With William Scott (q.v.) F E McWilliam is the most internationally distinguished artist to have been born in Ulster in the 20th century. The son of a doctor, he was educated at Campbell College, Belfast. In 1926 he entered the Belfast School of Art, and in 1928 went on to the Slade School in London, where he studied under Henry Tonks (q.v.) and Randolph Schwabe. He won a scholarship to Paris in 1931, and since then has lived in London. Though always averse to groups and manifestos, McWilliam exhibited with the British Surrealist Group in 1938, and held his first one-man-show at the London Gallery in 1939. During the War he served as an Intelligence Officer with the RAF in the Far East. He joined the London Group in 1949, and the Royal Society of British Artists in 1950. From 1946 to 1968 he taught sculpture at the Slade School. He was elected ARA in 1959, but later resigned. Many of his sculptures have been commissioned for public places, as for example the bronze *Princess Macha* (1959) at Altnagelvin Hospital, Londonderry.

---

81. *Collage*. 1946. (no. 4689).

Cut-out magazine photographs and crayon on black paper
38.7 × 24.8 cms / 15¼ × 9¾".
Signed b.r. "F E McW 1946".

Bought: Paris, Paul Renaud, 10 May 1985 (78).

The disturbing atmosphere of this collage reveals McWilliam's surrealist background. The forms in the top half certainly relate to McWilliam's sculptures over about a decade, in particular the Hopton Wood stone *Mandible* of 1938 (Penrose 1964 pl 8). In the mid 1940s, McWilliam was preoccupied also with the motif of the disembodied head resting upon another form (in this case an enormous shoulder). Many of his fragmented and disembodied figure sculptures date from these years.

The Ulster Museum has the following sculptures by McWilliam: *Man and Wife* 1948, *Head of William Scott* 1956, *Woman of Belfast no. 7* 1972, *Woman in Bomb-Blast* 1974 and *Crossed Legs* c 1928.

Bibliography:
Tate Mod Brit, Hewitt, Catto, Waters, Farr, Naylor and
   P-Orridge.
Roland Penrose: *McWilliam, Sculptor* Alec Tiranti 1964.
Belfast, Arts Council of Northern Ireland, and Dublin, Irish
   Arts Council: *F E McWilliam* catalogue essays by Judy
   Marle and T P Flanagan 1981.

WILLIAM SCOTT
Born Greenock, Scotland 1913

William Scott is the most celebrated of living Ulster painters. Born in Scotland of Scots-Irish parents, in 1924 he was brought to his father's native town of Enniskillen, Co Fermanagh. His father was a house painter and signwriter. While at school in Enniskillen he was given lessons in art, and introduced to the modern movement, by a remarkable young teacher, Kathleen Bridle (who is still alive). Scott entered Belfast College of Art in 1928, and in 1931 went on to the Royal Academy Schools in London. He never returned to Northern Ireland. After his marriage in 1937 he lived abroad, mainly in France. From 1941 to 1956 he taught at the Bath Academy of Art, where he became senior lecturer in painting. In 1953 he went as guest instructor to a summer school at Banff, Alberta, Canada. He then visited the United States and met Jackson Pollock, de Kooning, Kline, Rothko and Brooks. He was a Ford Foundation artist resident in Berlin in 1963-65, and in 1966 was awarded a CBE. In 1977 he was elected RA.

---

82. *1st Aegean Suite no. 1.* Jan 1969. (no. 2669).

Pencil, black ink, watercolour and white bodycolour on white paper
slightly irregular, 26.2 × 33.5 cms / 10¼ × 13¼".
Signed in pencil, b.r. "W Scott 68".
Inscribed on hardboard back of discarded frame: "28 May 69 / For John / William".

Provenance Sir John Heygate, Bellarina, Ballymena, Co Antrim.

Bought: Chester, Richard Heygate 1983, along with five other pictures by William Scott.

Exh London, Tate Gallery: *William Scott* 19 April-29 May 1972 (93 d), lent by Sir John Heygate.

William Scott's art, whether on an intimate or monumental scale, moves from the objective to the abstract. He also works in phases, each related to the previous phase. Sometimes his painting is entirely in monochrome greys, and then when he needs colour again he uses bright colour. He has quoted Leonardo in saying that "drawing is the art of correction", and in both his drawings and his large paintings there is an obvious element of erasure and re-statement. In 1955 he visited the Lascaux caves, and in 1970 he went to Egypt. The art of both cultures impressed him by its anonymity. A drawing like this is not a preparatory drawing for a particular painting, but relates to Scott's painting in the plural. He said to Lawrence Alloway in 1954: "I draw to shock myself out of a too-easy rhythm. I begin with no conception whatever. An image emerges; almost always any image that I am obsessed with. I rub it out, and begin again, searching for its counterpart. When it appears, I invariably find that the thing I draw is at my elbow; it is out of the window, or has been standing at my front door for a long time".

The Ulster Museum has nine paintings and drawings by William Scott, as well as a bronze head and torso of him by F E McWilliam (q.v.).

Bibliography:
Tate Mod Brit, Waters, Hewitt, Catto, Farr, Naylor and P-Orridge.
Herbert Read: *Contemporary British Art* Penguin 1951.
Lawrence Alloway: *Nine Abstract Artists* Alec Tiranti 1954.
Patrick Heron: *The Changing Forms of Art* Routledge 1955.
Herbert Read: *Great Britain in Art Since 1945* Thames and Hudson 1959.
Ronald Alley: *William Scott* Methuen, Art in Progress Series 1963.
Alan Bowness: *William Scott: Paintings* Lund Humphries 1964.
Edward Lucie Smith: *A Girl Surveyed: Five Poems with Drawings by William Scott* London, Hanover Gallery 1971.
Lou Klepac, ed. *William Scott: Drawings* New York, David Anderson 1975.
Hilton Kramer: *Painterly Subtleties fill work of Scott* New York Times, 6 Jan 1973.
Hilton Kramer: *Art: Seeing an Emotion's Shape* New York Times, 11 Jan 1975.
Belfast, Ulster Museum. Dublin, Guinness Hop Store, and Edinburgh, National Gallery of Modern Art: *William Scott* catalogue essays by Ronald Alley and Terence P Flanagan 1986.

LOUIS LE BROCQUY
Born Dublin 1916

One of the most successful living Irish painters, Louis le Brocquy was born in Dublin of Belgian extraction. He studied chemistry at Trinity College, and until 1938 worked in the family firm, the Greenmount Oil Company. He first exhibited at the Royal Hibernian Academy in 1937, and from that time exhibited regularly there. He held his first one-man-show at his studio in Merrion Row, Dublin, in 1942. In 1946 he moved to London, teaching at the Central School of Arts and Crafts, and exhibited for the first time with Gimpel Fils in 1947.

The same year he was included in the British Council exhibition *Twelve British Painters*, which toured northern Europe, and in an exhibition *Contemporary Irish Painting* in New York. He represented Ireland at the Venice Biennale in 1956. He has also produced some outstanding book-illustrations, in particular for Thomas Kinsella's translation of *The Táin* (Dundalk, Dolmen Press 1969, and Oxford University Press 1970). Le Brocquy is married to the painter Anne Madden, and since 1958 has lived mainly in the south of France.

---

83. Skilful boy. 1947. (no. 811).

Pen, black ink, wax, watercolour and bodycolour over pencil on white paper
12.2 × 15.2 cms / 4¾ × 6″.
Signed and dated b.l. "Le B./ April '47".

Given by the Contemporary Art Society 1964.

Exh Rosc '75 (87).

Between 1939 and 1945, le Brocquy's painting moved from academic realism, through a form of impressionism, to a linear style. Between 1945 and 1948, his early style of maturity was an expressionistic figure style, containing many images from the lives of Irish "tinkers" or "travellers". (There are no genuine gypsies in Ireland; the Irish tinkers are of Gaelic stock, not Romanys as are found in Europe and Britain). He himself stated: "...for me the travelling people represented, dramatically perhaps, the human condition" (Dublin Catalogue 1966 p 14). This group of children playing football, with a boy on the left heading the ball, is not explicitly a tinker scene, but is related to this phase, when le Brocquy produced many watercolours as well as oils. Sometimes he used scumbled wax to diffuse his Indian ink lines.

See Earnan O'Malley: *Louis le Brocquy* Horizon vol XIV, no. 79, July 1946, reprinted in Walker 1981, pp 71-76; and *Mr Louis le Brocquy's Watercolours* The Times, 26 May 1947.

The Ulster Museum has eight paintings and drawings by Louis le Brocquy.

Bibliography:
Tate Mod Brit, Arnold, Rosc '75, Waters, NGI, P of I.
Louis le Brocquy: *Music in Painting* The Dublin Magazine, Oct-Dec 1941.
Zurich, Galerie Charles Lienhard: *Louis le Brocquy* introduction by Robert Melville, January 1961 (includes a useful list of review articles).
Dublin, Municipal Gallery of Modern Art: *Louis le Brocquy: Catalogue of a Retrospective Selection of Oil Paintings 1939-1966* 1966.
Dublin, Dawson Gallery: *Louis le Brocquy* 1971.
Dorothy Walker: *Louis le Brocquy* introduction by John Russell, Dublin, Ward River Press 1981.

RICHARD HAMILTON
Born London 1922

Hamilton studied at the Westminster School of Art under Mark Gertler, and at St Martin's School of Art under Bernard Meninsky in 1936. However, he became an office boy in an advertising firm and then a display assistant before going on to the Royal Academy Schools in 1938-40. During the War he worked as an engineering draughtsman with EMI. He returned to the Royal Academy Schools in 1945-6, but was expelled for "not profiting by instruction". He then served as a sapper in the Royal Engineers at Aldershot, 1946-7. From 1948 to 1951 he studied etching under Buckland Wright at the Slade School. He was a design instructor at the Central School of Arts and Crafts 1951-53, lecturer in basic design, King's College, Newcastle-upon-Tyne 1953-66, and lecturer in interior design at the Royal College of Art 1957-61. Towards the end of his period in Newcastle he reconstructed Marcel Duchamp's *Large Glass*. Hamilton is regarded as the founder of British pop art, but his work is very various, and he constantly borrows or quotes from the work of other artists or writers. Since the late 1940s he has devoted much time to printmaking, and has produced an impressive array of published writings.

---

84. *Bronze by Gold.* 1948. (no. 2571).

Watercolour over pencil on white paper
Sight 56.7 × 38.7 cms / 22⅜ × 15¼".
Signed b.r. "R Hamilton".

Bought: London, Anthony d'Offay Gallery 1980.

Exh London, Anthony d'Offay Gallery: *Richard Hamilton: Drawings, Prints and Paintings 1941-55* 1979-80 (14) (reviewed by Anna Greutzner, Art Monthly no. 35, 1980, p 20). Belfast, Ulster Museum: *Alistair Smith: A Personal Selection* 1981.

Rep d'Offay catalogue 1979 (colour); Ireland of the Welcomes, James Joyce Centenary Issue, vol 31 no. 3, May-June 1982 p 4 (colour).

Hamilton describes his interest in James Joyce's *Ulysses* in a statement issued by Waddington Graphics in 1982: "The only benefit I experienced from eighteen months of enforced detention in our post-war army was time to read. An excellent regimental library of English classics from Chaucer to Hardy provided a staple diet. I also spent many hours in the barrack room reading and re-reading the two-volume Odyssey Press edition of Joyce's *Ulysses*. It was then, in 1947, that I first began to think about the possibility of illustrating *Ulysses*. It may be that an exhibition of French books at the National Gallery in 1946 fired me with enthusiasm to emulate the printmaking achievements of Picasso, Matisse, Braque, Rouault and others. With illustration in mind, my examination of *Ulysses* was more intensive than any book I have read".

The illustrating project came to nothing, as Hamilton goes on to explain: "There was some interest in my drawings when a few were shown in the Joyce exhibition at the ICA, but a meeting with T S Eliot, in his professional role as a Faber executive director, deterred me from taking my work further. He explained that the cost of resetting Ulysses for a limited edition would be prohibitive. It was then I understood the reasons for the School of Paris penchant for the illustration of poems: Villon, Verlaine, Rimbaud, Baudelaire created the kind of ten-line image that gave the artist a big picture - with minimal setting costs for the publisher".

The content of this watercolour illustration is described in detail by Alistair Smith of the London National Gallery, in his *Personal Selection* catalogue, Ulster Museum 1981, pp 37-8: "*Bronze by Gold* illustrates the chapter which starts 'Bronze by gold heard the hoofirons, steelyringing'. [Further on: 'Bronze by gold, Miss Douce's head by Miss Kennedy's head, over the crossblind of the Ormond Bar heard the viceregal hoofs go by, ringing steel.'] Miss Douce (identified by her initials on the heart-shaped pendant at her throat) and Miss Kennedy, the barmaids of the Ormond, stand before the 'mirror gilt Cantrell and Cochranes' - 'Bronzelydia by Minágold'. In the mirror are visible some of their customers, including Blazes Boylan - 'He touched to fair Miss Kennedy a rim of his slanted straw. She smiled on him. But sister bronze outsmiled her, preening for him her richer hair, a bosom and a rose'. The thoughts of the ladies are seen in the way they handle the beer-pulls. Hamilton's punning use of these reflects the extended use of this technique in the original. Also a linguistic pun is seen in the word *Cochrane* appearing from the barmaids' heads, like a thought.

171

"The most obvious source quoted for Hamilton's composition, with its use of the mirror, is Manet's *Bar aux Folies-Bergère*. The relationship between the ladies, the way one places an arm around the other, is, however, more akin to formulae used in early 16th century Venetian portraiture. The melancholic air reminds me more of Carpaccio's *Two Courtesans*.

"More important, however, is Hamilton's decision to render his subject in a style akin to *Neue Sachlichkeit* which brings with it an accurate 'period quality' (the first edition of *Ulysses* was published in 1922). This particular style was also much used for night-club scenes of an explicitly sexual nature, often with overtones of decadence or menace. The adoption of the style for the mildly flirtatious Lydia and Mina might be described as an example of satirical diminution, although Hamilton seems to view the ladies with some considerable affection."

In 1981, Hamilton returned to the *Ulysses* theme with his aquatint *In Horne's House*, the first study for which was made as early as 1949. Here he expresses Joyce's apeing of other writing styles in this particular chapter, by drawing the characters in the styles of different artists or periods. See the Tate Gallery catalogue *Richard Hamilton: Image and Process*, 1983, nos 64-71. The Ulster Museum has a print of *In Horne's House* (P680).

Bibliography:
Naylor and P-Orridge.
Richard Hamilton: *Hommage à Chrysler Corp* Architectural Design, March 1958.
Richard Hamilton: *Diagrammar: The Developing Process* Newcastle 1959.
Richard Hamilton: *Persuading Image* Design Feb 1960.
Richard Hamilton: *Artists as Consumers* BBC Radio discussion with Lawrence Alloway, Eduardo Paolozzi and Basil Taylor, March 1960.
Richard Hamilton: *The Bride Stripped Bare by her Bachelors, Even 101 1960.*
Richard Hamilton: *An Exposition of She* Architectural Design, Nov 1961.
Richard Hamilton: *Duchamp* Art International, Jan 1964.
Richard Hamilton: *The Bride Stripped Bare by her Bachelors Even Again* Newcastle 1966.
Richard Hamilton (with Mario Amaya): *Son of the Bride Stripped Bare* Art and Artists, July 1966.
Richard Hamilton: *Roy Lichtenstein* Studio International, Jan 1968.
Richard Hamilton: *Photography and Painting* Studio International, March 1969.
Richard Hamilton: *Collected Words* 1983.
Jasia Reichardt: *Pop Art and After* Art International, Feb 1963.
Charles Spencer: *Richard Hamilton, Painter of 'Being Today'* Studio International, Oct 1964.
Patrick Procktor: *Techniculture* The New Statesman, Nov 1964.
Gene Baro: *Hamilton's Guggenheim* Art and Artists, Nov 1966.
Lucy Lippard: *Pop Art* 1966.
Lawrence Alloway: *Popular Culture and Pop Art* Studio International, July-Aug 1969.
London, Tate Gallery: *Richard Hamilton* 1970.
Edwin Mullins: *Father of Pop Art* The Daily Telegraph Magazine, March 1970.
John Russell: *Richard Hamilton* Art in America, March 1970.
Cor Blok: *Richard Hamilton: Towards a New Definitive Statement?* Museumjournaal (Amsterdam) Sept 1970.
John Loring: *Not Just So Many Marvellously Right Images* Print Collector's Newsletter (New York) Nov 1973.
London, Tate Gallery: *Richard Hamilton: Image and Process. Studies, Stage and Final Proofs from the Graphic Works 1952-82* catalogue by Richard S Field 1983.

The following seven drawings by contemporary Ulster artists are at present in the collection of the Arts Council of Northern Ireland, which collects and exhibits work by living local artists. There is an arrangement by which these collections are, after a time, transferred to the Ulster Museum, where they will form part of the historical collections of Irish art.

TERENCE PATRICK FLANAGAN
Born Enniskillen, Co Fermanagh 1929; lives in Belfast

While at school in Enniskillen, T P Flanagan attended evening classes at the Technical College there, and received lessons from Kathleen Bridle, who also taught William Scott (q.v.). He went on to study at Belfast College of Art, 1949–53, then taught art in schools in Lisburn and Ballynahinch, and later at the Belfast College of Art. From 1955 he lectured in art at St Mary's College of Education, Belfast, and was head of the art department there from 1965 until his retirement in 1985. He was a trustee of the Lyric Theatre, Belfast, 1961–65. In 1970 he was commissioned to design an Ulster '71 postage stamp, and was by then established as one of the most successful painters in Ireland. In 1973–4 he spent a sabbatical year in the USA, and returned there for a lecture tour in 1976. He has exhibited widely, but principally with the Tom Caldwell Gallery, Belfast, David Hendricks Gallery, Dublin, and with the two Arts Councils in Ireland. From 1977 to 1982 he was President of the Royal Ulster Academy. His work contains many landscape elements from the Fermanagh lake country and Donegal.

---

85. *An Enniskillen Sunday*. 1982.

Pencil, black and grey chalk on white paper.
Sight 55 × 74 cms / 21⅝ × 29¼″.
Inscribed b.l. "An Enniskillen Sunday".

Collection: Arts Council of Northern Ireland.

Exh Arts Council of Northern Ireland: *Along these Lines I* 1983 (14).

This view, taken from a car park in the centre of Flanagan's home town of Enniskillen, shows the Roman Catholic Parish Church on the left, and on the right, the spire of St Macartan's (Church of Ireland) Cathedral. Flanagan shares with Basil Blackshaw (q.v.), his contemporary at the Belfast College of Art, a tentative sense of feeling for the subject through atmosphere, a quality found also in the older Ulster painter, Tom Carr (q.v.).

The Ulster Museum has six paintings and drawings by T P Flanagan: *Winter Lough* c 1960–62, *Bog Landscape* 1961, *Landscape with Five Trees* 1961, *Gortahork 2* c 1969, *Poppies and a Sepia Drawing* c 1975, and *Twilight on a Bog* 1982.

Bibliography:
Arnold, Hewitt, Catto, Anglesea RUA.
Drawings for *Cuchulain* by J J Campbell, 1957.
Gallery Programme *Contrasts* BBC Northern Ireland 1966.
Seamus Heaney: *Talking to T P Flanagan* Irish Times, 21 Sept 1967.
Aquarius Programme *The Other Belfast* London Weekend Television 1971.
Kenneth Jamison: *Painting and Sculpture* Chapter in *Causeway: The Arts in Ulster* Dublin, Arts Councils of Ireland 1971.
The Artists in Northern Ireland The Arts in Ireland vol 1 no. 1, Autumn 1972.
T P Flanagan: *Drawings of William Scott* The Arts in Ireland vol 1 no. 3, Spring 1973.
Gallery Programme *Painter – T P Flanagan* BBC Northern Ireland 1973.
T P Flanagan: *To Speak of Drawing* Introspect no. 1, Dec 1975.
Caroline Walsh talks to the Painter T P Flanagan Irish Times, 14 Aug 1976.
Belfast, Ulster Museum: *Personal Choice: T P Flanagan* 1980.

Enniskillen Sunday

BASIL BLACKSHAW
Born Glengormley, Co Antrim 1932; lives in Antrim

Blackshaw was brought up at Boardmills, Co Down. He attended the Methodist College, Belfast, and Belfast College of Art 1948–51. In 1951 he was awarded a scholarship by the Committee for the Encouragement of Music and the Arts (CEMA) to study in Paris. Since then he has worked mainly in the Lagan Valley. His work contains many landscape elements such as Colin Mountain and the Slieve Croob Hills. Horses, dogs, and their world of fanciers and breeders form another important part of his subject-matter. He has also painted formal portraits. The Ulster Museum owns his oil-paintings *The Field* (1953) and *Nude* (1973) as well as a charcoal drawing *A Road* (c 1960).

---

86. *Hill*. 1982.

Pencil, coloured chalks and crayons, watercolour and bodycolour on white paper.
Sight 55 × 74 cms / 21⅝ × 29¼″

Collection: Arts Council of Northern Ireland.

Exh Arts Council of Northern Ireland: *Along these Lines* 1983 (3).

There is a close relationship in subject matter and technique between Blackshaw's work and that of his contemporary, T P Flanagan (q.v.), particularly a feeling for atmosphere and weather in the constantly-changing Ulster climate. Here, with a surprising variety of materials, Blackshaw handles that most difficult of subjects to paint, rain.

Bibliography:
John Hewitt: *Portrait of a Young Man as the Artist* Threshold, Feb 1957.
Kenneth Jamison: *Painting and Sculpture*; chapter in *Causeway: The Arts in Ulster,* Dublin, The Arts Councils of Ireland 1971.
Belfast, Arts Council of Northern Ireland: *Basil Blackshaw Retrospective* 1974.
Dublin, Irish Arts Council and Department of Foreign Affairs: *Six Artists from Ireland: An Aspect of Irish Painting* essay on Blackshaw by Liam Kelly 1983.

177

DAVID CRONE
Born Belfast 1937; lives in Holywood, Co Down

David Crone was taught by Kenneth Jamison at Annadale Grammar School, Belfast, and attended Belfast College of Art 1956–61. In 1964 he was awarded an Arts Council Travelling Scholarship and visited Germany, Italy, Belgium and Holland. In 1963–75 he returned to Annadale Grammar School as an art teacher. Since 1975 he has taught the foundation course at the Ulster College of Art and Design. Though his work can come near abstraction, it almost always contains a figurative or landscape element, and he revels in impasto.

---

87. *Fields.* 1982.

Pencil, charcoal, watercolour and bodycolour, with surface-scraping, on white paper.
Sight 74 × 55 cms / 29¼ × 21⅝″.
Signed in ink, b.r. "David Crone. 82".

Collection: Arts Council of Northern Ireland.

The only bright note in this sombre watercolour painted at Slieve League, Co Donegal, is the acid green of the square field, low on the hillside. David Crone's watercolours, whether of figures reflected in shop windows, or, as here, pure landscape, are mostly gestural, expressive and heavily-worked-over. As with Blackshaw (q.v.), the dampness of Crone's colour directly reflects the perennial moods of the Ulster countryside.

The Ulster Museum has an oil painting by David Crone, *Rocks and Vegetation*, 1964, and a watercolour *Figures in the City,* 1985.

Bibliography:
Catto.
Belfast, Arts Council of Northern Ireland: *David Crone: An Exhibition of Paintings and Drawings* 1968.
Belfast, Queen's University Common Room: *David Crone* introduction by Kenneth Jamison, Michaelmas Term 1974.
Belfast, Arts Council of Northern Ireland: *David Crone* March 1980.

David Crone '83

CLEMENT MCALEER
Born Coalisland, Co Tyrone 1949

After working for six years on leaving school, Clement McAleer did the foundation year at the Ulster College of Art and Design, Belfast, in 1971–72. He went on to study at Canterbury College of Art 1972–5 and at the Royal College of Art 1975–8. Though he taught for a time at the Ulster College, McAleer has managed to live entirely by his painting. He shuttles between Northern Ireland and Liverpool, where he has a studio in the Bluecoat Chambers. He often paints landscape on a large scale.

---

88. Field and Forest 1982.

Black, yellow and white chalk on white paper.
Sight 55 × 74 cms / 21⅝ × 29¼".
Watermark: "T H SAUNDERS England".
Signed b.l. "Clement McAleer".

Collection: Arts Council of Northern Ireland.
Exh Arts Council of Northern Ireland: *Along these Lines 1* 1983 (13).

Landscape, both in Ireland and England, is the dominant theme of McAleer's paintings. The broad handling and big scale of his work in oil is present also in this bold chalk drawing with its tactile rubbings and erasings.

The Ulster Museum has two canvases by Clement McAleer, *Day* and *Night*, 1979.

Bibliography:
Belfast, Arts Council of Northern Ireland: *Clement McAleer* July 1979.
Liverpool, Bluecoat Gallery: *Viewpoints: Recent Paintings by Clement McAleer* October 1981.
Dublin, Douglas Hyde Gallery, Trinity College: *The Ulysses Project* 1982.
Belfast, Arts Council of Northern Ireland: *Clement McAleer: Paintings and Drawings* May 1984.

JOHN AIKEN
Born Belfast 1950

John Aiken is a sculptor. He studied at Chelsea School of Art 1968–73, and at the British School at Rome 1973–75. While there he became interested in renaissance military architecture and its use of pure geometry. Another abiding interest was archaeology with its application of geometric grids to irregular landscape features. In 1974–75 he taught at the New School in Rome, and during the following year was visiting lecturer at a number of art schools in Britain. He was appointed a lecturer in sculpture at the Art and Design Centre, Belfast, in 1976. He revived his interest in fortifications when in 1977 and 1978 he visited the D-Day Landing Zones in Normandy and the Maginot Line in Alsace and Lorraine. He used imagery inspired by these in Spring Show 2 at the Serpentine Gallery, London, in 1978 and in an exhibition at the Arts Council Gallery in Belfast. In 1978 he was awarded a bursary by the Arts Council of Northern Ireland. His large-scale sculpture has been largely of a transitory nature, often made of sand moulded by glass sheets; the construction and destruction of each installation has been recorded photographically.

---

89. *The line.* 1984.

Pencil and pastel on white paper.
Sight 83 × 78 cms / 32⅝ × 30¾″.
Collection: Arts Council of Northern Ireland.

The all-over pattern of this drawing, recalling some of the work of Paul Klee or Mark Tobey, has the quality of a sculptural relief, and contains motifs derived from the star-shaped bastions of military fortifications, one of Aiken's constant themes.

Bibliography:
Belfast, Arts Council of Northern Ireland: *John Aiken: Recent Sculpture* 5 Oct–4 Nov 1978.
Dublin, Oliver Dowling Gallery: *John Aiken: Drawing on Three Planes* 27 April–12 May 1984.

182

CAROL GRAHAM
Born Belfast 1951

Carol Graham was educated at Cambridge House School, Ballymena, and Belfast College of Art 1970–74, where she took her diploma in 1974 and spent a post-diploma year 1974–75. She was awarded an Arts Council bursary in 1976, and an Arts Council major award in 1980. Her paintings use a form of photo-realism and show a fascination with light shining through translucent materials such as fabrics. In a statement of 1981 she said "I paint intuitively and wish my work to both challenge and seduce the viewer".

---

90. *Garden, Ballywalter*. 1982.

Pencil on white paper.
Sight 28 × 31 cms / 11 × 12¼″.
Signed b.r. "Carol Graham 8/82. A.C.".
Collection: Arts Council of Northern Ireland.

Ballywalter is a coastal village on the Ards Peninsula in Co Down, some fifteen miles east of Belfast. This tightly-finished pencil drawing conveys the same qualities found in Carol Graham's oil paintings – stillness and luminosity. The wide range of tones possible in pencil is made to conjure up the August heat in an overgrown orchard, while the carefully-ruled but modulated perimeter line, and the wide margins, give the drawing the appearance of a line-engraving.

The Ulster Museum has Carol Graham's oil and acrylic on canvas, *Light Falls Within,* 1978. A portrait of the Belfast-born flautist, *James Galway,* was commissioned from her by the Museum in 1988.

Bibliography:
Belfast, Arts Council of Northern Ireland: *Carol Graham* 1981.
Brian Kennedy: *Carol Graham's Photo-Realism* Circa, July–Aug 1982.
Aidan Dunne: *Contemporary Women Artists,* essay in *Irish Women Artists from the Eighteenth Century to the Present Day,* Dublin, National Gallery of Ireland and Douglas Hyde Gallery 1987. (Carol Graham has a passing mention on p 64 but was not included in the exhibition).

185

FELIM EGAN
Born Strabane, Co Tyrone 1952

Now possibly the most successful young painter in Ireland, Felim Egan studied at the Ulster Polytechnic, Belfast, 1971–72, Portsmouth Polytechnic 1972–75, and as a postgraduate at the Slade School, London, 1975–77. He has since taught at the National College of Art and Design, Dublin, 1978–79. and the Art and Design Centre, Belfast 1980–81. In 1981 he returned to Dublin to teach at the National College of Art and Design. In 1979 he was awarded a scholarship by the Arts Council of Northern Ireland to the British School at Rome, and while there he started incorporating neon tubes into his work. Egan's paintings, drawings, constructions and gallery installations make use of linear calligraphy and forms derived from megalithic spirals. He plays Irish traditional music, and finds a visual analogy to its rhythms and counterpoints.

91. Plant Dance no 6. 1982.

Paper collage, pencil, watercolour and white bodycolour on white paper.
Sight 44 × 28 cms / 17¼ × 11".
Inscribed b.r. "Plant Dance 6".
Signed b.r. "Felim Egan 82".

Collection: Arts Council of Northern Ireland

The effect of cutting up one drawing and turning it into another produces unexpected results, accentuated by the fastidious neatness of the ruled pencil lines. Such qualities are found throughout Egan's work, often in large-scale canvases and works executed directly on gallery walls.

The Ulster Museum has an acrylic painting by Egan, *Line Composition – Blue,* 1979, and a canvas incorporating a shaped neon tube. *Score, 1981.*

Bibliography:
Dublin, Oliver Dowling Gallery: *Felim Egan* 1978.
Dublin, Oliver Dowling Gallery: *Seven Artists* 1979.
London, various venues: *A Sense of Ireland* 1980.
Dublin, Trinity College, Douglas Hyde Gallery: *Hibernian Inscape* 1980.
Belfast, Arts Council of Northern Ireland: *Felim Egan* catalogue introduction by Dorothy Walker, with two written statements by the artist, October 1981.

General Bibliography

Monographs and specialised works on individual artists are listed in full following the catalogue entries, whereas general works and reference books are listed by abbreviated titles as below. Works are published in London unless otherwise stated.

Anglesea RUA: Martyn Anglesea: *The Royal Ulster Academy of Arts: A Centennial History* Belfast, Royal Ulster Academy 1981.

Archibald: E H H Archibald: *A Dictionary of Sea Painters* Woodbridge, Suffolk, Antique Collectors' Club 1980.

Arnold: Bruce Arnold: *A Concise History of Irish Art* Thames and Hudson World of Art Library 1969, 2nd edition 1980.

Bénézit: Emmanuel-Charles Bénézit: *Dictionnaire Critique et Documentaire des Peintres, Sculpteurs, Dessinateurs et Graveurs* Nouvelle Edition, 10 vols, Paris, Librarie Grund 1976.

Binyon: Laurence Binyon: *English Water-Colours* Adam and Charles Black, Library of English Art 1933, 2nd edition 1944, reprinted 1946, 1962.

BM Brit Dr: London, British Museum: Department of Prints and Drawings: *Catalogue of British Drawings I: XVI & XVII Centuries* by Edward Croft-Murray and Paul Hulton, 2 vols 1960.

Bryan: *Bryan's Dictionary of Painters and Engravers* new edition revised and enlarged under the supervision of George C Williamson, 5 vols, G Bell & Sons 1918.

Catto: Mike Catto: *Art in Ulster 2: a History of Painting, Sculpture and Printmaking 1957–1977* with selected biographical notes by Theo Snoddy, Belfast, Blackstaff Press 1977. Companion volume to *Hewitt*.

Caw: Sir James L Caw: *Scottish Painting Past and Present 1620–1908* Edinburgh and London, T C & E C Jack, 1908.

Chaloner Smith: John Chaloner Smith: *British Mezzotinto Portraits* 5 vols and portfolio of prints, 1878–83.

Clarke: Michael Clarke: *The Tempting Prospect: A Social History of English Watercolours* British Museum Publications (Colonnade Books) 1981.

Clement & Hutton: *Artists of the Nineteenth Century* 1879.

Cordingly: David Cordingly: *Marine Painting in England 1700–1900* Studio Vista 1974.

Cunningham: Alan Cunningham: *The Lives of the Most Eminent British Painters* 6 vols, 1929–32.

DNB: *Dictionary of National Biography* edited by Leslie Stephen, 63 vols plus supplements, index and epitome, Smith Elder 1908, and 20th century supplements, Oxford University Press.

Edwards: Edward Edwards: *Anecdotes of Painters* 1806.

Elmes: Dublin, National Library of Ireland: *Catalogue of Irish Topographical Prints and Original Drawings* by Rosalind M Elmes, Dublin, Stationery Office 1943.

Farr: Dennis Farr: *English Art 1870–1940* Oxford History of English Art 1978.

Foskett: Daphne Foskett: *A Dictionary of British Miniature Painters* 2 vols (text and plates) Faber & Faber 1972.

Graves BI: Algernon Graves: *The British Institution 1806–67* 1875, Kingsmead Reprints, Bath 1969.

Graves Dict: Algernon Graves: *A Dictionary of Artists who have exhibited works in the Principal London Exhibitions from 1760 to 1893* 1884, 1895, enlarged edition 1901, Kingsmead Reprints, Bath 1969.

Graves RA: Algernon Graves: *The Royal Academy of Arts: A Complete Dictionary of Contributors and their Work, from its Foundation in 1769 to 1904* 4 vols 1905, Kingsmead Reprints, Bath 1970. Continued by *RA Exhibitors 1905–70*.

Graves Loan: Algernon Graves: *A Century of Loan Exhibitions 1813–1912* 5 vols 1913–15; reprinted in 3 vols, Kingsmead Reprints, Bath 1970.

Graves S of A: Algernon Graves: *The Society of Artists of Great Britain 1760–1791 and the Free Society of Artists 1761–1783* 1907, Kingsmead Reprints, Bath 1969.

Guichard: Kenneth M Guichard: *British Etchers 1850–1940* Garton and Cooke 1977.

Gunnis: Rupert Gunnis: *Dictionary of British Sculptors 1660–1851* Odhams 1953.

Hardie: Martin Hardie: *Water-Colour Painting in Britain* vol 1 *The Eighteenth Century*, vol 2 *The Romantic Period*, vol 3 *The Victorian Period*, edited by Dudley Snelgrove with Jonathan Mayne and Basil Taylor, Batsford 1968.

Hewitt: John Hewitt: *Art in Ulster 1: Paintings, Drawings, Prints and Sculpture for the last 400 years to 1957* with biographies of the artists by Theo Snoddy, Belfast, Blackstaff Press 1977. Companion volume to *Catto*.

Hughes: C E Hughes: *Early English Water-Colour* 1913, revised edition 1950.

Huish: M B Huish: *British Water-Colour Art* 1904.

Irish Portraits: Dublin, National Gallery of Ireland, London, National Portrait Gallery, and Belfast, Ulster Museum: *Irish Portraits 1660–1850* catalogue by Anne Crookshank and the Knight of Glin, published by the Paul Mellon Foundation for British Art 1969.

Irwin: David and Francina Irwin: *Scottish Painters at Home and Abroad 1700–1900* Faber & Faber 1975.

Johnson & Greutzner: J Johnson and A Greutzner: *The Dictionary of British Artists 1880–1940* Woodbridge, Suffolk, Antique Collectors' Club 1976, reprinted 1980.

Lambert: Belfast, Ulster Museum: *The Gordon Lambert Collection of Contemporary Art* introduction by James Johnson Sweeney 1976.

Lloyd Patterson: Belfast, Ulster Museum: *British Art 1900–1937: Robert Lloyd Patterson Collection* catalogue by Brian Kennedy, published by the Friends of the Ulster Museum 1982.

Mallalieu: Huon L Mallalieu: *The Dictionary of British Watercolour Artists up to 1920* Woodbridge, Suffolk, Antique Collectors' Club 1976.

Mellon: New York, Pierpont Morgan Library, and London, Royal Academy of Arts: *English Drawings and Watercolours 1550–1850 in the Collection of Mr and Mrs Paul Mellon* New York, Pierpont Morgan Library 1972.

Naylor and P-Orridge: Colin Naylor and Genesis P-Orridge, eds.: *Contemporary Artists* London, St James Press, and New York, St Martin's Press 1977.

Nettlefold: C Reginald Grundy and F Gordon Roe: *A Catalogue of the Pictures and Drawings in the Collection of Frederick John Nettlefold* 4 vols 1933–38.

NGI: Dublin, National Gallery of Ireland: *Illustrated Summary Catalogue of Drawings, Watercolours and Miniatures* compiled by Adrian le Harivel, introduction by Homan Potterton 1983.

OWCS: *The Old Water-Colour Society's Club* Annual Volumes from 1924.

P of I: Anne Crookshank and the Knight of Glin: *The Painters of Ireland c 1660–1920* Barrie and Jenkins 1978.

Pasquin: John Williams (alias "Anthony Pasquin"): *An Authentic History of the Professors of Painting in Ireland* 1797, reprinted with an introduction by Ronald Lightbown, Cornmarket Press 1970.

RA 1934: London, Royal Academy of Arts: *Exhibition of British Art* commemorative catalogue 1934.

RA Exhibitors 1905–70: *Royal Academy Exhibitors 1905–70: A Dictionary of Artists and their Work in the Summer Exhibitions of the Royal Academy of Arts* 6 vols, Wakefield, Yorkshire, EP Publishing Ltd 1973. Continuation of *Graves RA*.

Redgrave Cent: Samuel and Richard Redgrave: *A Century of British Painters* 1866, revised edition 1947.

Redgrave Dict: Samuel Redgrave: *A Dictionary of Artists of the English School* 1878; Kingsmead Reprints, Bath 1970.

Roget: John Lewis Roget: *History of the Old Water-Colour Society* 2 vols, Longmans 1891; reprinted in 1 vol, Woodbridge, Suffolk, Antique Collectors' Club 1972.

Rosc '75: Cork, Crawford Municipal Art Gallery: Rosc Exhibition *Irish Art 1900–1950* catalogue by Hilary Pyle 1975.

Stewart: Ann M Stewart: *Royal Hibernian Academy of Arts: Index of Exhibitors 1826–1979* Dublin, Manton Publishing, vol 1 1985, vol 2 1986, vol 3 1987.

Strickland: Walter George Strickland: *A Dictionary of Irish Artists* 2 vols, Dublin and London, Maunsel & Co 1913; reprinted with an introduction by Theo Snoddy, Shannon, Irish Universities Press 1968.

Tate Mod Brit: London, Tate Gallery: *The Modern British Paintings, Drawings and Sculpture* catalogue by Mary Chamot, Dennis Farr and Martin Butlin, 2 vols, Oldbourne Press 1964.

Thieme/Becker: Ulrich Thieme and Felix Becker: *Allgemeines Lexikon der Bildender Künstler von der Antike bis zur Gegenwart* 37 vols, Leipzig, E A Seeman Verlag. Reprint, Zwickau, F Ullmann 1972.

VAM: London, Victoria and Albert Museum: *Catalogue of Water Colour Paintings by British Artists and Foreigners working in Great Britain* revised edition by Basil S Long and F W Stokes, Board of Education 1927.

Supplemented by: London, Victoria and Albert Museum: *British Watercolours in the Victoria and Albert Museum: An Illustrated Summary Catalogue of the National Collection* by Lionel Lambourne and Jean Hamilton, Sotheby Parke Bernet 1980.

Vertue: George Vertue: *Manuscript Notes* published by the Walpole Society vols XVIII *(Vertue I)* 1930; XX *(Vertue II)* 1932; XXII *(Vertue III)* 1934; XXIV *(Vertue IV)* 1936; XXVI *(Vertue V)* 1938; XXIX *(Index to Vertue I–V)* 1947; XXX *(Vertue VI)* 1953.

Walpole: Hon. Horace Walpole (Earl of Orford): *Anecdotes of Painting in England* 4 vols 1765–1771; reprinted in 3 vols with Dalloway's notes, edited by Ralph Nicholson Wornum 1876; vol 5, edited by F W Hilles and P D Daghlian, Yale University Press 1937.

Waterhouse: Ellis K Waterhouse: *Painting in Britain 1530 to 1790* Harmondsworth, Middlesex, Penguin Books, Pelican History of Art 1953.

Waters: Grant M Waters: *Dictionary of British Artists working 1900-1950* 2 vols (text and plates) Eastbourne, Sussex, Eastbourne Fine Art 1975.

Williams: Iolo Aneurin Williams: *Early English Watercolours and some cognate drawings by artists born not later than 1785* The Connoisseur 1952.

Windsor: Adolf Paul Oppé: *English Drawings, Stuart and Georgian Periods, in the Collection of His Majesty the King at Windsor Castle* Phaidon 1950.

Glossary of Technical Terms

The most readable account of the materials and methods of the British graphic artist is contained in the introductory chapter *The Nature of Water-Colour,* in Martin Hardie's *Water-Colour Painting in Britain* vol 1 (Batsford 1966). This is the work of a man who was a practicing artist as well as being Keeper of Prints and Drawings at the Victoria and Albert Museum. Hardie was constantly making experiments with recipes taken from old manuals on drawing and painting. More up to date is the Tate Gallery catalogue *Paint and Painting,* an exhibition which was sponsored by the firm of Winsor and Newton, 1982. The comprehensive reference book on paper is Silvie Turner and Birgid Skiold: *Handmade Paper Today: a worldwide survey of mills, papers, techniques and uses,* Lund Humphreys 1988. Some suppliers of fine paper (e.g. Atlantis Paper, Gulliver's Wharf, 105 Wapping Lane, London E1 9RW, and John Purcell Paper, 219 Eversleigh Road, London SW1 5UY) produce catalogues of their stock with useful introductions outlining the history and care of paper.

AQUATINT

An intaglio printmaking method related to ETCHING, in that the image is "bitten" on to the wax-coated plate by acid; but where etching is a line process, aquatint is a tonal process. Tones are produced by laying a semi-pervious ground of resin globules. Pioneered in England by Paul Sandby, the process was used widely for books of topographical illustrations until in the mid-19th century it was superseded by LITHOGRAPHY. In the 1960s and 1970s it underwent a revival as a medium for autograph printmaking.

BLACK INK

In its primitive and purest form, carbon ink, this consists of an allotrope of carbon, lamp-black, ground with gum-arabic as a binding agent. Martin Hardie, following 18th century practice (Horace Walpole's "sut-water"), found that chimney-soot mixed with water contained enough natural binding materials to be used alone. Unlike IRON-GALL INKS, carbon ink is permanent and non-injurious to the paper. See INDIAN INK.

BODYCOLOUR

Watercolour mixed with LEAD WHITE or CHINESE WHITE. This destroys the transparency of pure WATERCOLOUR, making the paint opaque and viscous, so that the white paper plays no part in the luminosity. Bodycolour, while much used in conjunction with watercolour for striking effects in the 18th and 19th centuries, and today by designers and poster artists, lacks both the delicacy of pure

watercolour and the richness of oil painting. See GOUACHE.

BRUSH

From the 15th century to about 1850 artists' brushes were commonly called PENCILS. The best watercolour brushes are made of sable, cheaper ones of camel hair. Up to about 1850 the bristles were mounted in quills, according to size: lark, crow, duck, goose and (largest) swan. Later these were superseded by wooden handles with a nickel or aluminium ferrule.

BRUSH-LINE

A fine line drawn with a fine brush, commonly used in 18th century drawings and watercolours for such details as the rigging of ships. The untrained eye can easily mistake it for a PEN line.

CARD

Generally heavier and stiffer than paper, the better cards are made of rag, while inferior cards are made of wood-pulp and are highly acidic. More usually used for MOUNTING, cards are occasionally used from the 15th century on as supports for MINIATURE paintings or drawings. See LAMINATED BOARD.

CHALK

A soft form of limestone (calcium carbonate), usually white, which can be used as a drawing material in its natural state or mixed with a fixative binder like gum. See PASTEL.

CHINESE WHITE

Zinc oxide, first marketed under that name (for no good reason) by Winsor and Newton in 1834 as a white pigment intended especially for watercolour. Before that time LEAD WHITE was almost invariably used in both oil and watercolour. Zinc white or "Chinese white" has the advantage of not being nearly as subject as lead to change or blackening by the action of sulphuretted hydrogen from the atmosphere, since watercolour pigments are not protected by the medium as they are in oil paint.

COLLAGE

The practice, pioneered by Picasso and Braque, and perfected by Kurt Schwitters and Robert Rauschenberg, of sticking "found objects", newspapers, magazine photographs, linoleum or any other object onto the surface of their pictures to make a composition.

COLOUR-NOTES

Notes written by artists on their drawings or sketches made rapidly out-of-doors, to remind them of the colour of objects. Edward Lear's colour notes are particularly entertaining.

CRAYON

Loosely speaking, any drawing material made in stick form, such a graphite held in a metal porte-crayon (before about 1850, see PENCIL). Today it usually means coloured wax crayons with a chalk base.

CRIMSON LAKE

A crimson pigment used in both oil and watercolour, made from the root of the madder plant.

DAVID COX PAPER

A rough white flecked wrapping paper, manufactured in Dundee from old ships' sailcloth. It was discovered by David Cox, who liked it so much that he ordered a ream of it, and later regretted that he had not ordered more. When asked how he dealt with flecks in his sky areas, he replied "I put wings to them and they fly away" Later some paper-mills offered the same kind of paper specifically as artists' watercolour paper.

DRAGGING

See SCUMBLING.

ENGRAVING

The most arduous and exact method of intaglio printing from copper plates by incising the design in reverse using a hard pointed tool called a burin, which raises a needle-sharp sliver of copper which has to be filed away after each line is engraved. The plate is heated gently and ink is carefully forced into the engraved lines, then slowly wiped from the surface. Printing is done on a roller press something like an old-fashioned wringer. The method was used from the 15th to the 19th century for high quality printing and for reproduction of paintings in monochrome. See WOOD-ENGRAVING and ETCHING.

ETCHING

A less arduous way of incising a design on a copper plate for intaglio printing. The plate is first coated with a waxy varnish, in which the drawing is made with a needle. The plate is then immersed in a bath of acid, which bites the design into the plate. The varnish or ground can then be removed with a solvent and prints can be taken in the same way as with ENGRAVING. A line process, etching is sometimes used in conjunction with the tonal process of AQUATINT.

FOXING

A fungus which grows in paper and appears as small brown spots. It is encouraged by warm, damp conditions, and may be removed by bleaching and sterilisation.

GOUACHE

(French "gouache", Italian "guazzo") generally the same as BODYCOLOUR, i.e. a water-based paint with sufficient body to render it opaque. Gouache is usually made by adding white (LEAD WHITE or CHINESE WHITE) to watercolour. Distemper, a related medium, is made by adding isinglass jelly and size, and is normally used for theatrical scene-painting.

GRISAILLE

A generic term for any painting or design in near monochrome, limited to greys, grey-greens or grey-browns.

GUM-ARABIC

A vegetable gum obtained from the Acacia tree. It is readily soluble in water, and is the binding material for WATERCOLOUR, giving the paints their characteristic gummy smell. It also has the properties of a thin varnish, and can increase the luminosity of colours and strengthen dark colours. It became the practice in the 19th century to apply gum-arabic with a brush to the dark areas of watercolours to deepen the shades. It can easily be seen as it is shiny.

HATCHING

Shading by small strokes in pencil, pen, brush or engraving, so as to build up tones by a mesh of lines or strokes. Hatching can be bold, or in the case of MINIATURE painting, extremely delicate.

HOT-PRESSED

A term used in Britain to describe the finish of hand-made or machine-made PAPERS for artists. It means the smoothest surface, a glossy finish produced by placing the individual sheets between smooth zinc plates and applying pressure of several tons per square inch. No heat is used in the process. See NOT and ROUGH.

Impasto

Any paint, oil or water-based, which achieves its effect by being built up into a thick, tacky paste. This can be done with BODYCOLOUR or GOUACHE, especially in highlights. It is advisable to use impasto sparingly, as thick paint when dry can become brittle.

Indian Ink

(French "encre-de-chine", German "Tusche") a black drawing ink, carbon-based, originating in China, but so-called in Britain because it was imported through India by the East-India Company. The term "Indian ink" is used by Pepys in 1665. In the early centuries it was marketed in cake or stick form, later in liquid form in bottles. Dr Thomas Monro used to draw on wet paper with a dry stick of Indian ink.

Iron-Gall Ink

Brown inks used in the 17th and 18th centuries were often iron-based, and were used frequently by artists like Fuseli and Flaxman. Unlike the black carbon inks, iron inks are highly unstable, and contain sulphuric acid and gallic acid. This can attack the paper in time and penetrate right through it. Drawings affected in this way can only be treated by deacidification and strengthening or replacement of the corroded area with new paper.

Laid Paper

All PAPER before 1800 was hand-made; hand-made paper is still manufactured, it tears much less easily than machine-made paper and has a more interesting surface, thus the superior artists' papers are still hand-made. Before 1750 all hand-made papers were laid (see WOVE PAPER). Hand-made paper is made by teams of two skilled workmen, a vatman and a coucher; the vatman manipulates a mould in the vat of pulp, then passes it to the coucher who presses the film of pulp picked up by the mould onto a sheet of felt, forming a sheet of paper. Another sheet of felt is placed on top, and the process is repeated. The mould is a wooden frame containing a mesh of wires. Before the invention of WOVE PAPER the wires were always LAID at right angles to form a sheet, "laid" wires and "chain" wires crossing each other. The resultant paper when held up to the light shows a pattern of lines, the "chain" wires at roughly one-inch intervals, crossed by the "laid" wires at much closer intervals. The WATERMARK is worked into the wire pattern in the mould.

Laminated Board

In the early 20th century a number of paper manufacturers such as Whatman's offered "prepared boards" or "artists' boards", that is, rigid boards built up of laminated sheets of good quality paper, perhaps from two to six plies thick. These eliminated the tendencies of all paper to cockle when wet, did away with the necessity of straining or "drumming" paper, and proved more convenient for working out of doors than ordinary paper which would blow about.

Lead White

Basic lead carbonate, the usual white pigment for both oils and watercolour before 1834 (see CHINESE WHITE). Lead white, or "flake white" is highly poisonous. This is completely satisfactory for oil painting, where the pigment is protected from the atmosphere by the linseed oil. But in watercolour the pigment is unprotected and is therefore liable to blackening by the action of sulphuretted hydrogen. For this reason lead white in watercolour was superseded in the 1830s by zinc white or CHINESE WHITE.

Line Engraving
see ENGRAVING.

Lithograph

The principal means of reproductive printmaking of the 19th century. The process was accidentally discovered by Aloys Senefelder about 1800, and depends on the physical phenomenon of adsorbtion, and the fact that grease and water do not mix. The lithographer draws in greasy ink on a specially-ground block of fine-grained lithographic limestone. The process of fixing the image is too complicated to be described fully, but it enables a much larger edition to be printed than the copperplate processes of ENGRAVING and ETCHING. It also allows every nuance of the artist's drawing to be reproduced, and is the most versatile of printmaking processes. It is still widely used by both commercial and autograph printmakers.

Miniature

A painting, usually a portrait, "in little". The techniques derive from medieaval manuscript illumination. English "limners" of the Tudor period usually painted in watercolour or gouache on parchment, vellum or card. In the early 18th century, enamel techniques on metal, which involved many low-temperature firings, were developed. In the later 18th century, painters like Richard Cosway or Horace Hone often painted in watercolour on thin sheets of ivory. At the same time, tightly-painted watercolour portraits on paper are still classed as miniatures.

Mount

Drawings, watercolours and prints need to be protected by rigid card mounts within glazed frames. Normally these consist of a backboard to which the drawing is attached, overlapped by another card, usually hinged to the backboard, containing a bevelled aperture which allows the image to be seen while at the same time protecting it from the inside of the glass in the frame. Traditional English watercolour mounts have their apertures decorated by ruled lines and washes. In the Victorian period there was a fashion for gilded mounts. Modern museum-standard mounts are made of highest quality solid-plate rag board, as inferior wood-pulp boards are unstable and acidic and will ultimately attack and corrode the drawing.

Not

i.e. not HOT-PRESSED. A term used by British PAPER-makers to describe the intermediate finish of artists' papers, not so smooth as HOT-PRESSED, nor so coarse as ROUGH. The NOT surface is produced by pressing the newly-made sheets of paper against each other over a period of days, without the use of zinc plates.

Palette

The surface on which a painter lays and mixes his colours; it can take any form besides the traditional oil painter's mahogany kidney-shaped palette. Many modern painters use a sheet of glass over a sheet of white paper, or a table-top given several coats of hard gloss paint. In the 17th century, watercolour palettes were usually made of glass, shell or ivory. Porcelain saucers were also often used in the studio in the 18th and early 19th centuries. Mahogany boxes for outdoor use, containing cakes of watercolour and a marble palette, were advertised by Ackermann's in 1801. These were also offered by Winsor and Newton in 1832, when they introduced "Japanned Tin Sketching Boxes for the Pocket, with 6, 8, or 12 Colours, Pencils, Bottle, Cups etc. complete". This is still the pattern for the familiar watercolour sketching box of enameled tin, with one or two hinged palettes, a thumb-hole or thumb-ring, and compartments for pans or cakes of colour. Sometimes these boxes are made to slide into the top of a large box containing tubes of watercolour kept in a liquid state by the addition of glycerine.

Paper

As distinct from vellum or parchment (animal skin, therefore a protein substance), paper is a plant substance, consisting of a mass of cellulose fibres which normally originate from the cotton plant (either directly or by way of recycling rags). Cotton or linen rags are boiled with water to make a pulp, which is a suspension of cellulose fibres. This can be formed into sheets in three ways:
(1) Hand-made: that is by a vatman and a coucher working in pairs using a hand-mould and a pile of felts. See LAID PAPER and WOVE PAPER. Before about 1800 all paper was made by hand, but today only the best quality paper is made this way from the finest raw materials.
(2) Cylinder mould-made: this machine process was invented soon after 1800. The pulp is passed into a vat containing a rotating cylinder covered in a fine wire mesh. The fibre forms into a matt on the outside of the cylinder and the water drains away inside the cylinder. After each rotation a sheet of paper is couched off onto a felt. The machine is usually run very slowly and produces paper only slightly inferior to hand-made paper.
(3) Machine-made: the Fourdrinier machine, invented in France, was patented in Britain in 1801 and the first machine was set up in Hertfordshire in 1803. The Fourdrinier process is still recognised as the fastest and most economical method of manufacturing paper in large quantities. The pulp is poured onto a moving belt of metal web which pulsates from side to side, causing the cellulose fibres to interweave. Most of the water is then pressed out by a Dandy roll which also impresses the watermarks or LAID-lines. The process produces a continuous roll of paper which is dried by heated rollers and then wound onto a reel. Paper made this way is usually much cheaper and more easily torn than hand-made or mould-made paper.

After the sheets are made, the surface "finish" is applied: see HOT-PRESSED, NOT and ROUGH.

All freshly made paper is known as "waterleaf" and is like blotting paper; it can only be drawn or painted upon after treatment with size.

Parchment
See VELLUM.

Pastel

Sticks of CHALK-based dry powdered colour ground with just enough GUM-ARABIC to act as a binder. They can be made soft or hard. Pastel was much used by some French and English portraitists of the 18th century, and revived by Degas in the late 19th century as a serious drawing medium. Its main disadvantage is that the colours never solidify and must always be protected from smudging by glass. Another drawback is that the medium makes a favourable base for FOXING.

Pen

Before about 1830, all pens were usually either quills or reeds; each made its own distinctive line, and each needed frequent sharpening. The modern steel pen was invented in the 1830s, and had the advantage of durable interchangeable nibs of a variety of thicknesses and flexibility. See BLACK INK, INDIAN INK and IRON-GALL INK.

Pencil

Up to about 1850 the word pencil meant an artist's BRUSH. This usage is now archaic. The word now signifies what was formerly called a CRAYON, and commonly means a thin strip of graphite, one of the many allotropes of carbon, grey and exceptionally smooth, either encased in a cylinder of soft wood, or in a metal case with a tapering end ("porte-crayon").

Poster-Paint
Basically the same as BODYCOLOUR or GOUACHE. In this century it is widely used by poster-artists and designers and is readily available in sets of disks, cakes or liquified in bottles.

Rough

Like HOT-PRESSED and NOT, this is a term used in Britain to describe the finish of artists' hand-made or machine-made papers. The word is self-explanatory. The ROUGH surface is produced by applying no pressure at all to the freshly-made sheets of paper. They are merely piled in a heap and allowed to dry under their own weight for a matter of weeks until sufficiently flat.

SCRAPING

A means of lifting colour in watercolour to produce highlights. It can be done in many ways, with the colour dry or semi-dry, using a knife, a razor-blade, the finger-nail, or the end of the brush-handle. Turner and his 19th century followers used various methods of surface scraping with much freedom and invention.

SCUMBLING

The opposite of glazing in oil painting, or laying a WASH in watercolour. A slightly-damped brush is charged with dry colour and dragged on its side across the paper, giving a rough, textured effect. All the early 19th century English watercolour painters, the Varleys, Turner, Cotman, Bonington, Boys etc. frequently used this trick.

SEPIA

A warm brown pigment obtained from the ink-bags of cuttlefish, and used either as an ink or as a watercolour. It is barely distinguishable from bistre, a similar pigment made from burning wood.

SQUARING-UP

A time-honoured means of transferring a drawing from paper to canvas by ruling a network of squares which can be scaled up or scaled down as required. Sickert believed that squaring-up improved the look of a drawing, and the practice was followed by his associates, Gore, Gilman, Ginner, Bevan and Drummond and others.

STIPPLE ENGRAVING

A late 18th century method of ENGRAVING, practiced by Bartolozzi and various engravers after Angelica Kauffman and others, in which the tones are built up using minute dots as well as lines. The roulette and the mattoir were the instruments used. There is a small distinction between stipple engraving and "crayon-manner" engraving, the intention being to produce the effect of a drawing in chalk or crayon.

STOPPING-OUT

Highlights can be produced in watercolour by lifting colour from WASHES already laid. This is done by dropping blobs of water on the part required to lift, and removing the colour with blotting-paper, a handkerchief or breadcrumbs. This will leave the exact shape of the drop of water as a light area. The technique is clearly seen in the watercolour by James George Oben (27). Artists' colourmen of the early 19th century misunderstood this technique when they observed it in Girtin's watercolours, and thinking that it was produced by a method similar to the "stopping-out" techniques well-known in ETCHING, they marketed concoctions under the name of "Girtin's Stopping-Out Mixture".

STUDIO STAMP

A small wooden or rubber stamp, usually containing a monogram, used instead of a signature by artists, or, perhaps more often, by the salerooms in marking the contents of an artist's studio after his death. Some collectors of drawings and prints use similar stamps to identify items that have passed through their collections.

TINTED PAPER

Some artists like to work on coloured PAPERS, usually in BODYCOLOUR or CHALK. In the 18th century artists sometimes tinted their own papers by laying yellow, pink, brown or coffee-coloured WASHS before commencing. This practice is common in the work of William Gilpin and Paul Sandby. During the 19th and 20th centuries a wide range of tinted papers were manufactured, using the increasing choice of dyes that became available. These could be obtained from indigo, onion-skins, coal-tars or many other sources, but as some dyes use an acid mordant to bond with the paper fibres, they can be eventually injurious to the paper.

VELLUM (OR PARCHMENT)

Prepared animal-skin, a protein substance, usually sheep or goat, used especially by MINIATURE and GOUACHE painters, and in mediaeval times for illuminated manuscripts. Nicholas Hilliard's *Art of Limning* recommends "virgin parchment", i.e. the skin of an unborn kid, which had never grown hair, for the smoothness required for miniature painting.

VIGNETTE

A format for prints, drawings and watercolours which was fashionable in the first half of the 19th century, in which the composition does not fill the corners of the rectangular paper, but is "vignetted" or faded off to produce an irregular oval. The woodcuts of Thomas Bewick and the engraved illustrations after Turner are usually vignettes.

WASH

An even covering of dilute ink or liquid WATERCOLOUR, applied with a BRUSH using a liberal amount of water. Washes can be prepared in trays or saucers. In pure WATERCOLOUR the composition is built up by successive transparent washes.

WATERCOLOUR

Artists' paints in which the binder is usually GUM-ARABIC, the vehicle is water, and the support is PAPER. In "pure" watercolour, the white paper is used to make the highlights and no opaque white pigments are used (see LEAD WHITE and CHINESE WHITE). Colour is applied in liquid, transparent WASHES which allow the white paper to shine through. Great skill, rapidity and dexterity is required in the manipulation of washes. In hot dry conditions the water may evaporate too quickly and glycerine may be added to retard the drying process. On the other hand, if it is wished to accelerate the drying process, alcohol may be added, which in the 18th century was usually in the form of brandy, whisky or gin. Gall was often used to make washes run evenly over grease or impurities in the paper. Watercolours are supplied in sold cakes or pans, or semi-liquified in tubes; see PALETTE. When opaque white is added, the transparency of "pure" watercolour is lost, and the result is BODYCOLOUR or GOUACHE.

Watermark

The PAPER maker's symbol or trade-mark, worked in the wire of the paper-mould. It is impressed into each sheet of paper and can be seen when the sheet is held up to the light. Watermarks have been used since the 16th century in Europe. Sometimes they carry the year of the paper's manufacture.

Wax

As well as in the form of wax CRAYONS, wax in the 20th century is sometimes used with ink and WATERCOLOUR to produce interesting textures. Usually it is in the form of candle-grease rubbed onto the drawing, and worked over by pen and watercolour.

Wet Method

A method of WATERCOLOUR invented by the Scottish painter Arthur Melville (1858–1904) and used and described by his pupil Romilly Fedden (65). It involves taking WASH to its logical conclusion, and requires confidence and concentration to avoid a muddy mess. The whole paper is completely soaked in water, washes are applied and blobs of saturated colour are dripped onto the wet surface. With a bit of luck the end result can be brilliant.

Wood-Engraving

A relief-printing technique allied to woodcut, but while woodcut is done on the plank-grain of softwood, with a knife, wood-engraving is done on the end-grain of hardwood (usually boxwood), using engravers' tools such as the burin (see ENGRAVING). Unlike intaglio copper-engraving, the cut out parts of the wood-block will print as white. The process was pioneered by Thomas Bewick (1753–1828) of Newcastle-upon-Tyne, who used "white-line" as a convention. Later in the 19th century wood-engraving in the "black-line" style was used extensively for reproducing pen-drawings which sometimes were made directly onto the wood-blocks by artists, and were then pecked away by engravers, the true proletariat of the Victorian art profession. The *Illustrated London News* and *Punch* were entirely illustrated by wood-engravings, and many Victorian watercolourists like Birket Foster and Pinwell received their first training as reproductive wood-engravers. In the 1920s and 30s, the "white line" tradition was revived by Noel Rooke at the Central School of Arts and Crafts, and the technique underwent a revival in

the production of fine printed books with illustrations by Robert Gibbings, Eric Gill, John Farleigh, Gertrude Hermes and others.

Wove Paper

Before 1750 all PAPER was hand-made and LAID. In that year, a technique for weaving wire was discovered, and paper-moulds with woven meshes were produced. This resulted in paper with an overall woven pattern, without the criss-cross of lines found in LAID PAPER. The process was introduced by the Birmingham printer John Baskerville, who used wove paper for his edition of Virgil (1757) which, according to Macaulay, "went forth to astonish all the librarians of Europe".

Index of Artists